CROSSCURRENTS ALONG THE COLORADO

CROSSCURRENTS ALONG THE COLORADO

The Impact of Government Policy on the Quechan Indians

Robert L. Bee

THE UNIVERSITY OF ARIZONA PRESS
TUCSON, ARIZONA

About the Author

ROBERT BEE became interested in sociocultural change in Native American communities while doing research on a summer work project in the Quechan community at Fort Yuma. Following military service, he assisted in ethnographic studies of the Prairie Potawatomies of Kansas, and returned to Fort Yuma several times during the late 1960s and early 70s to do doctoral research on the processes of Indian policy. In 1967, Dr. Bee joined the faculty of the University of Connecticut, to teach courses on Native Americans and culture change and to continue his research into the relationships between Indian groups and federal policymakers.

THE UNIVERSITY OF ARIZONA PRESS

This book was set in 10/12 Videocomp Century Schoolbook

Library of Congress Cataloging in Publication Data

Bee, Robert L.
Crosscurrents along the Colorado.

Bibliography: p.
Includes index.
1. Yuma Indians—History. 2. Yuma Indians—Government relations. 3. Indians of North America—Government relations. I. Title.
E99.Y94B43 970.004'97 81-7446
AACR2
ISBN 0-8165-0558-6
ISBN 0-8165-0725-2 (pbk.)

Contents

MAPS

Preface

IN THE SPRING OF 1976, A PRESS CONFERENCE WAS CALLED in Washington, D.C. by some very angry Quechan (or Yuma) Indians, their attorney, and representatives from the Confederation of Lower Colorado Tribes. The federal government had at last issued a judgment in an attempt to resolve the competition for water and land in the Lower Colorado River area, and the Quechans, and ultimately their Indian neighbors to the north and south along the river, were the losers.

A few weeks earlier—after years of negotiations between the Quechans, their tribal attorney, BIA officials in the Phoenix Area Office and Washington, the solicitor's office in the Department of Interior, and personnel in the Justice Department—the Quechans had been sent a letter by the new solicitor declaring that there were no legal grounds for returning thousands of acres of former reservation land to tribal control. Only days before the letter was written, the Quechans had subsidized a delegation to Washington in the last of a series of efforts to remind the secretary of the interior of their intense desire to get some action on their negotiated proposal. This delegation had left the capital believing the secretary would at last approve the land's return.

The Indians and their advocates were convinced that the explanation for the Interior Department's abrupt and highly questionable about-face lay not in the land itself, but in the water flowing past it.

Greater water demands and needless seepage had made the Colorado a critical, but increasingly scarce, resource in the desert home of the Quechans. Large water-user interests in the region, such as the Central Arizona Project and the Imperial Irrigation District, along with state agencies in both Arizona and California, were said to be desperately anxious to prevent the diversion of additional Colorado River water for Indian use. Were the Indians to be given the land in question, it was feared they would then demand enough water to make the land arable in order to increase the limited economic potential of their community. However, tribal leaders and their attorney continued to work for a reconsideration through their contacts in Washington, and on 15 December 1978—a month after key federal congressional elections—the Carter administration's Interior Secretary Cecil Andrus and Interior Solicitor Leo Krulitz revived the case and quietly informed the Quechan president that 25,000 acres of the land would be restored to the tribe. The new decision still made no provision for additional water for the tribe, declaring only that any tribal claims for increased allocations must be handled according to procedures outlined in the earlier court decision in the *Arizona* v. *California* case. (An estimated 5,000 acres of the restored tract might be irrigable.)

THE IMPACT OF COLONIALISM

Colonialism involves political, economic and cultural domination of one group by another, usually as a result of military conquest. Once created, the colonial situation typically features an intermittent series of shifts in official policy for dealing with the dependent peoples and their resources. Inevitably each new shift is proclaimed the most humanitarian solution to the dependents' continuing plight. Just as inevitably, the actual results of the shifts tend to serve the interests of the dominant society.

Scholars have noted with increasing insistence that the development of federal Indian policies and their impact on Indian tribes constitutes internal colonialism of a most unsubtle sort (Thomas 1966/1967 and Jorgensen 1971 and 1972). To appreciate colonial relationships, however, we must understand the distinction between the ideology and intent of colonial policy at the highest administrative levels (Congress and the executive in this case) and the actual application and impact of that policy at the local, grass roots level.

My concern in this study is to describe the impact on the Quechans of a century of United States government efforts to "develop" their economic and social well-being. Federal efforts have been uneven at best, careening between extremes of almost total, aloof indifference and intense, but heavy-handed, manipulation of the

Quechans' daily lives. The impact of these efforts has therefore been uneven as well, and almost always different from that publicly predicted by policymakers in Washington.

More specifically, I have tried to explain the reactions of the Quechans themselves. To this end, I have found it useful to characterize their collective attempts to adjust to the shifts in federal policy as a series of "adaptive strategies" (see Bennett 1969), and to describe how these strategies were influenced by prevailing economic, political, and social conditions in the community. The strategies were not necessarily new responses to specific conditions at specific times. More frequently they tended to be distillations of past strategies the Quechans had developed in the face of persisting conditions. For example, Quechan reactions to the War on Poverty programs of the mid-1960s reflected both their knowledge of how the federal government had operated in previous years as well as past patterns for marshalling community resources for cooperative endeavors.

Presumably, the Quechans throughout their history have evaluated the advantages and consequences of major adaptive strategies during critical periods of transition and have selected those they felt would offer the greatest advantages and/or the fewest disadvantages (Bailey 1960 and Barth 1963 and 1967). Part of my task is to show how the strategies they selected were more advantageous than others—or else were the only options available to them. It should be noted that these strategies were never unlimited in their range but existed in a particular context, limited by economic, social, political, and attitudinal conditions that emerged during the history of the Quechans' contact with aliens.

If conditions and patterns for the Quechans are much the same for the Cherokees, Navajos, or Prairie Potawatomis, so much the better for comparative studies. Perhaps more significant, however, are the differences in patterns that may exist between tribes.

SOURCES OF INFORMATION

This book is the result of thirteen years of intermittent research on the Quechan tribe. My information was gleaned in part from extended visits to the reservation in 1961, 1962, 1966, 1969, and 1974. These visits included attendance at public gatherings, sacred and secular, festive and solemn. I also interviewed individuals and families, some of them repeatedly and at length, and found it gratifying that their own interest in uncovering details of the tribe's past was sometimes aroused by my investigations. My interviews with those who spoke only Quechan had to be conducted through an interpreter, but, except for a few of the oldest Quechans, most of the people were able to express themselves in English.

In addition to the personal interviews, I devoted several weeks in both 1961 and 1966 to door-to-door surveys, using a prepared questionnaire. Although most of the people were consistent in their descriptions, they were often hazy about dates. For putting recalled events in a proper time perspective, I found documents in local newspaper files and the National Archives, as well as those belonging to individual Quechans, most helpful. The complete census of the reservation taken in 1972 by tribal members and students affiliated with the American Medical Association was also very helpful, as were the figures in recent Program, Planning, and Evaluation Reports provided by the Fort Yuma Subagency of the Bureau of Indian Affairs in 1974.

COMMUNITY POPULATION

In 1974, it was necessary to distinguish between the Quechan reservation community—those living on the reservation itself or sufficiently close to it to participate regularly in its social networks—and the Quechan tribe, including all people of Quechan descent regardless of where they lived. There was not always a need for such a distinction. In the late 1800s, the tribal population was probably about the same size as the community population. During the entire 1884–1974 period, the population of the Quechan community remained relatively stable, despite declines from a flu epidemic in 1917–18 and a period of endemic syphilis in 1935 [A. M. Halpern, personal communication]; the tribal population, however, had increased dramatically by the mid-1900s.

During the 1960–74 period of my field investigations, various Quechans estimated their reservation community population at "about a thousand," but this estimate was higher than population figures compiled by a tribally-sponsored community census in 1972. The census listed 874 reservation dwellers: 707 Quechans, 91 other Indians, and 76 non-Indians. These totals did not include Quechans living in nearby towns who were either regular participants in reservation life or spent much of their free time on the reservation. Of the total that was included, 414 (just over 47 percent) were seventeen years of age or younger.

The 1972 figures were very close to the total population of 826 recorded in 1905 by the Fort Yuma Indian Agency. Population figures for intervening years show similar consistency, although earlier figures tend to be more erratic and generally higher; in the eighteenth and early nineteenth centuries, the tribal population was estimated at about 3,000 by both Spanish and American sources (Forde 1931:103). It seems safe to conclude that for my purposes in this study, the Quechan community included between 800 and 900 tribal members between 1884 and 1974, plus perhaps another 100 Indians and non-Indians.

In contrast, the modern Quechan tribal roll—listing all persons of Quechan ancestry regardless of residence—showed a total of 1,544 persons as of 1 April 1968.

I have used the term Quechan tribe ambiguously to refer to reservation inhabitants, plus those Quechans living in towns nearby and, in rarer instances, to all those voting in tribal elections whether they are reservation dwellers or not.

THE CONTINUING STRUGGLE

Tribal politics during the last half of the 1970s were particularly unsettled. Three different tribal presidents served during that interval, and there were five successful recall elections against tribal council members in the 1975–76 period.

The political turmoil has since simmered down, and the tribe has plans for developing the newly restored land. Although some of the constraints are different and the options more restricted, the Quechans' development needs in 1980 remain essentially the same as they have been for the past hundred years: a role of relative power in regional economics; capital for development and operation; and a reliable source of lucrative wages. The fact that the Quechans' resource base has been augmented, and that it remains ultimately (if not always effectively) under tribal control, give cause for continuing hope that some sort of meaningful development will occur.

Robert L. Bee

Spelling and Pronunciation of Quechan Words

QUECHAN (not to be confused with the Quechuan language of the Incas) is not a written language. Abraham Halpern (1935) and Daryll Forde (1931) both produced guides to pronunciation and spelling of Quechan words, but they have not used identical symbols and there is disagreement between them as to the precise sounds of certain Quechan vowels. I recommend Halpern's work to those wishing an expert linguistic rendering of Quechan pronunciation.

The following spelling-pronunciation guide, based on Halpern's version, is intended for the general reader rather than the trained linguist:

VOWELS

a	as in father
e	as in met
i	as in pin
o	as in hot (approximate)
u	as in boot

A raised dot immediately following a vowel (example: a·) indicates that the sound is of slightly longer duration than undotted vowels.

CONSONANTS

Most of the Quechan consonants are pronounced as in English except for the following:

c	intermediate between ts and ch
d	as in *th*is
k^w	as in *qu*ick
l^y	approximates the ly sound in Lewel*ly*n; uncommon in English
r	a rolled or trilled sound not found in English; common in Spanish, as in amo*r*
š	as in *sh*ine
ţ	not found in English; pronounced with tip of the tongue touching the top of the gums
v	intermediate between boy and voice; more like the Spanish v as in *v*aca
x	not found in English; similar to the Spanish x as in Me*x*ico, or German ch as in i*ch*

The symbol ˀ indicates a glottal stop, such as occurs in the pronunciation of "bottle" in some dialects of English in the northeastern United States: "botˀl". An accent mark " ˊ " indicates the accented syllable of the word.

I have left the spellings of Quechan personal names as they appear in original historical documents. Usually these are rough approximations that were first written by non-Quechan speakers. Quechan personal names are capitalized only on the initial element (e.g. *Akes ha ar*) and are set in italics throughout the text.

Introduction: The Land of the Quechans

THE SETTING FOR THIS NARRATIVE is the narrow, fertile floodplain formed by the junction of the Gila and lower Colorado rivers, on the boundary between California and Arizona. White men's dams have tamed the Colorado now, but in times past its annual floods deposited rich layers of silt across the plain, an important ecological blessing for the Indians who had settled there. Just a few miles downstream from the confluence, the river channel narrows briefly. In 1974, automobile and railway bridges spanned this gap, recognized for centuries by both Indians and whites as a logical spot to ford the river when it was not at its flooded maximum. The narrows have proved a mixed blessing for the Indians, because a succession of Spanish, Mexican, and Anglo intruders have tried to control the crossing for their own purposes, either through cooperation with the original inhabitants or forceful intimidation of them.

At the narrows on the river's northwestern bank, a small bluff juts up from the surrounding flatness of the floodplain, providing a commanding view of the area for those standing on its levelled summit. "Indian Hill," as it is known to local inhabitants, was for years the site of the Fort Yuma Subagency and other administrative installations of the modern Indian community. Earlier, the hill was capped by Fort Yuma, whose remaining buildings have been refurbished to lure tourists. Earlier still, in 1780–81, the hill may have been the site of a Spanish settlement known as Concepción—which met a cataclysmic end at the hands of enraged Indians (Forbes 1965:201 ff). Some eight miles to the south and west of Indian Hill, but still on the river's western bank, is a much larger peak known as Pilot Knob. At its base, the Indians settled in large numbers through the first decade of this century (Forde 1931:101).

The river cuts a fertile gash through the surrounding Sonora Desert, a forbidding combination of sandy soil and jutting brown rocks, broken by scrubby ironwood, spider-like ocotillo shrubs, and palo verde and mesquite trees. About ten miles west of the confluence, the desert disintegrates into a large stretch of sand dunes, devoid of vegetation. Motion picture producers have found in these dunes a cheap but convincing substitute for the Sahara, and travelers from the time of the peripatetic Spanish padres have found them to be troublesome—even treacherous. Temperatures throughout the area are those expected in a desert, ranging between a high of 120 degrees Fahrenheit and a recorded low of 22 degrees. Rainfall is a scant 3.44 inches annually (Castetter and Bell 1951:16–17).

Physically, the modern Quechans, like their Indian neighbors on the lower Colorado, are large people whose skin is somewhat darker than that of other American Indian groups. The men stand about six feet tall, with broad, heavy shoulders and stout waists and hips. The women are also tall and large boned. Both sexes show a tendency toward increasing corpulence in middle age, but the oldest Quechans attribute this to a combination of modern diet and a relative lack of prolonged physical activity. In the past, these older tribal members recall, members of both sexes were better able to maintain trim figures.

The exact time that the Quechans moved into the confluence area is not known. No group of that name is mentioned by the Spaniard, Alarcón, reportedly the first European to pass through the area when he was on his way to meet Coronado's expedition in 1540. Spanish records of the late seventeenth century make the first reference to the Quechans by name, but by then the Indians were already settled in the confluence area, as well as north and south along the Colorado and east along the Gila.

The Quechans themselves tell of a southward migration from a sacred mountain they call Avikwame (Newberry Mountain, located north of Needles, California). A deity, Kukumat, created them there, along with the Cocopas, Maricopas, Kamias, and Mohaves. Kukumat, according to the legend, later died from sorcery worked upon him by his daughter Frog, who, in a pique, stole a portion of his excrement and devoured it (Forde 1931:214). The mourning ceremony for Kukumat became the prototype for the *karˀúk,* one of the Quechans' most important and spectacular rituals. Although all

Yuman speakers must have descended from a single ancient aggregate, anthropological evidence suggests that the Yuman tribes are the result of an amalgamation of smaller bands between the thirteenth and eighteenth centuries. The bands' amalgamation was fostered in part by nearness to each other along river bottoms during the horticultural seasons, by similarity of languages, and by the effects of incessant warfare (see Forbes 1965:36 ff., and Steward 1955:159–61).

Unlike tribes such as the Cheyennes or Cherokees to the east, the Quechans have not been pushed out of their home territory by the pressures of shifting colonial policy or white settlers—although such pressures have certainly been applied. In 1974, tribal members could still glance at the solitary mass of Pilot Knob in the southwest, or at the pillar called Picacho in the north, as did their ancestors, and recall legends about the goings-on of humans and spirits on those heights.

CHAPTER 1

The Pre-Colonial Setting: 1540-1852

THE SPANISH WERE THE FIRST EUROPEANS to make contact with the Quechans in the confluence area. Contacts were sporadic between 1540 (if the Quechans were in the area that early) and 1770, being limited to brief exchanges with traveling missionaries and explorers. By the 1770s, however, the Spanish had become convinced that an overland route between Mexico and California was essential. To their way of thinking, the confluence area occupied by the Quechans would be the best point to ford the Colorado for entry into California. A Quechan leader, Salvadore Palma, together with his brother and two other members of the tribe, were invited by the Spanish captain, Juan Bautista de Anza, to Mexico City, where they were "entertained, baptized, and indoctrinated in hopes they might help secure the Spanish position on the Colorado River" (Forbes 1965:177).

In 1780, the Spanish escalated their consolidation efforts by starting construction on two pueblos (village settlements made up of immigrant farm families, soldiers, and Franciscan padres) near the confluence. When completed, these pueblos were to become bases of operation for farmers and soldiers, and centers of religious indoctrination for the Indians. By early 1781, the Quechans had already been brought into what the Spanish hoped would be a long tutelage in the tenets of Franciscan catholicism. But it was not long before the Quechans learned that such traditional practices as a man taking more than one wife or the sick calling on specially endowed native curers for relief were not at all to the liking of the new order. Indians sympathetic to the Spanish cause were used to punish their recalcitrant tribal members. Further, the settlers in the new pueblos created a severe strain on the area's food supplies, most of which were apparently being provided by the Quechans themselves.

On 17 July 1781, the Quechans decided that they had endured an increasingly intolerable situation long enough. Both pueblos were attacked almost simultaneously by the Quechans and a few Mohaves. The buildings were gutted and some ninety-five Spaniards, including four priests, were either killed or captured (Forbes 1965:175–200). The event was still remembered by the Quechans in the 1960s as a successful instance of retaliation in what they regarded as a long record of exploitation by whites. Some even chafed at the monument to one of the slain priests that stood at the entrance to the Catholic church on Indian Hill, remarking that it conveyed scant impression of the conditions culminating in his martyrdom.

The lower Colorado crossing was used in the early nineteenth century by various trappers, adventurers, and military detachments, but it was not until the California gold rush in the late 1840s that intensive and protracted Quechan-white contact was reestablished—this time with Anglos. In order to protect the forty-niners and others against possible Indian depradations, a small military post was established on the Colorado's west bank, opposite the mouth of the Gila River. Three companies of the Second Infantry, under Brevet Major S. P. Heintzelman, pitched camp but were soon forced to withdraw because of difficulties of supply and threats from local Indians (Heintzelman 1857:34). In February 1852, the Anglos returned to build a garrison on Indian Hill,with the original troops augmented by an additional infantry company. Heintzelman (1857:34) proudly wrote:

> Since . . . [the building of the garrison], the navigation of the Colorado by steam has been assured, and it is now in a fair way of being a permanent station. It is the most important in southern California, as it protects the southern route of American emigration into California . . . controls numerous tribes of warlike Indians, and commands the passage by land on the Pacific side into Sonora and the Mexican republic. It is also spoken of as a point on the great Pacific railroad.

From that time on, contacts between Quechans and outsiders were no longer sporadic. The Anglos had come to stay.

TRADITIONAL QUECHAN LIFEWAYS

In order to describe the effects that Anglo contact had on the lives of the Quechans, it is necessary to describe their probable patterns of living at the time Major Heintzelman established his *pax Americana* in the confluence region. But it is also necessary to note that the Quechan culture had already been influenced by years of often tumultuous contact with aliens. Heintzelman and his Second Infantry were confronting a people who knew something about the ways of whites and, doubtlessly, recognized the importance of their territory to the white intruders.

The Quechan people lived principally on plant foods they could gather and grow. The rugged desert terrain bounding the fertile river bottoms only grudgingly yielded game, and at a relatively high cost in human effort, so that hunting was not an important subsistence pursuit (Forde 1931:107, 118). The fish in the river were bony and unpalatable, and the Quechans were apparently unenthusiastic fishermen. (Older Quechans, recalling ancient enmities, still speak disparagingly of a "fishy smell" among some Cocopas, who apparently depended more on fish as a dietary staple than did the Quechans.) The ratio of cultivated to wild foods in the early Quechan diet has not been estimated, but Spanish records indicate that horticulture was "no mere accessory" to gathering (Forde 1931:115–16). Estimates of the percentage of cultivated foods in the diets of Colorado River peoples in general range from a low of about thirty percent for the Quechans' southern neighbors, the Cocopas, to a high of about fifty percent among the Mohaves, the Quechans' allies to the north (Castetter and Bell 1951:238). Occasionally the Colorado-Gila overflow was not as extensive as usual and the Indians were subjected to near famine conditions. There were also instances when late flooding destroyed already sown fields (Forbes 1965:189; Castetter and Bell 1951:8). But all in all, before the modern dam system controlled the river waters, the flooding of the river and the resulting richness of the surface soil made farming a relatively low-risk enterprise with a high potential yield—and all for relatively little physical effort.

Some of the Quechans' fields could be planted several times during the year. Small amounts of maize and some melons were planted in February and did not depend on the natural river irrigation for growth and eventual harvesting (Forde 1931:109). But the primary horticultural effort began with the clearing of brush from the fields prior to the spring flooding, and planting was done when cracks appeared in the surface of the flood-deposited silt as it began to dry—usually in July. The people first sowed teparies, maize, and watermelons, then black-eyed beans, pumpkins, and muskmelons (Castetter and Bell 1951:149). Fall was the time for sowing winter wheat, to be harvested just before the river flooded the following spring. The Quechans also planted the seeds of wild grasses on less fertile lands, grinding the harvested seeds into meal and baking or drying them into cakes.

The farm work was not particularly demanding or time-consuming. The people did not bother to weed the wheat fields. Teparies were weeded once during the season; pumpkins, maize, and black-eyed beans were weeded twice. Able-bodied members of large family households often cooperated in the weeding chores, men doing the heavier work such as clearing the brush from the fields and digging the planting holes, women sowing the seeds and storing the harvested foods. But the division of labor was by no means strictly sexual, and both women and men could work at agricultural chores of their choosing.

The sweetish pods of mesquite and screwbean were the Quechans' primary source of wild food, mesquite being the more popular as well as drought resistant (Castetter and Bell 1951:179). The pods were ground into a pulp, dried, then ground into flour and mixed with water to make cakes that could last indefinitely. Crushed pods could be steeped in water to make a nourishing drink that, after fermentation, was mildly intoxicating (Castetter and Bell 1951:186). These wild foods were probably the main source of sustenance when there were crop failures or occasional food scarcities between harvests. Families did not own groves of mesquite trees unless they grew close to the family shelter, but family groups tended to return each year to the same grove to harvest the ripe pods. The Quechans and their neighbors used other wild plants also and an extensive list appears elsewhere (Castetter and Bell 1951:187–88).

SETTLEMENT PATTERNS

The Quechans recognized themselves as a single tribe, but the people were geographically separated into a number of settlements scattered north and south of the confluence along the Colorado, and eastward along the Gila. Strictly speaking, these settlements were not villages in that their arrangement, composition, and location shifted from year to year, and even from season to season within the year. The large families forming the basic units of the settlements dispersed to their farmlands on the river bottoms during the planting and growing seasons, then clustered together on high ground, away from the flooded area, during the winter and spring (Bee

1963:209). The geographical arrangement of the settlements was thus closely geared to the condition of the rivers and the techniques of bottomland horticulture. The threat of enemy attack may also have been a factor, particularly in the eighteenth and nineteenth centuries. Like the Mohaves, the Quechans may have launched their most massive war expeditions after the annual harvests (Fathauer 1954:98; Stewart 1947), when a settlement's family units were less dispersed and therefore probably less vulnerable to surprise counterattacks by the enemy. In recalling patterns of nineteenth century warfare, old Quechans in the 1930s described their targets as enemy settlements rather than isolated families, possibly indicating that the nature of warfare, like that of the settlements, depended in part on agricultural cycles and—ultimately—on the river itself.

Each settlement contained several hundred people. The largest, called Xuksíl^{y} by the Quechans, was located at the base of Pilot Knob and numbered over 800 individuals, according to Spanish estimates of 1774 (Forde 1931:101). Members of the same settlement considered themselves related and, in spite of their ultimate tribal allegiance, felt their own settlement group was somehow superior to the others (Bee 1963:209).

The families in the settlements were what anthropologists call composite families, consisting not only of parents and their children, but also grandparents, some aunts or uncles and their children, and perhaps more distant relatives who had moved in. This composite family made up the basic cooperative group for farming, although it was not uncommon for several such families to pool their labor for the more demanding agricultural tasks of clearing brush, weeding, and harvesting (Castetter and Bell 1951:140). The families lived in small brush shelters while farming the bottomlands, then moved into either brush shelters or larger and more substantial earth-covered houses on high ground to wait out the winters (Forde 1931:120).

The Quechans believed it was most proper for young brides to move in with their husband's family group, but a young couple was usually free to decide which set of in-laws—his or hers—they wanted to live and work with. Yet it was clear that a couple was to move into a composite family; unlike modern Anglos, newlyweds apparently were not anxious to go off alone or have a place to themselves. Regardless of a Quechan couple's wishes, they probably would not have been wise to go off on their own, for the composite family made a perfect grouping for the techniques of bottomland farming. It was a cooperative work force that was large enough to spread the heavy labor among a number of individuals, yet small enough to minimize squabbles over personal versus family economic interests. Leaving open the issue of whose relatives a newly married couple would live with gave the composite family flexibility in incorporating new workers for the labor force.

The patterns of land ownership were not clear. One report (Forde 1931:114–15) describes farm plots as being individually owned by males. But given the importance of the composite family in the farming operation, this seems odd. It seems even more odd in view of the fact that when a man died, the land that he and others farmed was not passed on to heirs but was abandoned by the entire composite family. They sought replacement plots among bottomlands not being utilized by others, leaving their original holdings for the future use of others who were not close kinsmen. It is perhaps safest to conclude that "land ownership was little formalized" (Castetter and Bell 1951:144). This conclusion, together with the practice of abandoning plots at the death of family members, conveys an important implication: that during the traditional period, land was not particularly scarce, even though occasional interfamily brawls erupted over the precise locations of family plots when floodwaters washed away boundary markers (Forde 1931:114–15). But whatever the traditional conditions may have been, in time and under the influence of Anglos, land for the Quechans became a vital and critically short economic resource.

During the traditional period, the inheritance of other kinds of property probably did not cause conflict either, because such inheritance was practically nonexistent. All possessions of the deceased (including the family shelter) were either destroyed or given away to nonrelatives, in the family's attempt to obliterate painful reminders of their former member. Often this left the survivors in destitution, to be provided for by friends and settlement leaders until they could recoup their material losses.

KINSHIP GROUPS

Besides the composite family, the Quechans recognized a series of clans, whose membership was inherited through males. What roles these groups played in traditional life are not entirely clear. The clan name was borne only by females, but all members felt themselves to be associated with one or more namesakes or totems (e.g., corn, frog, red mud, red ant, moon, coyote, rattlesnake). It is certain that the clans regulated marriage, in that two persons belonging to the same clan were forbidden to marry. They may also have been ranked in order of prestige; in the 1960s people still recalled *xavcá·c kʷacán* as the "leading" clan or the "real Quechans" (Forde 1931:142). And there is a suggestion that some of the clans operated as special units during mourning ceremonies (Bee 1963:217; cf. Forde 1931:145). Clan membership did not necessarily correspond to membership in a settlement, but there was a tendency for one clan to predominate numerically in some of the settlements of the late nineteenth century (see chapter two). This was only to be expected, however, given the fact that residence was ideally with the groom's family and clan affiliation inherited through the male line.

Some clan names were either alien or made reference to alien groups in the Quechan language; others were shared with groups such as the Mohaves, Maricopas, and Diegueños (Forde 1931:142–43). However, if the anthropological theory of the emergence of tribal groups in the region is correct, it would support the conclusion that Quechan clans were at one time small, relatively autonomous, local groups that merged into a larger tribal group at some cost to their autonomy and importance. The mystery of the whys and whats of the Quechan clans continues, tantalizingly. Modern Quechans assert that "they're just names." Yet at one time they were certainly more than that.

THE TRIBE

Quechan families and settlements merged into a tribal grouping in large-scale war expeditions against neighboring tribes, when what mattered were one's skill in the use of a particular weapon, one's sex, and the fact that one could claim to be "a Quechan." Settlement or clan affiliations, for purposes of warfare, were not relevant. Settlements also came together for annual tribal harvest celebrations of feasting and visiting, each family contributing food or labor to the common enterprise. And almost every year there were tribal mourning ceremonies, in which the participants' activities were delegated according to sex and clan membership (Forde 1931:221ff.; Bee 1963:217). The tribe was not a continually obvious grouping. It formed and dispersed according to the activities of its members, just as the Cheyenne and Teton tribes farther to the east were, for much of the year, scattered into groups of roving hunters that came together only in the summer for large ceremonies and massive bison hunts, or when confronted by a large and well-armed adversary such as the United States Cavalry.

MATERIAL CULTURE

Perhaps because property was not inherited, the early Quechans were not concerned with the accumulation of material items beyond the immediate needs of the family or demands of ritual.

Settlement headmen usually had control of surplus food that could be handed out to needy persons or consumed during ceremonies. This surplus was accumulated through contributions of settlement families, who donated a portion of their harvest to the common larder. However, there were no marked gradations of material wealth among the families; not only did the mourning practices prevent such accumulation, but there was also tremendous popular sentiment against hoarding wealth when others were destitute (Forde 1931:137).

Nor were the Quechan people particularly preoccupied with technological or decorative elaboration beyond the demands of utility, although at least one Anglo was impressed with the painted geometric designs on late nineteenth century pottery (Trippel 1889:575–76). Their arrows, propelled from simple unbacked bows, did not have much penetrating power—especially when used (as they frequently were) without points. Stout wooden staffs served as digging sticks or, when cut in longer lengths, as effective weapons in close combat.

Neither males nor females needed much clothing in the desert environment. Women wore two-piece aprons made of the inner bark of willow. Men often wore nothing. When the weather cooled, the people would carry glowing firebrands close to their bodies (Forbes 1965:49) or wrap themselves in rabbit-skin robes and blankets obtained from the Hopis through trade. Males were veritable dandies in arranging their long hair. Either they rolled it into thin, pencil-like rolls treated with mesquite sap, or they plastered it with reddish mud—not only decorative, but effective in discouraging the growth and spread of insect pests. Both sexes were proud of their long hair and, as an act of profound sacrifice, shortened it only when mourning the loss of a loved one. Both sexes were fond of painting their faces with yellow, red, white, black, or green pigment (Trippel 1889:565), and men daubed light pigment over their entire body for warfare. Male adolescents endured the pain of having their nasal septums pierced, then, as adults, used the perforation (as well as holes punched in the tissue of the ears) for attaching bits of decorative shell or stones. Both sexes also wore facial tatoos, either on the forehead or in the form of vertical lines descending from the corners of the mouth. For most of the year, the Quechans had no need for substantial housing; their brush shelters served adequately in the warm temperatures and low precipitation of the desert climate. The relatively few earth-covered lodges served as more than adequate winter quarters.

Clearly, in this state of fairly low food-production anxiety, the Quechans focused on other than material aspects in their traditional way of life.

LEADERSHIP

Spanish and early Anglo records pertaining to the Quechans consistently mention two sorts of tribal leadership positions, one *(kʷaxóṭ)* dealing with civil affairs, the other *(kʷanamí·)* dealing with tribal warfare. Each settlement group also selected one or more male members to serve as local headmen (*paˀi·pá· taˀaxán*—"a real man") (Forde 1931:139). The Quechans' own conceptions of tribal leaders may not have been so unambiguous. Abraham Halpern's informants gave him the impression that the *kʷanami·,* while a brave warrior, was not considered a leader in the strict sense, and that the *kʷaxóṭ* was not a civil leader but a man known for his generosity and "superior spirituality" (Halpern, personal communication). This means that leadership at both the settlement and tribal levels was in the hands of the *paˀi·pá· taˀaxán.*

Neither the local headmen nor the tribal leaders commanded their positions by authoritarian might. Their authority was extremely limited by popular support and they were allowed to serve in their positions only as long as they were able to demonstrate competence to do so. Consensus was the rule in deciding on courses of action, both within the settlements and at the tribal level. In making vital decisions, a leader's speaking ability was every important, because the better and more forceful speakers were able to swing consensus in their favor during the hours of deliberation. Even in the 1960s, a leader's effectiveness was reckoned partly on his ability to express himself publicly, using a quiet but rhythmic oratorical style reserved for solemn public declarations in native Quechan.

The primary criterion of good leadership, however, was competence. Competence, the people believed, came from a personal power that was bestowed on some individuals by special types of dreams. A candidate for a leadership position quite literally dreamed his way into office. A group of elderly men first listened to a candidate's own accounts of his dreams, then decided whether or not the man was fit to become a powerful leader. But dreams alone were not enough; their power had to be demonstrated in an individual's behavior. A leader had to make the right kinds of speeches at the proper times, for example, regardless of the contents of his dreams. And he always had to be kind and generous to his people (Forde 1931:137).

Leadership tended to run in a few families; that is, it was usually hereditary—but only when the criterion of competence could be met by the incumbents.

One hot afternoon in 1961, I went to visit an old man who had lived among the Anglos for many years while working as a house painter and movie extra (he had portrayed an Arab and an African, but never an Indian), and who had also served as a policeman on the reservation. We began talking about the special dreams leaders were required to have had in the old days. He seemed to know a good deal about the subject and confided that he had had such dreams as a young man, but that they were always flawed in some way. He recalled one of them:

> It is said that if somebody dreams of a little hill up there [north] by Laguna Dam [on the Colorado], he will wake up with the power to be a great speaker or philosopher. I dreamed I was there once, and I saw a great big coiling road, sort of like a stairway, stretching up to heaven. I started to climb the stairs, but only got about halfway up when I looked back to the ground and saw a bunch of people there, all working some kind of magic tricks with bits of white paper. I wanted to keep climbing, but I also wanted to find out more about what those people were doing down there. So I decided to go back down to them. Later I found out that if I had just kept going up, I would have had the power of a speaker. As it was, I woke up without the power.

The *kʷaxóṭ* was the caretaker of enemy scalps and captives, although he seldom took part in battles once he assumed office (Forde 1931:137). He also had the power to make rain, both for confusing the enemy and for helping plants to grow. And, although he did not participate directly in the planning of tribal cermonies, he always made the best speeches at the ceremonies. "For it was by his speeches that people knew he had great power and was *kʷaxóṭ*" (Patrick Miguel, quoted in Forde 1931:137).

The proper sorts of dreams were also requirements for other special roles in Quechan life—singers, funerary speakers, and curers. Still other individuals predicted the success or failure of proposed undertakings on the basis of their dreams, and dreams provided both good and bad omens of things to come. There were still those in 1974 who refused to abandon their belief in the power of dreams.

WARFARE

The Quechans focused much of their attention and energy on war. War was considered a vital source of the tribe's life stuff, its spiritual power (Forde 1931:161). Their myths and rituals were based on accounts of past battles and reenactments of battle tactics. The planning and execution of most community activities has been characterized as almost nonchalant (cf. Forde 1931:161–2), but warfare was an exception. Preparatory to some of the larger military expeditions, for example, combat units were divided up on the basis of various warrior functions: the first group behind the leader comprised the spear- and club-men; behind them came the archers; next came a few horsemen armed with spears (when horses were available); and, finally, there followed a number of hefty Quechan women armed with stout staffs to finish off the enemy wounded (Bee 1967:16; Forde 1931:167). The war club of the Colorado River peoples was a unique and formidable weapon of heavy wood, pointed at the base of the handle for disemboweling the adversary and rounded on the opposite end into a heavy, sharp-rimmed cylinder for crushing his face. It looked very much like the "potato-masher" hand grenades carried by German soldiers in World Wars I and II.

The Quechans distinguished between two kinds of warfare: the major war party ("going to the enemy") and the small raiding party ("waking the enemy"). The latter was supposed to be a surprise attack, not perhaps so much to kill as to stir up trouble and maybe steal some horses or bring in some captives. Usually these raids were launched by younger men from individual settlements. An old Quechan in 1961 remembered one account of such a raid, told years earlier by his grandfather, a man of considerable strength and prestige:

> One day about twenty-five young people didn't know what to do with themselves. One of them said, "Let's go to Cocopa country" [to the south]. They arrived at a Cocopa settlement early in the morning and found two old couples living in a little hut. The youths awoke the old people and shouted, "You'd better get up—your enemies are here! Sing some songs quickly, before they get you!" Then the youths got together in a line, facing a line of Cocopa warriors. The Cocopa leader was kneeling in front of his men. One of the Quechans broke ranks, ran to the kneeling chief, and hit him in the head with a club. The Cocopas got mad and chased the Quechans back toward their own area. The Quechans ran fast, each man splitting off in a different direction so it wouldn't be so easy for the Cocopas to get them all. My grandfather ran too, and was chased by a Cocopa on a horse. He attempted to kill my grandfather with a club but he missed, and his horse carried him past my grandfather. My grandfather shot him in the back with an arrow. The other Cocopas continued the chase all day. That night my grandfather dug a hole in the bank of the river and covered himself with leaves. The next day he returned home to find that none of the twenty-five Quechans had been lost. My grandfather [laughter]—he always liked to do a lot of mischief!

The larger parties were tribal rather than settlement affairs, launched ostensibly as revenge for Quechan losses suffered earlier.

At times, these encounters were eminently chivalrous, including prearranged appointments for combat, agreement on types of weapons to be used, delayed attacks until both sides had drawn up in battle formation, and a stylized exchange of insults before the battle began (Forde 1931:162 ff.).

Warfare, although probably continual over the years, was not usually costly in lives. Often, one side would disengage itself from the fray if it appeared that too many of its men or women were being lost. There were occasions, however, when the battle dragged on until one side was all but obliterated. The last such clash to the death is said to have occurred in 1857, just after Heintzelman had established a teetering Anglo hegemony in the confluence area; the Quechans were the losers in battle with the Maricopas (Forde 1931:163–64).

The Cocopas and Maricopas (who sometimes allied themselves with the Pimas) were the Quechans' major enemies. The Quechans frequently joined forces with the Mohaves, striking out against tribes to the east of the Colorado, although they were also good friends with some of the Sand Papago groups (Castetter and Bell 1951:58–59).

It is possible that warfare among tribes on the Colorado and Gila rivers increased in scale and intensity during the eighteenth and early nineteenth centuries (Forbes 1965:134). The factors in this escalation seem to have been in part economic: to gain captives for trade to the Spaniards or alien Indian groups in exchange for horses or other goods (Dobyns et al. 1957:48ff.). If this was the case, then the assertion that the river people's warfare was not motivated by economics (Forde 1931:161) must be amended. The Quechans and Mohaves reportedly also joined forces to drive the Halchidomas out of the Colorado River valley north of the confluence, then settled there themselves (Stewart 1947:257; Fathauer 1954:111–112; Forde 1931:103). The Quechans later moved out of this area to lands closer to the confluence. During the same period, however, neither the Mohaves nor the Quechans showed much interest in occupying the lands of their enemies to the east and south. Again, the inference is that population pressure on available farm land was not very heavy at that time.[1]

MOURNING

The commemoration of the dead was as important in the Quechans' traditional way of life as patterned dreaming and warfare. By far the most important mourning ceremony was the *karˀúk,* usually performed when important leaders died or there was an accumulation of deaths of lesser persons, whose families wished to dedicate a ceremony to their memories.

Like the rituals of most societies, the *karʔúk* was a sort of microcosm of the ideal Quechan way of life. It kept alive the memory of how the Quechans were created and reminded them that it was a reenactment of the original *karʔúk,* staged after the death of the creator Kukumat. Corn, one of the staples in the Quechan diet, was the element of ceremonial purification, and women sprinkled it liberally over participants, buildings, and other paraphernalia at intervals in the proceedings. Tasks were assigned on the basis of the ideal but flexible sexual division of labor and also, perhaps, on the basis of clan affiliation. Older men, some of whom had dreamed of their ritual roles (Forde 1931:204), assumed important leadership functions, just as in nonceremonial activities their wisdom was called upon to solve problems, validate dream power, or cure illness. An important element in the *karʔúk* was a sham battle, including the major tactical steps used in a real foray against the enemy.

The *karʔúk* was also, in effect, a second funeral for the deceased, complete with copious wailing (a distinctive, high-pitched series of nasal whimpers having an eerie effect upon those hearing it for the first time), destruction of property and ritual items at the climax of the rite, and the cremation of elaborately dressed images that represented the dead (although the making of images may have been borrowed recently from the Diegueños to the west (Forde 1931:229). The *karʔúk,* like the war party, required more elaborate organization and coordination than the usual Quechan group activities, but, even so, it was more flexible than the ceremonies of groups such as the Pueblos, living farther to the east.

It was upon this traditional milieu that Major Heintzelman and his soldiers imposed themselves when they established their post on Indian Hill—the first representatives of the United States government's Indian policy.

CHAPTER 2

From Garrison to Reservation: 1852-1900

FOR THE FIRST HALF OF THE NINETEENTH CENTURY, the United States government regarded native American Indian tribes as "foreign" nations, free to pursue their way of life without interference from invading Anglos, yet entitled to such freedom only if it didn't interfere with the expansion of America's western frontier. Mass removal of many Indian tribes from their traditional homes in the east to less bountiful territories west of the Mississippi was well under way by 1830. By the mid-1840s, however, it became clear that, even after removal, the Indians were still an obstacle in the Anglo path to progress. What to do?

Extermination of the Indians was one alternative actively and publicly pursued by some Anglos, but the national conscience would not stand for a deliberate and protracted extermination. Most Anglos felt that a far better answer was to push tribal groups onto smaller blocks of land that were even further removed from the major routes of Anglo commerce, and to keep them there by force if necessary. In restitution for seizing large areas of Indian territory, the government agreed to provide the Indian tribes with the means for development or specifically, development into farmers, along the lines of industrious but small-scale Anglo farmers. It was believed that once exposed to Anglo civilization, the Indians would sooner or later abandon tribal ways and adopt the new image. In time, it was rationalized by government policymakers, they would surely be

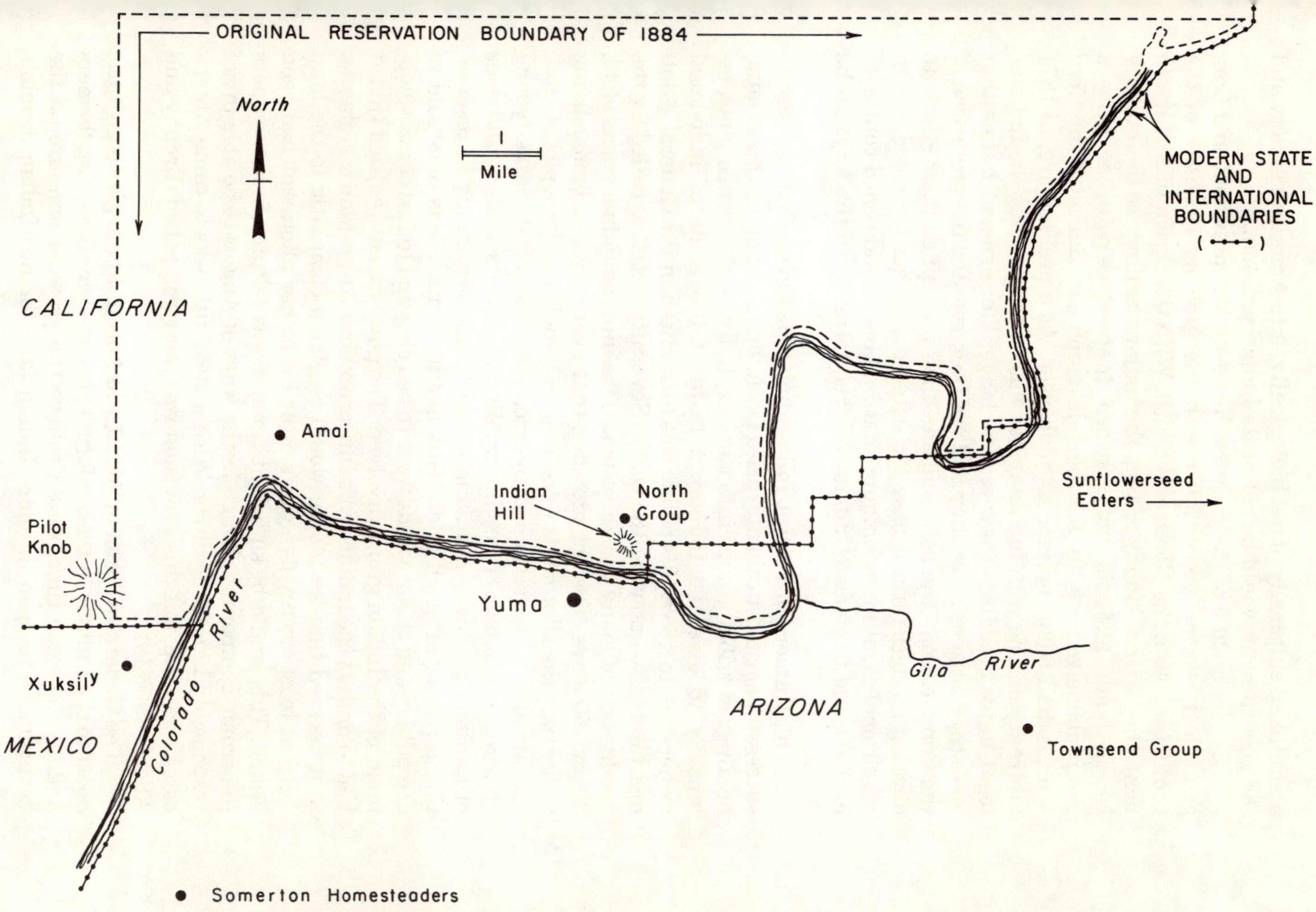

Approximate Location of Quechan Settlements During Non-Agricultural Months, 1880–1900.

assimilated culturally (if not biologically) into American society and the government would be rid of its Indian problem.

By the middle of the century, however, the president and Congress had become preoccupied with the growing intensity of the conflict between the North and South. With the threat of war imminent, they wished simply to keep the Indians confined to their diminishing lands and did not concern themselves with devising a comprehensive program for their development. But after the Civil War, Indian policy became more focused. As a preliminary, in 1871 all treatymaking with Indian tribes was halted, leaving the Indians' legal status muddled. They were no longer "foreigners," but neither were they citizens since they had not been granted the protection of the Constitution. The policymakers then intensified their efforts to develop an agricultural base for tribal economies (or meddle with traditional farming techniques that had been established centuries earlier), and to educate Indian children formally in the ways of the Anglos.

The framers of federal Indian policy believed that the key to successful agricultural enterprise lay in breaking up the mass landholdings of tribal groups into smaller, individually owned plots, ostensibly to give the Indians a taste of the pride of individual ownership. In 1887, this policy was formalized in the General Allotment Act (also known as the Dawes Severalty Act) that called for the subdivision of many Indian reservations into individual tracts of 40, 80, or 160 acres. The act provided that every tribal member living at the time the allotments were assigned would receive a plot of land, the amount to be reckoned by age, sex, and social status (young children and females receiving smaller allotments; male adult heads of families generally receiving larger). Land remaining in reservation territory after all allotments had been made was to be sold to the public, and the proceeds were to be relegated to further development of the Indian group involved. The government realized that it had to protect the Indians from unscrupulous Anglo land merchants, so it decreed that no Indian would receive a clear title to the land until at least twenty-five years after his or her allotment had been issued. This would be sufficient time, if was felt, for Indian owners to become competent enough in the ways of Anglos to be able to act responsibly in land dealings. With a clear title was to come American citizenship, but this provision was later postponed (Brophy and Aberle 1966:19).

The General Allotment Act, it was hoped, would give a gigantic boost to the Indians in their efforts to become small-holding farmers and, at the same time, would relieve the growing pressure on the government to open up more Indian land for non-Indian development. However, the act did not provide for farm implements and other supplies, placing the Indians at a disadvantage at the outset; it did not halt the drastically spiraling loss of Indian land to non-Indian settlers; nor did it make provisions for developing local leadership which would eventually be free from federal manipulation.

The idea of political self-sufficiency was anathema to the notion of Indian assimilation. Not only were the Indians to be shown the ways of Anglos, they were to be divested of the symbols of their former distinctiveness, including language, dress, ritual, and any tribal cohesiveness that might be spurred by encouraging the authority of local Indian leaders. Once subdued (or eliminated), men such as Red Cloud, Sitting Bull, and Chief Joseph were replaced by "tame chiefs"—appointed by Anglo administrators and useful to government agents as advisors and executors of policy, but seldom influential in formulating policy.

During Grant's administration in the 1870s, the responsibility for teaching Indian children was turned over to various Christian groups, one denomination per reservation. The government furnished the school buildings and supplies, and the religious aggregates provided teachers from the ranks of their missionaries. Ignoring the principle of separating church and state, the authorities made Christian dogma a regular part of the school curricula (Spicer 1962:437). It was felt, apparently, that a strong dose of Anglo religion would speed up the general process of Indian assimilation.

The goal of Indian assimilation was to assimilate Indian individuals, divested of tribal identity. The federal programs for economic development were clearly based on Anglo notions of private enterprise and private ownership; and the educational programs, by insulating young children from the effects of prolonged contact with their families, further abetted the push for anglicization of the Indian individual. The policy was overtly couched in humanitarian terms, but, in practice, the humanitarianism was at best narrow-minded and biased; at worst, it was a masquerade, performed to justify continuing Anglo land grabs and neutralize the ability of the Indians to resist.

HEINTZELMAN'S HEGEMONY

Major Heintzelman had trouble reestablishing his influence in the confluence area after his forced withdrawal in 1851. The Quechans were launching intermittent attacks on Anglo civilians as well as troops, while continuing their running conflicts with the Cocopas and enemies to the east, all of which made the area very unsettled in 1851–2 (Forbes 1965:323 ff.). But there was no major flood in 1851 and, as a result, the Quechan harvest was meager. Heintzelman shrewdly decided to add to the effects already wrought by nature. In 1852, he dispatched a series of patrols into the scattered Quechan settlements with orders to burn what crops there were, destroy shelters, and otherwise make it difficult for the Indians to build up resources for resistance. By the end of 1852, the Quechans were in no condition to challenge Anglo control of the area. There is no clear evidence, however, that the hostilities were concluded by a formal treaty, nor even that an understanding was reached concerning Quechan land cessions.[1]

After gaining the upper hand over the Quechans, one of Heintzelman's first acts was to meddle in their internal politics. Two principal Quechan leaders during the hostilities were Santiago, whom Heintzelman thought to be both a civil chief and "chief priest" (i.e., a *kʷaxóṭ*), and Cavallo en Pelo, who was identified as a "war chief" (*kʷanamí·*). The major wrote to his superiors in 1853:

> I deposed them for commencing the war, and directed the nation to choose a principal chief. They chose Macedon, to whom I gave a writing to that effect. (Macedon was, however, killed shortly thereafter in a fight with some Cocopas.) He was an excellent man, and a good friend to the Americans. No one has been appointed in his place. They are now busy planting; when that is over, I will try again to get at their polity [Heintzelman 1857:46].

He later certified a man named Pasqual as the principal tribal chief, although there were reportedly several other men who also wanted the title and raised a "violent opposition" when Pasqual was appointed (Trippel 1889:567). By his action, Heintzelman drastically revised the Quechan political process. From then on, whether or not a seeker of tribal chieftaincy met the Quechans' traditional criteria of dream power and competence was beside the point; his ability to stay in office was determined by the impression he made upon representatives of the American government.

The military regime at Fort Yuma seemed content merely to insure that the Indians kept the peace. Between 1852 and 1884, there was no mention of any plans for Quechan development. The government had established a reservation for the Mohaves and other river tribes in 1865, but the Quechans lived well to the south of it and refused to move into its confines (Department of Interior 1874:289). They remained at Fort Yuma and adapted themselves to the presence of the garrison and the growth of a small town nearby. Some, for example, came regularly to the fort to beg or pilfer from the troops; some worked as woodcutters for companies that fueled the growing fleet of riverboats plying up and down the Colorado. But for the most part, the Indians continued to live according to their traditional patterns.

The civilian town began inauspiciously on the south bank of the Colorado, directly opposite the fort. Presumptuously dubbed Colorado City, it consisted in 1857–8 of "but a few straggling buildings, the principal of which [were] a store, blacksmith's shop, and tavern" (Ives 1861:43). It stood squarely on the southern immigration route into California, however, and was thus destined for bigger and better things—but not before being washed downstream by a major flood in 1862. A new town, rechristened Arizona City, was built in its place shortly thereafter. As early as 1858, a Butterfield stage route ran through the town and westward into California. By 1873, five river steamers carried goods from the mouth of the Colorado up to Arizona City and farther north, and Arizona City, boasting a population of 1300, "chiefly Mexicans" (Lauderdale and Rose 1875:557–8), became the major point of debarkation for freight and passengers traveling the sea route from San Francisco to the Colorado River. Two years later, the name was changed again and Arizona City became Yuma, Arizona Territory, and was a major stop on the southern route of the new east-west railroad (Castetter and Bell 1951:4).

The Quechans resisted none of these developments. On the contrary, more and more of them were attracted to the growing town for low-paying jobs as barroom janitors, steamer deckhands, and woodchoppers. In fact, by 1883, their behavior had become so docile that the government decided a military detachment at Fort Yuma, to ensure the safety of Anglo townspeople and the river crossing into California, was no longer necessary.

On the other hand, the Quechans had neither moved nor died off but were still a presence to be reckoned with. They had become something of an embarrassment to the Anglo gentility—such as it was in Yuma at that time—and there was concern about their morality (particularly their dress—or lack of it), gambling, prostitution, and panhandling. In addition, they still controlled a large amount of rich river bottomland. Yuma's settlers and railroad interests, wishing to increase the town's commercial importance, most likely pressured the government to reduce the Indians' holdings. When disbanding the garrison became imminent in 1883, the government, by executive order (6 July 1883), finally set aside land on the east side of the Colorado for a reservation for the Quechans. The Indians were unhappy with the location and asked the superintendent of the Colorado River Agency to intercede with the president to have the reservation plotted on the west side of the river, extending north and west from Fort Yuma (*Arizona Sentinel* 1 March 1884). The government was agreeable and issued another executive order on 8 March 1884 to establish the reservation on the California side of the river. The reservation covered a large tract of land—over 45,000 acres—and included a broad band of fertile land along its eastern and southern borders, even though much of its interior soil was alkaline. The garrison was disbanded that same year, and administrative responsibility for the Quechans was transferred from the military to the Office of Indian Affairs in Washington. The stage was thus set for some marked changes in the settlement patterns and relative cultural autonomy the Quechans had maintained for so long. The reservation was to become their only rightful domain as far as the government was concerned; Anglo officials even tried to induce members of outlying settlements to resettle within the new limits.

Administrative problems arose almost immediately. Local jurisdiction over the Quechans was first assigned to the agent of the Colorado River Reservation, some ninety miles to the north. In 1884, he reported that it was difficult to administer to the Quechans because of their distance from his headquarters, so he recommended that a subagency be established at Fort Yuma (Department of Interior 1884:5). But instead of accepting his proposal, the federal government transferred responsibility for the Quechans from the Colorado River Agency to the Mission Agency in Colton, California—even farther from the confluence area (Department of Interior 1888:10).

The government did, however, establish a boarding school in 1886 in Fort Yuma's vacated buildings and awarded the contract for school staffing and administration to the Catholic church. Although it was not technically a subagency, the school performed many of the same duties. The first school superintendent was a nun named Mary O'Neil (Sister Ambrosia), who was designated as disbursing agent for the Quechans. This gave her responsibilities and authority that far transcended her narrow religious and educational concerns.

The school offered the children the three "Rs," as well as vocational training (shoemaking, tinsmithing, and carpentry for boys; washing, ironing, sewing, and cooking for girls), and Catholic catechism. No Anglo farming skills were taught, because the superintendent felt the effort would be wasted without some man-made irrigation system on the reservation to make farming a more reliable enterprise. As in other government schools, students were discouraged from speaking their native tongue and taught to use English. Boys had their hair cut short and were outfitted in uniforms of caps, light shirts, and knickers. Girls wore long "Mother Hubbard" dresses, characteristic of Anglo fashions of the period.

The first reactions of the Quechans to this new experience were not recorded, but it is evident that they soon objected to the school's pervasive influence. For one thing, the school routine required children to be away from family groups for long periods, a situation not at all to the liking of the children or their parents. (One old woman was able to recall, in the 1960s, her intense homesickness when, as a young student at the Fort Yuma school, she watched the activities of her family from the confines of the school grounds on top of Indian Hill.) For another, the superintendent put the pupils to work at cleaning and refurbishing the old fort's buildings. Tribal leaders, Mary O'Neil reported (Department of Interior 1888:250), did not want the students to do such work, but wanted them to spend more time in the classroom instead. Their reasons were not recorded, but it is likely that they felt the students were being exploited in cheap and involuntary labor. And, finally, Quechan parents soon began hearing reports of brutal punishments being inflicted on disobedient children by the school's staff. Truancy was a means of avoiding these unpleasantries and, before long, Superintendent O'Neil sent the first of a series of requests to the commissioner of Indian Affairs for authority to appoint Indian police to "see that the children of school age be kept out of town and in regular attendance at the school" (Department of Interior 1889:349).

The school also brought youngsters from the several different settlements together for extended periods of face-to-face contact. Earlier interaction had been limited to occasional visits to relatives in other settlements or tribal mourning and harvest ceremonies. The commingling at the school created close intersettlement friendships among the children and sometimes more intimate associations that eventually led to marriage. "That school kind of mixed us [the several settlements] up," a former student said. She also recalled that several families in her settlement had moved closer to Indian Hill after the school opened, to be near their children and the town (Bee 1963:211).

Thus, in 1886, there were three sources of pressure for an amalgamation of the formerly separate and somewhat chauvinistic Quechan settlements: the reservation and corresponding conviction of government administrators that it represented the total extent of Quechan territory; the growing town which offered employment and also not-so-gainful but pleasurable activities; and, finally, the boarding school with its mandatory attendance of children from all settlements.

It is necessary to take a closer look at the settlements as they existed around 1884, because much of what was to happen in the following years reflected back to contacts between and within these earlier groups.

There were six distinguishable settlements in the 1880s, despite considerable shifting both in location and composition over the years. The first was that of the "north dwellers," or *matxáḷʸ cadóm.* Its members lived within the boundaries of the reservation, scattered in family groups along the river banks during the agricultural season and clustered in the vicinity of Indian Hill at other times. It was the settlement occupied by the tribal chief, Pasqual, in the 1880s. The families living closest to Indian Hill were called the "coffee drinkers" by others in the settlement, because they spurned the traditional Quechan herbal tea in favor of the white man's coffee and allegedly were more concerned with activities in Yuma than traditional Quechen pursuits. One old Quechan offered a glimpse of the variety of relatives living in her family group within this settlement; the family was collectively known as the Sahentes, an anglicization of the Spanish word for sergeant (*sargento*). The woman lived with her parents, two of her siblings, her father's grandfather, her mother's father and mother, two female cousins of her mother's father, and her mother's mother's brother with his wife and four small children. Like the members of all settlements, these sixteen people lived in temporary shelters near the banks of the river when planting and harvesting the crops, then moved to higher and drier ground (farther west in this family's case) when the river flooded (Bee 1963:209). The Sahentes' land was bounded by that of other families in the settlement, and the farms of these north dwellers extended for some seven miles along the west bank of the river.

Another large settlement was Xuksílʸ, located south of Pilot Knob and across the international boundary near the modern village of Algodones, Mexico. The name in Quechan refers to a kind of hard, sandy hill. Early in the 1880s, it was under the leadership of a man known as Captain Cleveland (*capitán* being the title conferred on settlement headmen, [*paˀi·pá· taˀaxán*] by the Spaniards and retained by the Quechans into the Anglo period). The inhabitants of Xuksílʸ were known as the "south dwellers," *kavé·ḷʸ cadóm*. This settlement was to become a source of frustration for school superintendents who were anxious to impose the benefits of Anglo civilization upon as many Quechans as possible.

The members of a third settlement, the "Somerton homesteaders," were also known as *kavé·ḷʸ cadóm* to other Quechans and were said to the be related to the people of Xuksílʸ (Bee 1963:209). They had split from the larger group as early as 1872 and had moved to an area about two and a half miles north of the modern town of Somerton, Arizona (T. F. Wilson to Fort Yuma Agent, 15 January 1904). In the 1880s, the group included about forty families under *Ametta coup,* known as Captain Thomas to the Anglos. These families did in fact become homesteaders, which is both interesting and significant in view of later government schemes of development.

A fourth settlement was made up of immigrants from the area of Blythe, California, who had been forced to move southward because of increasing Anglo pressure in the Blythe area. Shortly before leaving Blythe, the group had included about fifty families, under the leadership of Captain *Akes ha ar* (Miguel 1951:3).[2] In the later 1880s and early 1890s, they moved to a western site on the reservation and occupied a portion of the elevated mesa above the floodplain. Their new domicile was called Amai (high), probably because of its height above the bottomlands, but the people themselves retained the name "Blythe group."

The "Townsend group," another settlement, lay south of the Gila River, some six and a half miles east and south of Indian Hill, near an old stagecoach station (and in the 1960s a small store) known as Gila Center, Arizona. About twenty families were living there in 1887, under the leadership of *Amil lav oau* (or Captain José).

And finally, the "sunflowerseed eaters" made up a settlement that, like Xuksíl^y and the north dwellers, showed considerable vitality and stability over a period of time. It was probably the "San Dionisio" visited by Kino, the Jesuit missionary, in 1700 (Forbes 1965:120), and the "water-reed place" mentioned by others (Forde 1931:101).[3] Patrick Miguel, a gifted Quechan and one of the principal figures in the reservation turbulence of the 1950s and 1960s, wrote in 1951 that water reed place

> . . . was a lake, and old bed of the Colorado, northeast of Yuma and on the east side of the river. This is the home place of a band of Quechan who were nicknamed "Aket ke ma'ts" (Sunflower eaters) . . .

In 1966, other Quechans supported Miguel's statement by describing a small, flat-topped hill known as Squaw Peak, about fifteen miles northeast of Indian Hill on the east side of the river, where, they said, the sunflowerseed eaters once lived and where other Quechans gathered squawberries. In the 1880s, this settlement included about fifteen families under *Hessee kwa no kum,* or Captain Chino.

As intimated earlier, the fact that settlement residents considered themselves members of the Quechan tribe did not necessarily mean that they or their leaders got along well with each other. Pasqual's chieftaincy was challenged by others, presumably from other settlements. And there was the chauvinism that persisted even in the 1960s. "My people, *matxál^y cadóm*—we acted like we were so much better than the other people in a way," one old woman recalled. "People from *kavé·l^y cadóm*—they're friendly, but they're so loud. I guess they can't help it. They were all one family" (Bee 1963:209). She meant by her last comment that the members of a settlement had tended to marry each other rather than seek mates from other settlements. This in-marriage was reported by others also (e.g., Trippel 1889:573).

Two social-structural conditions could have resulted from the Anglos' increased intervention in the confluence area. The settlements could have formed a united front of tribal resistance by suppressing their tendency toward local chauvinism and intersettlement competition. This tactic would have been aided in time by the mingling of school children from different settlements. Or, the tribe could have split into feuding parts along the more obvious social and geographical cleavages, and, ultimately, into smaller arenas for individual antagonisms. When the school first opened, it appeared that tribal harmony would prevail, but such harmony did not last very long.

THE DEATH OF PASQUAL

In 1887, Pasqual, the tribal chief appointed by Heintzelman, died. During his last years, there were indications that he had assumed a more authoritarian role than was characteristic of the leaders in traditional life, a change apparently due to contact with the Anglos. He ordered drunks to be flogged publicly and, when confronted with a Quechan accused of burglary, "the disgusted chief disowned the criminal for disgracing the tribe and sent back word that he would be delighted if they 'would throw the d——d thief into the river!' " (Trippel 1889:567). Such behavior, if accurately reported, must have won him the respect of the moralistic Anglo townspeople.

Whether Pasqual would have enjoyed such a long tenure as chief if he had not received the written support of the military authorities and affirmation of local Anglos is an open question. That is, the tribe might not have allowed Pasqual to get away with such high-handed measures if the Anglo military forces and townspeople had not been present to support his behavior. However, over the years of contact with the military, many Quechans had come to regard official papers as a validation of leadership. So, while traditional leadership criteria were perhaps not entirely cast aside, the new Anglo criteria were certainly influencing the Indians in the late nineteenth century and were to become even more crucial in ensuing decades.

According to some Quechans, Pasqual's behavior as leader did not mean that he had sold out to the Anglo authorities, but that he recognized a need to learn their ways so as to fight further encroachment (Halpern, personal communication); certainly the traditional Quechan patterns of defense were no longer possible. The behavior of Pasqual's ally and successor suggests that using Anglo gambits to preserve Quechan autonomy had become the favored strategy.

The old chief died on the night of 9 May 1887, during the final stages of a measles epidemic that had taken the lives of nearly a hundred of his people (*Arizona Sentinel* 14 May 1887). Mary O'Neil, the new school superintendent, had been on the reservation only a few months, busily organizing the school, rounding up Indian children, and attempting to foster some sort of consistent relationship between the Quechans and the government. Then this new crisis arose. She wrote to the commissioner (12 May 1887):

> Sometime before his [Pasqual's] death he designated 'Captain' Miguel as his successor. Miguel's assumption of the authority, however, met with the decided opposition of the older and less progressive element of the tribe. This element is bitterly antagonistic to education and anything else tending towards civilization and progress. They are wedded to the ways of their ancestors, which is tantamount to perpetual poverty, ignorance, starvation, and depradation.

Miguel was formerly a captain at Xuksíl^{y}, but he moved his family to the settlement of the north dwellers after being designated by Pasqual as the next chief.

Unsure of her own authority, Superintendent O'Neil proposed that the government authorize an army general to select a successor to Pasqual, noting that, "It would be no infringement of Indian individual or political rights as they *prefer* that the Government should settle their disputes and appoint their chief" (italics added). Then, ten days later, she seemed more sure of her position and telegraphed the commissioner: "I recommend Miguel. Think he would make the best chief." Miguel was duly appointed the official successor to Chief Pasqual. In the interval, Mary O'Neil had been assured by Miguel that he would aid her in her efforts to make the school a going concern.

Opposition to Miguel, attributed by the school superintendent to the "older and less progressive element of the tribe," came initially from Captain José, headman of the Townsend group settlement just south of the Gila River, and his supporters. There is no evidence that José and his group were either older or less progressive than Miguel. In fact, they had wisely enlisted an Anglo Wells Fargo agent, O. F. Townsend, to aid them in their resistance. In

October 1888, Townsend sent a petition to the commissioner of Indian Affairs to seek the removal of Miguel and appointment of Captain José as tribal chief. Neither the basis for José's claim nor the reasons for Townsend's interest in it are clear. But trouble between Miguel's supporters and the Townsend group continued.

One Anglo writer, E. J. Trippel, had an opportunity to gather firsthand reports on how Miguel operated as tribal chief. Miguel came up for reelection annually, Trippel wrote, "at the annual council of prominent men"; but he could hold office "only at the pleasure of the tribe and until he gives dissatisfaction" (1889:568). He was aided by a subchief, a sheriff, and a three-man judiciary. The subchief acted as an advisor to Miguel, conferring with him on "all important questions." The sheriff "usually enforces the sentences [of the judges] upon offenders and takes charge of their persons previous to trial."

Trippel then described the judicial process (1889:570):

> [The judiciary's] deliberations are held in a large shed especially devoted to their uses. When in session they squat upon the ground at one end of the structure, the witnesses and spectators grouping in convenient positions around them.
>
> So far as can be ascertained, the trials are limited to murder, theft, and drunkenness, all of which are punished with swiftness and extreme severity. Murder is punished with death by the club, arrow, or gun, at the hands of the sheriff; theft, by flogging with a blacksnake whip,—twelve lashes for the first, fifteen for the second, and twenty-five for the third offense. On conviction, the culprit is stripped, and his arms drawn high above the head and fastened to a tree. The sheriff then administers the castigation in the presence of a jeering crowd that congregates to witness the shame of the misdemeant. . . . For each glass of intoxicating liquor drunk, the drunkard receives three lashes for the first offense, which is increased for every subsequent dereliction.
>
> When brought before the chief by the district police [Anglos?], the accused is turned over to the judges, who examine the witnesses at their pleasure. He is never suffered to testify in his own behalf, but is sometimes allowed to question his accusers, and, upon their evidence alone, is his conviction or release determined. Differently from us, the prisoner is considered guilty until proven innocent, and so, as a logical consequence, his chances to escape punishment are exceedingly slim, he being unable to show mitigating circumstances through his personal testimony.

Anthropologist Daryll Forde, who visited the Quechans in 1928, was unable to find any material that would substantiate Trippel's account of leadership in the 1880s, noting that "the alleged titles are unknown at the present time, and the whole scheme is foreign to the native attitude toward government" (1931:140). Yet, on 23 November 1892, Chief Miguel himself sent a petition to President Cleveland that listed tribal offices similar to Trippel's, including a chief, two captains, three constables, two judges, and an interpreter. Thus, Forde's challenge may be warranted for the period prior to the 1850s, but the "scheme" was obviously not foreign to the Quechans after some thirty years of increasing Anglo influence.

From the advent of the Spanish and continuing through American military leadership into the early reservation period, non-Indian officials insisted on instituting a vertical authority structure among their wards—that is, on creating a line of influence by vesting authority in a single chief and, through him, exerting influence on the tribal mass (cf. Ortiz 1962:8; Shepardson 1963:45). By increasing the apparent authority of tribal chiefs and making them and their advisors responsible, in part, for maintaining discipline among their people, government representatives were relieved of some of the burden and expense of their own responsibility; thus, it was convenient for these representatives to support a local chief who was supportive of government policy. Although Trippel's account hints that the older ideal of rule by consensus still persisted (even if it was not followed in actual practice), Miguel was actually "giving dissatisfaction" to some portions of the tribe from the time of his first appointment, once again indicating that government authority, rather than traditional ideals or approval from the Quechans themselves, was ultimately what kept a man in office. (The Indians also realized this, as Mary O'Neil pointed out, assuming her observations were accurate; we cannot know if the Indians who preferred "that the government should settle their disputes and appoint their chief" represented all parties in the issue.) It was therefore to be expected that Pasqual would deviate from the traditional leader's behavior, and that his successor, Miguel, would deviate still further if he wished to remain in the position of tribal chief for very long.

For the Indians, Mary O'Neil was the United States government—on the reservation. Her written orders were laws to be obeyed and her approval was necessary for any legitimate development or political activity the Quechans wished to undertake. She, not Miguel, was the locus of administrative power. She was supported in her position by her immediate superior, the Indian agent at the Colton Agency, and by the vast bureaucratic structure at higher echelons. That is, she followed Anglo instructions, not Miguel's. And when there was a problem she could not solve readily, she called on the agent for help—not Miguel. She could, and did, control the amount and type of

Anglo intrusion into the Quechan community (e.g., Anglo merchants who set up small general stores on the school grounds). She also controlled to some extent the amount and kinds of exposure to Anglo ways the Quechan children received. And she, not Miguel, handled the distribution of whatever material benefits came to the tribe as a result of government munificence. All she needed to make this power even more pervasive was a handy group of armed men who would serve as a coercive force when her authority was challenged; and this was to come very shortly.

Miguel was forced to choose a course of personal action in a situation in which his predecessor, Pasqual, had never really been involved. The military detachment that represented government authority during most of Pasqual's chieftaincy had not interfered in Quechan life except to maintain law and order. Miguel, on the other hand, was subjected to pressure by military and other authorities from the day he was appointed tribal chief. He soon found it difficult to satisfy both his Quechan supporters and the Anglo officials.

The school year that began in September 1887 went well, as far as the superintendent was concerned. Eighteen eighty-eight, however, was another disastrous year for the Quechans' crops; there was no flooding that spring and the harvest was very poor. The agent at Colton requisitioned $3,000 worth of provisions for the tribe, to avert a major famine (Department of Interior 1888:11; 1890:16), but apparently the Quechans living in Captain José's settlement in Arizona did not share in the rations distribution. In September 1888, O'Neil sent a letter to the commissioner reporting that only twenty-four students had appeared at the school. She singled out the Wells Fargo agent, O. F. Townsend, as the source of the problem. He had allegedly advised José's people not to send their children to school, unless the government provided rations for their settlement on the same basis as the others. By their reaction (no rations, no school attendance), these Quechans indicated that they considered the provisions of rations as an obligation of the government, and the government had failed to fulfill this obligation. O'Neil angrily wrote, "This meddlesome interference with the policy of the Government should receive its well deserved rebuke, hence I desire that you [the commissioner] should know the truth. . . ." But Miguel, living on the west side of the river, was not encouraging school attendance either. As the months passed, Miguel became even more adamant in his refusals to assist in the return of absentees.

By the early 1890s, things had really become difficult for Miguel. In 1891, he was implicated in the murder of a shaman (medicine man) who, unfortunately for Miguel, was a member of the settlement headed by his rival, Captain José. There was a trial of the alleged murderers and one of Miguel's sons (as well as one or two other Indians) was found guilty. All were reportedly given life sentences in prison. Miguel himself escaped prosecution on "a technicality" (J. A. Leonard to commissioner, 22 March 1893), but by then he was also receiving stiff opposition from another source: Joe Palma, old Pasqual's son, had become yet another contender for the status of chief.

In November 1892, Miguel and his lieutenants hired an Anglo attorney in Yuma to draft a petition to President Grover Cleveland to protest the "wrongs" in the Fort Yuma school, particularly the severe punishment of children who misbehaved. Miguel still sounded conciliatory, but he was clearly vacillating between the consensual authority pattern of the past and the authoritarian role of the government model of tribal chief:

> I guess I will have to get the children back into school. The Indians on the reservation if they don't like me, can get another man to take my place, when I go wrong, but not now. . . . I can't tell how soon I can get the children back into school, I will have to talk to the people. I will get the children as soon as I can. My Captains will have to talk to their people [Miguel to President, 23 November 1892]

But he was wrong. The government, represented by Mary O'Neil, decided to get another man to take Miguel's place. In February 1893, in response to her pleas, the commissioner sent an ambiguous telegram pointing out that the Indian office was now discouraging the appointment of tribal chiefs, but that she should appoint whomever she felt was best qualified to succeed Miguel. In justifying Miguel's dismissal, O'Neil later reported that,

> imbued with that spirit of pagan savagery that relegates to the field of drudgery the females of the tribe, he [Miguel] bitterly opposed the return after vacation of the larger girls and in every way possible influenced other Indians to keep their children from school [O'Neil in Department of Interior 1893:405].

She had estimated Miguel's following to be 1,000 persons in 1888, as opposed to fewer than 100 for Captain José of the Townsend group (O'Neil in Department of Interior 1888:250). Less than five years later, Miguel's followers had dwindled to some forty people, according to an unofficial estimate (*Arizona Sentinel* 3 June 1893).

In March 1893, the Indian office sent J. A. Leonard, one of its education supervisors, to settle the difficulties at the school. While Leonard insisted that he lacked the authority to appoint a new chief in Miguel's place, the Indians clamored for him to do so, and to give them "a paper" of the formal appointment. The man the group wanted was Pasqual's son, Joe Palma (*Mato qui sam*). Leonard reported to the commissioner (22 March 1893): "I talked with him [Palma] concerning school matters and found he meant to carry out the wishes of the Government." Leonard wrote a letter of support for the new chief, reminding its recipients that Palma had agreed to "use all proper effort to prevent drunkenness and to encourage education and all other civilizing agencies among his people. . . ."

There is no official record of the number of Indians favoring Palma, nor of their particular settlement affiliations. Patrick Miguel, a young adolescent at the time, later recalled that the support came from the Townsend group, living on the Arizona side of the border under Captain José (Miguel, et al. 1937:1). The negotiations were probably held on the school grounds, which were located in the middle of the north dwellers' settlement, the new chief's place of residence. Miguel had been a former headman among the south dwellers at Xuksíl^{y}. Whether Xuksíl^{y} was represented is not known, but it is possible that the conclave was loaded with north dwellers and people from the Townsend group, who were acting partly on the basis of old anti-Xuksíl^{y} antagonisms.

But ex-Chief Miguel, as he was thereafter known, was by no means willing to give up the political battle. Knowing that the government would react adversely to his continued politicking, he turned to his fellow Quechans for support, portraying himself as guardian of their best interests. In a notarized letter to the commissioner on 12 May 1893, he warned

> Now I speak the truth, if the Yuma tribe want some other chief, I say all right. But I say no one but the Yumas can make a chief of the Yumas. If there is trouble come, I want you to know how it is.

The government's response was to continue to discredit Miguel's activities. The new superintendent of the Mission Agency in California wrote

> In coming into office I found ex-Chief Miguel, of the Yumas, selling the young women of his enemies to the whites for immoral purposes. To prevent this I have established a police system which has worked very effectually. The sheriff at Yuma reports that the police are doing good service and that the evil is practically at an end [Department of Interior 1893:125].

J. W. Dorrington, a local newspaper editor in Yuma, also attacked Miguel repeatedly, with perhaps his most sarcastic offering coming on 3 June 1893:

> Oh, no Miguel, retire to your lair, repent, reform, and come forth a new Indian, with a new dress, a re-constructed heart, with no brass buttons, but with a cane if you wish, no "G" string or furs, and then we may listen to your tale of woe. It is not quite time for you to assume to run the general government. Just at present Washington is too well posted on your case, to more than courteously listen to what you have to say. Your assault upon the press, because it publishes the facts in your case, and which could have said much more, and truthfully; your attack upon the management of the school, upon the worthy Mother Superior and her able associates, and your manifestation of a revengeful spirit against others, are entirely uncalled for, and place you in a worse position than you were before. You have picked up this fight, and we throw you down our gauntlet [*Arizona Sentinel*].

Obviously, the citizens of Yuma did not remain aloof from reservation affairs but, on the contrary, were a vociferous source of pressure on Quechan leadership.

In late September 1893, the Indian police suddenly rounded up ex-Chief Miguel's lieutenant, Walter Scott, and put him in the jail on Indian Hill. Some time later (recollections range between several hours and three days), Miguel himself and seven other men were also arrested. Miguel and Scott had been protesting the increasing number of land surveyors and engineers on the reservation over the preceding two years. With the help of a Yuma lawyer, George M. Knight, and one of his Los Angeles associates, C. N. Wilson, the Indians had succeeded in getting the government to stop the suspicious survey work. But rumors of an impending allotment of Quechan lands still spread rapidly.

Why the arrests? The *Arizona Sentinel* (7 October 1893) reported that Miguel and several others were taken into custody when they stormed the jail and fought with the Indian police in an effort to help Scott escape. Miguel's son later wrote that Miguel was arrested at Knight's law office in Yuma, where he had been during the fracas on Indian Hill (Miguel et al. 1937). Years later, Scott himself recalled why he had been arrested, as well as other unpleasant details:

> Mother O'Neil . . . ordered three [Quechan] policemen . . . [to come and tell me] I was under arrest. I said all right. Each had a gun and a policeman's star. They handcuffed me

> and took me before Mother O'Neil the Superintendent. When I appeared before her, Mother O'Neil told me that I was interpreting for those Indians [ex-Chief Miguel et al.] and writing to the Government and I was a trouble-maker. For that reason she told me I was arrested, and ordered the policemen "Take him to jail and lock him up." Next morning she ordered the same policemen to go and bring me out, so they did . . . They bound both of my hands, raised both of my hands to the ceiling and tied them there . . . Poncho Lachero got orders from Mother O'Neil to give me twenty-five lashes with a blacksnake. Poncho Lachero in turn, being the Judge, gave orders to Pelon to give me twenty-five lashes . . . He proceeded to whip me . . . [thirteen] lashes. He got tired and quit. The Judge ordered Omel to go ahead with the whipping. He took the blacksnake and proceeded to whip me. On the fifteenth lash, I pretty near fainted but got back to my senses again. He finished the remainder of the count of twenty-five lashes. Towards the end . . . he was pretty well tired out, so he took the heavy end of the whip and pounded me until he was through. Then the Judge . . . stood me there before a throng of fifty or more, all looking on. The Judge said that tomorrow I would be taken to Los Angeles to the County Jail . . . That same day I was arrested, eight more men were arrested. Four more besides me were whipped the twenty-five lashes, and four were not whipped. We all were sent to jail [Walter Scott signed statement of 7 November 1935].

Their escort was Agent Estudillo of the Colton Agency and two deputy United States marshals. The timing of the arrests may have been coincidental to other rapidly developing issues on the reservation, but it is far more likely that the timing was deliberate, and that the arrests were a device to get Miguel and his associates temporarily off the reservation.

What drastic action in a dispute ostensibly kindled by squabbles over school attendance! Considerably more was certainly involved, but the school issue was by no means irrelevant. The school was not just a school; it was the embodiment of the federal government's presence and control over the Quechan tribe. To fight the school was to fight the government's increasing authority in more than routine educational matters.

In view of these facts, one wonders why Miguel fought to hang onto a chieftaincy that was, in effect, an arm of the school. There were, of course, the baubles of the office, such as cast-off military uniforms. (Miguel's "brass buttons," so offensive to the *Sentinel* editor, were on an old blue army coat.) But there is no evidence that the chief received any significant monetary or other material rewards for his work, even though such rewards may have existed. Higher prestige may have been another incentive. But again, whatever prestige or authority accrued to the office was determined by the government and therefore was subject to hostile challenge by other candidates. Strong men like Miguel undoubtedly relished the eternal and divisive conflict and probably sought it out; weaker men simply sold out to the government and let it protect them from their angry tribal members.

The most obvious, albeit incomplete, explanation of why Miguel and his followers jockeyed for power is that they genuinely feared the effects of continued government encroachment and believed that the right chief, once appointed, would reduce the power of those who appointed him. Their fears of encroachment were justified, for, while Miguel and the superintendent were haggling over school problems, the government was deep in much more drastic plans for the Quechans' development. When Miguel became aware of these plans, he opposed them. He had to be removed.

THE 1893 AGREEMENT

In 1890, Agent Rust of the Mission Agency in Colton recommended to the commissioner that the Fort Yuma Reservation be subdivided into individual farming plots of ten acres each, with provision for water, to give the people some "economic incentives." He lamented the fact that once the children finished school there was nothing for them to do, and also reminded the commissioner that in 1888–89 there was no flood and thus no crops, so the government had had to send $3,000 worth of foodstuffs to the Indians. Private farms with good irrigation systems, he concluded, would keep the Indians gainfully occupied, assure their food production, and give them something to look forward to once they left the school (Department of Interior 1890:16).

During the next three years, 1890 to 1893, pressure mounted on the government to allot Quechan land. Promoters of an ambitious, privately built irrigation system in the area, who had formed the Colorado River Irrigation Company, launched a successful drive to obtain an agreement giving them right-of-way through the reservation; otherwise they would have to contemplate an expensive detour of their canal around Indian land. The promoters were also anxious to see a major influx of Anglo settlers into the area, to boost the proceeds from the irrigation network.

The Quechans, at least, were also anxious to have a canal built and were willing to cede some of their land in return for access to water and the means for improving their harvests. In a petition allegedly signed by 104 of them in July 1893, they asked the president and Congress to give them "part of our lands . . . in severalty and *under a ditch,* and that the proceeds of the sales of the lands of our reservation not appropriated to our use as above be set apart as a fund for our benefit" [italics added]. They clearly recognized the need for irrigation water for their farming ventures to succeed. They also recognized the economic impact of opening up portions of their reservation for eventual Anglo settlement: "If this ditch could be built it would improve our chances of securing labor while building and among settlers after its completion, and also furnish us with water for our land." But the key to their offer was clearly the construction of an irrigation canal.

The petition had an aura of suspicion about it. For one thing, it was notarized (and presumably polished up) by O. F. Townsend, the Wells Fargo agent who had been so active in furthering the cause of the Townsend group against the leadership of Miguel, and who was hardly a disinterested bystander in local reservation affairs. For another, many of the names appearing on the document, according to Quechans in 1974, were not recognizable Quechan names, even though Joe Palma's name and those of several well-known settlement leaders were included. Nonetheless, the petition made a certain amount of economic sense.

Public interest in the prospect of allotment was aroused among Yuma townspeople three months later by the *Sentinel,* whose editor evidently smelled a rat. On 28 October 1893, two weeks after Miguel and his lieutenants had been shipped off to jail, an article in the paper noted rumors in town to the effect that the reservation was to be "cut up" into allotments.

> The statement is also made that they (the Yumas) have petitioned for this change on the condition that they are supplied with water for irrigation. It is rumored on the streets that the big canal company across the river [i.e., on the reservation side] are at the bottom of this matter. When it secured its right-of-way through the reservation, *it was upon the conditions that the company furnish the Yuma Indians with all of the water that was necessary to irrigate their lands.* If the canal is to be built, why should the Indians seek any other sources for water [i.e., why should it be necessary to make a special plea for a clause for irrigation water from sources other than the canal company]? Are these lands to be settled by actual settlers [i.e., Anglos], or is the scheme one that seeks to gobble up these fine valley lands as a speculation. It will not be amiss for our people to look into this matter carefully and see what actually lies at the bottom of it [italics added].

By early December, however, the *Sentinel's* tone had become less suspicious. Three commissioners appointed by the government, accompanied by Agent Estudillo of the Mission Agency, had arrived on the reservation and had held public meetings to introduce the Quechans to the allotment agreement. The agreement was apparently to be based on the general principles of the Dawes Act of 1887 (although this was never made explicit), with special deviations recommended by Rust to allow for local conditions on the Fort Yuma Reservation. There was some debate among the Anglo townspeople about the quantity of land each Indian family should be given, and the *Sentinel* offered some timely suggestions (2 December 1893):

> Should each family be allowed 160 acres, each single Indian 80 and each single woman 40 acres, as in the case of some of the reservations on the coast, there will be but little left for any one to gobble up, if indeed they are permitted to do so. This may not be too much, in the present condition of the land, but in case a canal is ever built through this tract and water sufficiently supplied for irrigation, 10 acres is an abundance for any family, 5 acres for any single Indian, and 2 1/2 acres for any single woman.
>
> Should the Indians be allowed to sell their lands whenever and to whomsoever they please, in five years but few of them will have a garden spot left them. Some restriction should be placed on them in this regard.

The warning in the last paragraph would, in theory, be nulled by the twenty-five-year trust patent provision in the Dawes Act.

The agreement itself was drafted in late November 1893. Briefly, it called for the allotment of five acres of land to each living Quechan, with no additional consideration for family groups or family heads. Individuals (or parents, in the case of children) were to select their lots within sixty days after the arrival of a special agent to organize the allotment process, or they would have parcels chosen for them by the agent. Remaining reservation land would be sold to the Anglo public at the appraised value or higher, and the profit would go "by order of the President for the payment of water rents, building of levees, irrigating ditches, laterals, the erection and repair of buildings, purchase of tools, farming implements and seeds, and for the education and civilization of said Yuma Indians" (1893 Agreement, Art. IV). The government—not the Indians—had decided how the land-sale profits would be spent.

There was no further statement concerning irrigation water, and thus no written guarantee of free irrigation water for the new allotments. Yet, Article IV clearly stated that charges for water would be paid for out of the profits of the excess land sale, implying that, for as long as the money lasted, individual Indian landholders would not be held responsible for water rents.

Irrigation water was crucial to the plan; without irrigation, the land beyond the river's edge would not be productive—no matter how many acres were granted to individual tribesmen. Both the Indians and Anglos realized this. But a man-made irrigation system would be expensive to construct and would require continued maintenance to keep it from clogging up with river silt. The Indians were worried about the maintenance factor and wanted government assurance that they, as individuals, would not be saddled with large water-use bills in the future. (Their worst suspicions were to become cruel fact twenty-five years later, and indeed—if the Indians had only known—were incorporated into the version of the agreement finally ratified by Congress on 15 August 1894 (28 Stat. 332).

The only obtainable record of the Indians' reaction to the agreement during the signing procedure is a document that was prepared in 1937 by Patrick Miguel (ex-Chief Miguel's son) and other tribal members. They gathered together a series of eyewitness accounts, as an argument against the validity of the agreement for determining land-management policy on the reservation (Miguel et al. 1937), which painted a picture of coercion, misunderstanding, and fraud—characteristic of many land cessions in the nineteenth century. Miguel wrote:

> The agreement as it is understood by the Yuma Indians, in 1893 was this: That the U. S. Government would allot the Yuma Indian Reservation in severalty; that each member of the tribe would receive five acres of land; that all expenses for the building of the dam [probably Laguna Dam, completed in 1909] across the Colorado River, the levee and [irrigation] laterals would be borne by the government; that the Yumas would be given *perpetual free water* for use on their lands and that money derived from the sale of part of their reservation would be used to build homes for them; that they would be furnished with all farming implements, seed, and educational facilities [italics added].

Strictly speaking, these conclusions could have been drawn from the wording of the agreement. But the procedures for getting the Indians' approval of the plan were more suspect:

> ". . . the Indians did not come to the table and sign the document of their own volition. They were singled out by the interpreter (Bill Mohave) and as their names were called out they were escorted to the table by one or two Indian policemen. There the Indian was asked his name and he either gave his own or it was given by the interpreter and quite frequently by a policeman and written down.

> There were a few of us in a group which one of the policemen approached us and ordered us to move to the table [sic]. Seeing that we did not move, the policeman reminded us of the feed we had that day at the expense of the government. This policeman took one of the young men to the table and gave his name and it was written down. I was the next man to be ordered to the table by the same policeman and my name given. I did not know that I was signing away the biggest portion of the Indian reservation, in fact I did not know what it was all about." [Statement of Juan Chicken in Miguel et al. 1937.]

And another eyewitness, Jim Chaleco, recalled:

> "The officials ordered that all the Indians be gathered together at the Agency [then school] grounds so that they might all see and hear. According to their order the Indians were herded in from all over, that is, on the campus.
>
> "One of the commissioners stood up and made the announcement to all of the Indians, that the government had sent them to allot the reservation. . . . So the five acres story we knew nothing about.
>
> " 'If any of you refuse to obey the orders, that I am giving, the police will see to it that you do.' After this [commissioner's] announcement some of the Indians began to sneak away and the police went after them and brought them back and some others sneaked away in spite of all of it."

At the end of the day of signing, the commissioners allegedly had not received enough signatures to validate the agreement. So that night, according to the Miguel document, "the commissioners, the agent (Estudillo), the [school] physician (Dr. Heffernan) and the interpreter [Bill Mohave, a Mohave Indian] retreated to the office of Dr. Heffernan and there most of the fictitious names were supplied by Bill Mohave, who boasted at the same time that the deception would never be discovered by the Indians. Hence, the 203 names on the agreement." (Miguel et al. 1937, paraphrasing the statement of John Williams, a Quechan who, at the time of the signing, was a cook at the school.)

Chief Joe Palma himself objected to the small amount of land to be granted to each person, declaring that with a house, yard, barn, corral, outhouse with proper drainage, and so forth, little would be left for farming. According to those who heard his speech, he continued:

> "Then again you may not think it good argument to mention this fact but we Indians have a custom of cremating our dead as near to our homes as possible. If we allotted lands

> we cannot go and cremate our dead in the other man's allotment. It will be necessary for us to have a private cremation grounds and this in time will take up much of the five acres of land" (Statement of George Chino in Miguel et al. 1937).

Well before public meetings on the reservation got under way, ex-Chief Miguel and his supporters had been visited in the Los Angeles County Jail by the commissioners. The *Sentinel* reported (18 November 1893) that the government men went to "learn Miguel's views". Patrick Miguel recalled that the ex-Chief had even been asked to sign the agreement at that time, but had angrily refused (Miguel et al. 1937). Walter Scott, who was in jail with ex-Chief Miguel, agreed with Patrick Miguel:

> Bill Mohave told us these men [the commissioners] wanted our names. Chief Miguel answered saying "I am not going to give my name." Peter Brady [a commissioner] spoke up and said "If you don't give me your name I am going to send all of you to San Quentin." Chief Miguel spoke up again and said, "We are in jail now, you can do as you please with us" [Scott statement 7 November 1935].

The document, then, had been drawn up in final form before any public meetings were held with the Quechans to explain its provisions; the commissioners were on the reservation to sell rather than negotiate.

In spite of the Indians' reactions, the agreement was forwarded to Washington in early December 1893, bearing the marks of 203 Quechans out of an estimated population of 1600 (but this figure seems too high in retrospect). It was approved by Congress in August 1894 (28 Stat. 332), but a special proviso had been added: that the secretary of interior would have the authority to fix the rate of water rents paid by individual Indians. Each adult male would be granted free use of water for one acre of his allotment for ten years, as long as the free water was used for growing crops. After ten years, and for larger tracts, he would be required to pay water rent. No one bothered to inform the Quechans of this proviso until much later, and, in 1969, some of them were still insisting on free water for their fields.

By early 1894, Miguel and his associate, Walter Scott, were back on the reservation. Accounts of the results of their trial in Los Angeles are contradictory. Mary O'Neil, the school superintendent, wrote that they had been found guilty of their crimes (conspiracy and assault) and had served a three-month jail sentence (Department of Interior 1894:366). Quechans themselves (Miguel et al. 1937) believed Miguel had been acquited of the charges and had simply been languishing in jail while waiting for the case to be heard. Walter Scott claimed that there had never been a trial, and that one Quechan had even died in prison from the whipping he received. But the important fact is that Miguel and his supporters were out of the way during the critical period when the agreement was introduced to the Quechans and their "support" was obtained. Had Miguel, Walter Scott, and the others been present at the meetings, it would have been more difficult, if not impossible, to conduct the questionable business.

But now the ex-chief was back and still spoiling for a fight. Patrick Miguel's narrative of the events continues:

> When Miguel returned home [from prison] he called a tribal meeting with reference to the agreement. At the meeting the Indians and Chief Joe Palma denounced the agreement and the Arizona Indians [allegedly part of the Townsend group under Captain José] who helped force it through. For this, Joe Palma was deposed [by the government] after being in power a little over a year.

There is no surviving official correspondence describing Palma's removal as chief; his name simply disappeared from the school reports. There followed a period of about three years during which no official mention was made of anyone serving as tribal chief. It is interesting to note in Patrick Miguel's narrative that Palma's allegiance and sources of support shifted during his brief tenure in office: Palma had originally opposed Miguel and had been at least provisionally acceptable to Captain José's Townsend group. The haggling over the 1893 agreement apparently changed all that.

By mid-1894, the agreement had temporarily faded as a locus of political friction. The actual allotment process was not to begin for several years, probably because of the ponderous functioning of the bureaucracy. There was no rush by Quechans living outside the reservation to move within its boundaries to select their plots. Older issues began to reemerge as sources of conflict, focusing as before on the treatment of children at the school and tribal leadership.

To do battle with the school authorities, Miguel and his group were forced to confront some of their fellow Quechans who, as Indian police appointed by the superintendent, served as protectors of school personnel and policies. The police force had finally been authorized in 1893, following repeated pleas to the commissioner from Superintendent O'Neil. Members of the force were sent by her to fetch truant students from their homes—by force, if necessary. The Quechans looked on the police as misguided tools of the school authorities, who were thus hostile to their own people. The superintendent couldn't have been happier with her new helpers and regarded any attack on the police as an attack on the government. In 1894, she wrote:

> . . . increased attendance is due largely to the active support given by the [Indian agent] . . . in explaining to the adult Indians the advantages of an education, and enforcing his opinion by the aid of a reservation police force, who carry out the wishes of the management in bringing children to school [Department of Interior 1894:366].

And again the following year:

> Comparatively speaking there has been no trouble caused by children playing truant. Doubtless the presence of an efficient police force, which is always available to return them, acts as a restraint. It seems strange that it should be necessary to employ force to return a child to school. Parents, however, manifest supreme indifference as to the future benefits from an education, and I fear many of the children who attend regularly would remain away if it were left to the discretion of the father or mother [Department of Interior 1895:358].

But in this same report, she admits that Indian parents may have had good reason to be indifferent about "the future benefits from an education":

> . . . I desire to express regret that no encouragement is offered the pupils after graduation. The field of labor here being circumscribed, they of necessity return to the reservation, and retrogression cannot be attributed to lack of education. Neither is it wholly the fault of the individual; necessity forces him to it, the needs of the body acting as a powerful factor in this retrograde movement.

Between 1894 and 1899, Miguel's tactic of urging Quechans not to send their children to school thrust the school's Indian police into continuous conflict with parents. It also placed Miguel in the role of defender of Quechan rights against the government—at least for those who still followed his suggestions and supported his claims of leadership.

The continuing existence of the Xuksílʸ settlement of the south dwellers offered a decided advantage to those wanting to keep their children out of school. Since Xuksílʸ was situated across the international boundary in Mexico, those wishing to escape the Indian police could simply move over there (again, Miguel had been a leader in

Xuksíl^{y}). For awhile, it was a haven for conservative Quechans and fugitives from government authority, but the days of its existence were numbered.

Miguel and his allies preferred to remain on the reservation where they could keep close watch on their battle with the school personnel. By 1898, Superintendent O'Neil had designated a new tribal chief, although none of the official details surrounding the appointment have survived. The new man, Pancho LaCherro, was thoroughly under the wing of the school administration and, consequently, was unpopular with most Quechans. LaCherro had been one of Miguel's accusers in the murder of the shaman in 1892 and was the Indian judge who had ordered the whipping of Miguel, Walter Scott, and others in 1893; needless to say, his ascendance to chieftaincy was especially resented by Miguel's followers. Miguel convened a series of meetings among his supporters to seek LaCherro's replacement by someone more sympathetic to his cause. Indian police reported the meetings, and also the rumors about Miguel's designs, to Superintendent O'Neil, and she relayed the information to her superiors at the Mission Agency. By then, she was fed up with Miguel's interference and requested that the agent remove "Miguel and his henchmen" from the reservation permanently (O'Neil to Mission Agency 22 September 1897).

The superintendent was convinced, with justification, that Miguel was being supported by Anglos in Yuma, at least one of whom was an attorney. The reasons the Anglos became involved are not known; they may have been sympathetic to the cause for Indian autonomy, or they may have felt they could turn their help into large personal profit once the allotment situation was settled. The attorney, at least, probably anticipated a fee from the Indians. The specific nature of the Anglo help is not clear either, but it almost certainly involved advice on drafting petitions and letters, and perhaps some coaching on federal Indian law.

As was true of reservation politics elsewhere, Miguel's staunchest supporters were his own relatives: his sister, Maggie; her husband, Walter Scott; and Miguel's sons—first the one sent to prison for the murder of the shaman, then Patrick Miguel. Patrick was sixteen years old when the 1893 Agreement was signed and was branded as a troublemaker by the superintendent even then. By the late 1890s, he was emerging as the most vigorous and outspoken member of his father's group. He had, for example, exchanged several letters with the president of the Southern Pacific Railroad in an attempt to get free passage for Quechans on the company's trains.[4] He completely circumvented the school superintendent and agency when doing this but circulated the railroad's conciliatory letters and accounts of his own role in "getting something for the people" among the Indians (O'Neil to commissioner 11 April 1899).

The Mission Agency had taken no action on O'Neil's request to remove Miguel and some of his followers from the reservation in 1892, and the angry meetings among the Quechans had continued. By 1899, Miguel had joined forces with a man named Frank Pasqual, old Chief Pasqual's nephew, and had begun agitating to have Frank become the new chief. Frank's people were north dwellers, indicating that another coalition between the north dwellers and those originally from Xuksíl^{y} had formed to resist the influence of the Townsend group, now represented by the tame chief LaCherro. Rumors reaching the ears of the superintendent via her policemen had it that the plotters wanted to rid the reservation of the superintendent and her teaching staff, as well as two other Anglos—John Gandolfo, who operated a small store on the school grounds, and Louis Jaeger, who had obtained a patent to a quarter section of reservation land.[5]

Matters came to a head when a fire destroyed several school buildings on 14 March 1899. The superintendent's faithful police reported that they had heard the fire was part of the Miguel group's plan. The superintendent sent her report to the commissioner almost a month later (O'Neil to commissioner 11 April 1899):

> I learned [from the police] that Patrick Miguel boasted in the hearing of several Indians who were disposed to be friendly, that he had started the fire and expressed a desire to see more burn. The Indians also threatened to bodily harm to the chief [sic] and to the policemen and fearing trouble I requested Agent Wright [of the Mission Agency] to come at once.

On this hearsay evidence, Patrick Miguel was arrested by the superintendent's police and charged with arson. Patrick's father and others promised vengeance and threatened to attempt to release him by force, but they were frustrated by a squad of deputy United States marshals, and Patrick was transported to jail in San Bernardino, California, to await trial.

Thus rid of Patrick, the superintendent again petitioned—this time the commissioner—to have the ex-chief and his supporters removed from the reservation "for the preservation of peace and unity" among the Quechans (O'Neil to commissioner 11 April 1899). "Until this is done," she wrote, "I am of the opinion dissension and trouble among the Yuma Indians will exist and continue to grow worse. The evil effects of which will be an interference with the best interests of this school and tend to destroy the benefits of educational work among the Yuma Indians."

NINETEENTH-CENTURY DEVELOPMENT IN RETROSPECT

There was considerable irony in the superintendent's solemn prognosis to the commissioner. During her tenure in office, there had been dissension and trouble among the Quechans, with or without Miguel and his followers, and the benefits of the educational work —whatever they were—were squandered in an economic and social structure in which formal education bore little relationship to existing jobs. Old Quechans in the 1960s recalled that in late-nineteenth-century reservation life, there was neither the need nor the equipment to put school-taught skills such as shoemaking or how to bake 150 loaves of bread at one time to productive use. In short, one economic structure was needed to keep the school going, and another was needed to help people make a living on the reservation.

The only real economic opportunities available to the Quechans at this time were unskilled labor jobs in the neighboring town and farming on their own family plots, using traditional techniques. And both of these had drawbacks. The Quechans had to compete with poor Anglos and emigrant Mexicans in the former, and the latter depended on the river's capriciousness; disastrous flooding in 1884 and no flooding in 1888 had ruined the harvests and prompted government aid. But neither were the two alternatives mutually exclusive, and many Quechans worked both for wages (when such work was available) and at subsistence farming, selling a limited amount of farm produce and chopping wood to supplement their net income. Neither the farming nor wage work was a direct result of the government's programs for economic development, however.

There was a third moneymaking project also—that of seasonal or permanent emigration from the reservation for work that would put the school's training to better use. But there is no indication that the Quechans seriously considered this alternative. They wanted to stay with the people and customs they knew best and thereby locked themselves into the economic opportunities that existed locally.

Education as extolled by the government policymakers in those early years was not only economically irrelevant; it was culturally irrelevant to adult life on the reservation. In time, of course, traditional culture would inevitably adapt to the ever present school and the knowledge imparted there. And certainly leaders like Miguel were finding that speaking, writing, and reading English were important tactical skills in their continuing battle with the government. But no continuity of the Quechan world view or style of life carried over to the Catholic boarding school, and there was no agreement between the Quechans and the nuns on the meaning of life or what values were or were not desirable. Conflict between the two world views was inevitable. More important, in terms of development, was the government's attitude that this conflict had to be resolved by eliminating the Quechan way and replacing it with the way of the Anglo middle classes. This could best be done, it was thought, by imposing the new way on children, while isolating them as much as possible from the influence of their parents. (This explains in part why the superintendent was so anxious to have a police force and why it was so essential that only those tribal leaders who embraced the new order enthusiastically, or at least kept their noses out of school business, be supported by the government.) But no matter how well the Quechan children learned Anglo middle-class ways, the reservation was by no means an Anglo middle-class community, nor did it possess the economic basis for becoming one —even if its members had wanted it to. Ultimately, the indoctrinated children resolved the contradiction of life-styles by returning to Indian ways. The reversion was not complete, however, because the students had been intensively exposed to Anglo behavior and had acquired, in some measure, the techniques for dealing with it.

To repeat another important point about the government's development scheme of the time: it was not at all concerned with developing autonomous Indian leadership in the community. Instead, Anglo administrators tried to establish a line of Quechan go-betweens who were sympathetic to the school and its personnel —persons who would opt for the wishes of their Anglo superiors rather than those of their own people. These men were not policy or decision-makers but were executors of policies and decisions made by Anglo officials. Miguel, for one, chose not to play this "tame" role and so was removed from his chiefly status by the school superintendent.

This is a typical example of a classic colonial situation, as anthropologist J. A. Barnes once observed (1966:229). After distinguishing between politics (policymaking) and administration (carrying out policy), he wrote:

> Under almost any scheme of colonial administration, the recognized chiefs, headmen, and councillors, are intended to be mainly, if not wholly, administrators, like their superiors in the hierarchy. In the traditional society prior to contact, positions of leadership call for the exercise of political

> rather than administrative skill. . . . Official reports contain many instances where a chief or leader had shown that, however courageous a warrior and adroit a politician he may have been, he makes an ineffective subordinate administrator.

The superintendent and agents had no doubts about where the real political power ought to lie. But Miguel and his adherents, as shown by their continued struggle, hoped the power base could be manipulated to their own advantage, if not shifted altogether.

Both principal parties in the power dispute—Miguel and the superintendent—did what they had to do, given their positions vis-à-vis each other. That is, the superintendent could not have yielded any of her decision-making power to local leaders who might prove inimical to her or the school; otherwise she might have lost her position for failure to push hard enough against "tribal heathenism." So there was no possibility of a "free" election of chiefs without threat of a government veto, and there was no chance that Miguel could continue to do battle with the school while serving as an officially endorsed leader.

In his tactics, Miguel was forced to deal with opposition from both the government and his fellow tribesmen. Violence, in skirmishes with Anglo marshals and Indian police, proved unproductive, so his only hope lay in discrediting the school administration. By publicizing alleged atrocities against students, he could keep attendance down and at the same time enhance his image in the eyes of his people. Publicity was not a problem on the reservation where word of mouth was a rapid, if not too accurate, means of spreading information. But he also had to get accounts of the atrocities and his displeasure about them to higher administrative echelons in the Office of Indian Affairs, without involving the local school superintendent and Indian agent at Colton, California. For this, he needed outside (i.e., Anglo) technical assistance, at least until his son Patrick or other Indians could become skilled at drafting resolutions and interpreting existing federal Indian law. There was no way Miguel could get such assistance from school authorities, so he was forced to seek aid from Anglos in Yuma—as Captain José of the Townsend group had been doing since 1887. In short, Miguel could play politics against the school only by going outside the local official channels to get to the decision-makers in Washington.

Miguel probably understood that the Indian office tended to close ranks when its policies and programs were under general attack. But whatever his understanding, his tactic of pitting officials within the system against each other (by his reports to higher policymakers of local incompetence and cruelty) was a way to combat the bureaucracy without appearing to challenge it as a whole. For example, there is no record of his ever speaking out against the presence of a school, or against the policy of Anglo education for Indians; it was this particular school, and more precisely, its administrators, that irked him. And there was never a call for the total withdrawal of the government from reservation affairs, but rather a series of petitions to remove some of its individual representatives.

In the last years of the nineteenth century, the Indian office showed no signs of vulnerability to such attack, at least in terms apparent to the Quechans. Nonetheless, their plotting and struggling continued, but often with a division of tactical opinions that led to factional divisions among settlement and kinship groups. The alternating splits and mergers among the various factions should have given a measure of flexibility to the Quechans' position in that, theoretically, the tribe would not become fossilized in its ideology or tactics. In actual practice, however, factionalism further diminished the political power of the tribe by practically assuring a lack of consensus on major issues, thus reducing the amount of pressure that could be put on government power-holders. Three outcomes seemed possible: first, the continuing political powerlessness of the tribe vis-à-vis the government would increase the severity of the factional rifts, because no power-gaining tactic could succeed, and therefore there would never be a firm basis for consensus. Or, secondly, the tribe would begin to pull together as a unit, once the feasibility of mass resistance was recognized—something it had not done since the reservation was established. Or, thirdly, the powerlessness would reduce the Quechans to a politically apathetic mass of individuals who passively adjusted, without resistance, to shifts in federal policy. This last condition was what the government apparently desired. Mary O'Neil wanted Miguel removed from the reservation "for the preservation of peace and unity on the Yuma reservation" (O'Neil to commissioner, 11 April 1899). For "peace and unity," she could just as easily have substituted "political apathy."

The government's feeble development schemes of the late nineteenth century were not working. Instead, the Quechans were undergoing a kind of antidevelopment that included not only the debilitating feuding among factions for power they could never gain, but also confusion and frustration which resulted from the government's forcing middle-class Anglo ideals on them—a way of life they didn't have the means to achieve. Although the government schemes for instilling Western civilization were not relevant to the tribe's social and economic context, time plus a mutual agreement of development objectives between the two cultures could have perhaps resolved these inherent contradictions. Time was certainly not a problem; the Quechans had plenty of it. But colonial powers have never been noted for their willingness to accommodate their objectives to those of their colonized subjects. And as anthropologist Robert Thomas, himself part Cherokee, has written (1966/67:39), an Indian reservation "is the most complete colonial system in the world that I know about."

CHAPTER 3

Amalgamation, Allotment, Paternalism: 1900-1934

THE FIRST TWO DECADES OF THE TWENTIETH CENTURY were ones of consolidation and florescence of major Indian-policy principles forged during the late 1800s. The land-allotment system methodically proceeded to break up masses of tribal land. Government schools and agency superintendents continued their efforts to stamp out old tribal ways and replace them with something like the American protestant ethic, aided by a set of official guidelines that denied the Indians a number of rights that were normally guaranteed to American citizens. The government, working through its agency superintendents, continued to decide what was best for its wards, handing down important decisions to various tribes without enlisting their active participation in the decision-making process.

Much of the bureaucrats' attention was directed to land-management problems, and with very good reason: the allotment policy was not only breaking up tribal blocs, but was also reducing total Indian landholdings at an alarming rate. Public sales of Indian land, considered excess after all the tribes had received their allotments, accounted for some of the loss. Other tracts were claimed by the government for flood control or other purposes. And loopholes in the allotment act itself permitted Anglos to buy up large amounts of land from Indian allottees before the twenty-five year trust period expired—something humanitarians had long feared would happen. These factors caused Indian-held land to shrink from 132 million

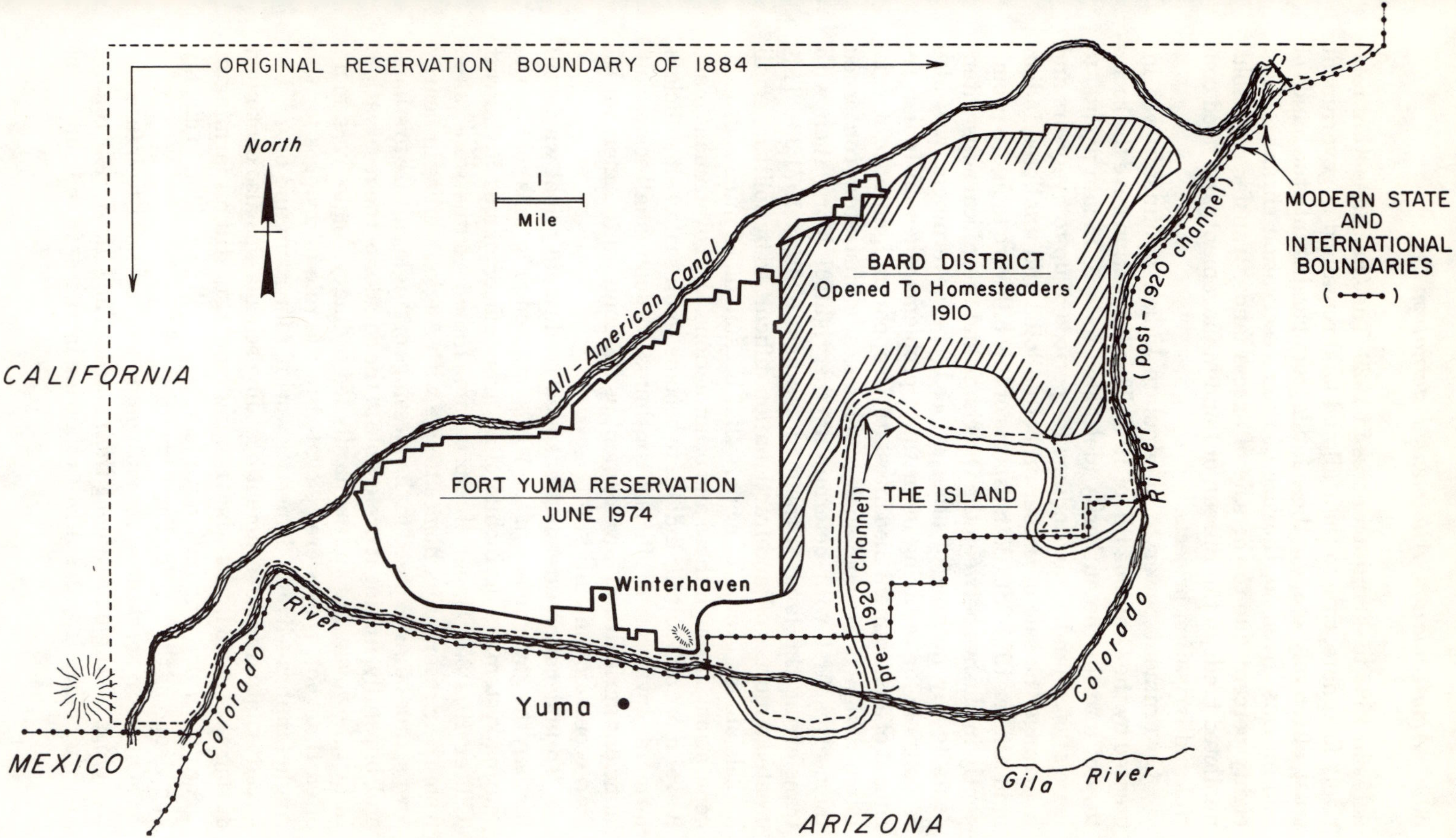

Relative Amounts and Locations of Loss to Quechan Land Holdings, 1884–1974.

acres in 1887 to 30 million acres in 1929. The Quechans were relatively fortunate; title to their alloted land remained in government trust, effectively keeping these lands from passing into the hands of non-Indians. Even so, the size of their reservation shrank almost eighty percent due to the sale of excess lands, transfer of unsold, unalloted lands to the Bureau of Land Management, and flood control and irrigation projects.

Government power to manipulate Indian allotments was increased by the Omnibus Bill of 1910. This legislation gave the secretary of interior the authority (delegated to local Indian agents) to lease alloted land to non-Indians for periods of up to five years and to arrange the sale of timber on both alloted and unalloted Indian land (Officer 1971:38). (Both aspects of this bill were to figure prominently in clashes between the Quechans and their local superintendents to say nothing of other tribes.) The government was also responsible for resolving inheritance problems when an Indian recipient of an allotment died intestate. In apparent ignorance of legislation designed to avoid such problems, administrators concerned themselves first with determining the rightful heirs, then with transferring the land to them in common (Officer 1971:38). This created a morass of land fractionation difficulties by splitting small parcels among groups of owners that became more numerous each generation. Through these and other actions, the government made it ever more difficult for Indians to become small-scale, self-sufficient farmers; government officials continued to push small-scale, self-sufficient agricultural development as the solution to American Indian economic difficulties.

To undermine already weakened traditional tribal ways still further, the government in the 1880s imposed programs such as the "outing system," a brainchild of an army officer named R.H. Pratt (Officer 1971:35). Under this program, Indian youths were taken from their reservation homes to live with Anglo families in nearby towns, thus being exposed to the blessings of Anglo culture firsthand and, hopefully, finding it preferable to the squalor of the reservation. In fact, however, the youths hardly led ordinary Anglo lives; more often than not, they were relegated to the role of drudges for the Anglo families—live-in domestics working for room and board. Enforced isolation in government boarding schools was also continued during this period, with the training emphasis still on farming or domestic service, and Indian students were still forbidden to display knowledge of their traditional heritage.

On the reservations, Indian agents worked hard to infuse the trappings of Anglo life among their wards. They laced their reports to higher officials with statistics showing increases in the number of frame houses (as opposed to hovels) built during their tenure, the number of Indians who were becoming fluent in English or who wore Anglo clothing, or the number of Indian couples who had been induced to get married legally rather than continue to live in the bonds of Indian-style marriages. The Indian office found traditional religious practices particularly loathsome, so it developed its own "code of religious offenses" as justification for forbidding several varieties of religious gatherings among the Indians (Spicer 1962:175, 359).

Indian policy and Indian agents continued to stifle Indian political development as well. By the turn of the century, the Indian office had officially discontinued the practice of appointing local chiefs—even tame ones—because of the obvious relationship between chiefly status and old tribal ways. The agents, using their Indian police as paid enforcers, continued to wield exclusive political authority. Indian political activists may have schemed and petitioned the federal government, but it was wasted effort against the closed ranks of the agents and their supporting bureaucracy.

In short, the means for absolute political, economic, and social control lay in the hands of the agents, just as it had during the previous period, but now control became even tighter as the tentative procedures of previous years were refined, reapplied, and thus made routine. The objectives of Indian policy were still basically assimilationist, but, given government administrative tactics, the Indians could never hope to be assimilated as the equals of Anglos. As late-nineteenth-century policies became crystallized in the early twentieth century, dependent isolation—not assimilation—seemed the more likely result.

However, just as the public conscience mobilized against extermination of Indian people in the 1870s, so too public displeasure in the 1920s against the repressive policies of the Indian office coalesced into a protracted pressure drive. In 1922, Anglo activists found the issue they needed to launch a general protest—the government's questionable handling of the problems of Pueblo Indian landownership in the southwest. Nongovernment radicals like John Collier of the Indian Rights Association joined forces with several congressmen to expose the case and publicize other examples of graft and deceit that violated Indian rights (Downes 1945:334–335).

It was perhaps partially in response to this growing offensive that Congress passed the Indian Citizenship Act in 1924, placing Indians under the protection of the Constitution (although it was not until years later that full constitutional privileges were extended to all Indians).

The citizenship act did not deflect the popular protest. Still more pressure was placed on Congress to investigate the Indian office's handling of the oil-rich lands of Oklahoma Indians in 1925–1926. The Department of Interior responded by ordering a full-scale probe of the conditions of Indian life in 1926. The result was the Meriam Report, a careful and scholarly analysis of conditions as well as a statement of recommended policy reform, delivered to the interior secretary in 1928. Very soon thereafter, probably sensing that its continuing approval of Indian office procedures could become a political liability, Congress sent its own members to the various reservations to find out just how deplorable reservation life had become.

All this activity put the Indian office administration on the defensive—from the commissioner down to local agents. Everyone wanted to avoid adverse publicity and was therefore eager to implement token programs, but did not want to undertake a general policy overhaul. The commissioner of Indian affairs between 1921 and 1929 was Charles H. Burke, a former congressman from South Dakota who, in the midst of the public outcry, stood staunchly in defense of his individualistic policy for Indians. In 1923 he said, "I believe in making the Indian take his chance, just the same as white folks do. . . . Don't fool yourself. The Indian makes good when he has the chance." (quoted in Downes 1945:343). He left unstated the real dilemma of the Indians at that time: they were being made to take a chance by having their traditional economic patterns shattered, but they were not being given the means to make their enforced gamble pay off.

The Meriam Report laid the blame for Indian lack of development on poor education. Some of the first reforms of the 1930s were therefore aimed at improving vocational training in Indian schools (Downes 1945:333, 349). But in the Quechans' case, poor education was only a small part of the problem. Much more fundamental was the fact that they were being denied the economic or political means to develop, either on their own terms or those imposed by the government.

A CHANGE IN FORT YUMA SCHOOL ADMINISTRATION

The policy of contracting the operation of Indian schools to Christian mission groups had been terminated for several years before the impact was felt at Fort Yuma. It was not until a few months after the school fire and the arrest of Patrick Miguel that the Catholic superintendent and her staff were replaced by civil servants. In October 1899, the new superintendent, J. S. Spear, arrived for the start of the school year. He also carried the title of "acting Indian agent," because Fort Yuma had become an Indian agency. For Spear and his successors, this meant freedom to make decisions about local administration without having to consult some distant authority.

Spear seemed sympathetic to local conditions when he took over his new positions. He wrote that the Quechans were industrious but that there was little work available; that they had a "contempt for authority" but that, in general, they were "good Indians and deserve more consideration than they get." But he soon displayed a greater sympathy for federal regulations than for his Quechan wards: "Last year one of our best boys ran away from school to work for his grandfather who was old and nearly helpless. While I sympathised with the boy I could not overlook his infraction of the rules of the school" (Spear to commissioner 30 July 1900). He also reported that:

> The conditions of the school, when I took charge last October, were peculiar and, to me, embarrassing. Though a Government school, it had for fourteen years been under the management of the Sisters of St. Joseph, all of this time, too, under one superintendent. It is needless to say that they had stamped their character upon the whole school, and that their religion permeated all their work [Department of Interior 1900:479–480].

Over the protests of the remnants of the Catholic staff, Spear's first administrative acts included serving meat at school meals on Fridays and ending compulsory prayer periods and church services. But Spear was no less dogmatic than his predecessors in his belief that school attendance should be compulsory:

> I gave the [Indian] police emphatic instructions that when they went for a child that they should bring it, in spite of the protests of the parents—that if parents objected for any reason they might come along and take their protests to me, and I would be the judge whether the child should come to school or not. A number of parents came as thus directed—most of them irate [Spear to commissioner 7 May 1901].

In fact, Spear felt it would be best to lower the mandatory attendance age to four years, to get the children out of their "poor homes" even earlier.

There was no real reason, then, for the Quechans' attitude toward the school to become more conciliatory after the Catholic administration ended; the government had merely sent fresh replacements into the struggle. From the Quechans' perspective, the basic issue was still whether their authority or the government's would rule the reservation, and conflict still focused on the question of who was to become the officially sanctioned chief.

THE EMBATTLED AGENTS

During the first thirty years of the twentieth century, no other issue on the Quechen reservation generated more correspondence than that of political authority. Spear and his successors at Fort Yuma were too preoccupied with keeping law and order on the reservation and too little concerned with education and economic and social development. But, from their perspective, law and order had to receive top priority; otherwise, any programs the government attempted to impose would simply become new arenas for confrontation between the Indians and agents.

During this time, a policy shaped by direct consultation with the Indians and a sensitive assessment of their actual needs was considered unthinkable. Yet, as individuals, the agents at Fort Yuma were in a double bind. They had to establish themselves as able administrators with their superiors if they wished to keep their positions, which meant avoiding unfavorable attention by the Indian office; but this was difficult to do in the face of bombardments of petitions and letters from irate Indians demanding government redress of their functions as agents. In other words, by following orders, the agents antagonized the Quechans; by ignoring orders they lost their jobs.

Some notion of how Spear and his successors coped with this dilemma emerges from the following accounts of political skirmishing that have survived in the written records. These accounts reveal that the Quechans doggedly clung to a hope of eventual victory, despite setback after frustrating setback. Except for brief flashes of ingenuity, they kept repeating the strategies they had established late in the nineteenth century as there seemed to be no other alternatives. And, as the skirmishes and setbacks continued, factionalism emerged to destroy any potential for effectiveness that their strategies did have.

In the late 1890s, ex-Chief Miguel and his kinsmen joined forces with a group supporting Frank Pasqual, old Chief Pasqual's nephew, for the position of tribal chief, thus actively opposing the official but less popular chief, Pancho LaCherro, and his followers from the Gila valley, east across the Colorado. Spear took over while the struggle was going on and swiftly declared his support for the official chief. He therewith assured himself of one of the most conflict-ridden records in the history of the Fort Yuma agency, because the Quechans were still far from becoming politically apathetic.

Spear had been in office only about three months when the Miguel-Pasqual group clamored for the election of a new official chief. A brawl erupted and Spear ordered some of the group arrested.

Remaining protestors immediately complained to the commissioner (Indians to commissioner 2 February 1900), but the tame Chief LaCherro retained his office for the time being.

One of the instigators of the protest was Patrick Miguel. Patrick was actually away from the reservation, having been sent to Carlisle Indian School in Pennsylvania for disciplinary reasons after his arson trial in San Bernardino. But, by mail, his father and others kept him informed of events on the reservation, and Patrick responded with a series of letters scathingly critical of the new agent, whom he had never met. Members of the Miguel-Pasqual group read his letters, then passed them on to the Fort Yuma agency in an obvious attempt to rile Agent Spear. The attempt succeeded. On 22 February 1900, Spear complained to the commissioner that "these letters [of Patrick's] are believed here, and are the cause of innocent but misguided Indians getting into trouble." He enclosed the latest of Patrick's writings, one that Patrick had specifically requested be given to him:

> Dear father,
> . . . I am sorry to hear that troubles [over Frank Pasqual's legitimacy as chief] are not settled yet but I hope it [sic] will soon. I have seen the Commissioner about it & he promised me & the Yumas that he will communicate to Spear about it. I also wrote to Mr. Spear, & told him not to touch the Indians again unless he wants to be reported, so I think he will very likely change his mind and accept the new chief [Frank Pasqual]. Spear is not a Sheriff, nor a Judge, but Agt. & Supt. of the School & of the Res. but if he wants to loose [sic] the position like Mary O'Neil, he can just keep on playing Sheriff & Judge, & it won't take me long to report him, but I think he will change his mind after he gets the Commissioner's letter. I have given him fair warning & at the same time very good advise [sic] [P. Miguel to ex-Chief Miguel 13 February 1900].

Patrick's tone was brash, just as his father's had been, but his position was clear: the agent was there to help the Indians, to accede to their wishes (or, more accurately, to the wishes of those representing the Miguel-Pasqual faction); the Indians had the ultimate authority, not the government. Patrick, then twenty-three years old, had issued Spear a warning that was actually a familiar threat: if the agent did not toe the Indians' line, they would circumvent the local agency and make complaints or requests directly to Washington, attempting to discredit the local agent in the eyes of his bureaucratic superiors. And finally, Patrick did not miss the chance to build popular support by enhancing his own role in the removal of the

Catholic school officials, just as he had claimed credit earlier for intervening with the Southern Pacific Railroad to get free passes for the Indians.

Another major confrontation came only five days after Patrick's letter reached the agent. Spear had earlier imposed on the Indians a plan for rationing the supply of wood on the reservation by designating certain areas for immediate cutting and others to be left for the future. This was at the order of the Indian office in Washington. On 27 February, defiant members of the Miguel-Pasqual faction went to one of the restricted areas and chopped the wood "in a particularly wanton manner" (Spear to commissioner 7 April 1900). Spear dispatched his Indian police to arrest the choppers, but the Miguel-Pasqual group drove them away. The alarmed agent wrote for authorization to hire some Anglo police, because his tiny force of five Indian police could not enforce his orders among the hostile population. He also wanted permission to remove ex-Chief Miguel and his followers from the reservation, the third such request to the Indian office in three years.

While Spear waited for the commissioner's reply, Frank Pasqual, the self-proclaimed chief, drafted an angry letter to the commissioner complaining of Spear's behavior in the confrontation. The sale of wood, he wrote, was necessary for the welfare of the Quechans. At the time, about fifty Quechans were in debt to an Anglo, E. F. Sanguinetti, who ran a small general store near the school, and needed cash to pay off the debts. Pasqual declared that he had no need for "polices to watch or guard over me and my people, . . . nor sherifs" (Pasqual to commissioner 8 March 1900).

Without commenting on Spear's own urgent appeal, the Indian office forwarded Frank Pasqual's complaint to him for explanation. Spear replied that Patrick Miguel's letters and ensuing events on the reservation had strengthened the dissidents' conviction that Patrick was right in declaring that the agent had no right to meddle in the Miguel-Pasqual group's affairs. Spear wanted the commissioner to write to the Indians directly and tell them that he did have such authority and that Patrick was lying. Spear also lamented that the Quechans had not become dependent on government rations for survival. If they had, Spear declared, the dissidents could easily be brought to heel by cutting off their food supply, "but I have not that leverage here" (Spear to commissioner 15 March 1900). Finally, months later, the letter Spear had requested arrived from the Indian office. Spear quickly and publicly used its contents to refute those of the Patrick Miguel letters, confident that he had thereby destroyed Patrick's credibility among most of the dissidents. The skirmish was briefly broken off.

Sometime during the following year and a half, the official chief, LaCherro, lost his position. None of the details have survived; he simply was no longer mentioned as a tribal official. Frank Pasqual's name and writing appear frequently in the correspondence of the period, but Spear never referred to Pasqual as the official chief. This did not discourage Pasqual from referring to himself as "chief of the Yuma tribe" in all his letters to Washington.

In September 1902, open hostilities resumed. The Miguel-Pasqual group again resisted the efforts of Spear's Indian police to return truant children to school, and another fight broke out. This time the police managed to arrest several troublemakers. Spear tried them at the agency and sentenced them to have their hair cut short and to spend thirty days in jail. Spear ordered the haircuts to keep faith with an Indian office directive urging Indian agents to discourage the wearing of Indian clothing, body paint, and (for males) long hair.

The Quechan men were still very proud of their long hair, banged in front and rolled into long, pencil-thin rods at the back. Spear's sentence was thus particularly resented by the dissidents, and, in retaliation, they chose a course of action that was thoroughly Anglo: they hired an Anglo attorney in Yuma to file a suit against Spear in the federal courts. One man, *Aguhis,* was named as plaintiff in the case. The issue dragged on for about two years, with both Spear and the Indians marshalling their support. The Indians solicited the help of an Indian rights association known as the Sequoia League, in an effort to get travel funds for witnesses against Spear (the government had refused to pay their travel expenses to the scene of the trial), and Frank Pasqual launched a series of protests to Anglo lawyers, congressmen, and the commissioner, urging that Spear be removed as agent. Spear, for his part, solicited the help of prominent Anglos in Yuma. Thirty-five of them, including the mayor, district attorney, and publisher of the *Sentinel,* sent a petition to the commissioner urging that Spear be retained in his post, much as some of these same citizens had rallied behind Mary O'Neil in the 1890s.

There is a tantalizing lack of information about what happened at the trial (if there ever was one). Spear was, of course, merely following orders from the Indian office in rounding up truants and cutting their hair as punishment for misdemeanors; this may have earned him acquittal. Whatever, Spear did not long remain as agent. He was gone from Fort Yuma by March 1906—apparently without ever having laid eyes on Patrick Miguel.

Spear probably had to go if the troubled waters were to be calmed, and the Miguel-Pasqual coalition could claim much of the credit for his departure, even though they lost most of their confrontations with him. But victory was probably less important than the fact that the confrontations had occurred. Confrontation, combined with attempts to discredit government appointees, was about the only strategy left to the Quechans—their only means of getting action on local issues from the Indian office inner sanctum in Washington. The dissidents shrewdly chose to dispute those policies that were most distasteful to the Quechan majority, hoping to win the maximum possible grass-roots support for their position. By choosing their issues carefully, they could also count on the support of sympathetic outsiders and organizations to apply still more pressure on the government. The greater the popular pressure, the more likely the Indian office would be to take action—even if it always fell short of shifting the power from the local agent to the Indians. The Indian office was goaded into finding another agent to replace Spear. Whether this would shift the locus of power was something the Quechans were anxious to determine. With Spear in command, they had had no maneuverability; with the appointment of a new agent, there was at least a chance that the administration might loosen up a bit.

THE RETURN OF PATRICK MIGUEL

Patrick Miguel left Carlisle about the same time Agent Spear left the Fort Yuma Agency. But instead of returning to the reservation, Patrick went to Los Angeles for three years and was not seen on the reservation until October 1909. The new agent at Fort Yuma, Anna C. Eagen, was not at all happy to have him back. She accused him of immediately starting to go "in and out amongst his people endeavoring to acquire for himself prestige as a leader, and intent always on stirring up trouble" (Eagen to commissioner 10 December 1910). He contracted with Anglo farmers to clear their lands, then hired needy Indian men to do the work. He functioned as an advisor to an Anglo attorney who unsuccessfully attempted to get two Quechan youths acquitted of charges of breaking into the girls' dormitory at the school. Both actions were designed to enhance his importance as a champion of the people. But in mid-November 1910, he was handed the opportunity to build this image on a much grander scale.

The Miguel-Pasqual group had decided to send a member of the tribe to Washington, to talk to the commissioner about the impending land allotments and the problem of tribal leadership. In a series of meetings, the group had raised $190 for the trip, being careful that the agent was kept ignorant of their intentions until the plans were complete. Patrick was told by his supporters that he was to be the envoy, so he bought a train ticket to Washington. To Frank Pasqual's followers, however, Frank was still the tribal chief—no matter what the government said. They angrily trooped up to the agency to complain to Agent Eagen that "if anybody went to Washington it should be the Chief" (Eagen to commissioner 10 December 1910). This apparently was the first she had heard of the plan. She quickly called a meeting of all Quechan males to vote on the issue. A small majority favored Patrick as the envoy, and he was on the next train going east. The government immediately notified Eagen that she should not let Patrick leave, because he had received no Indian office authorization to meet with the commissioner (commissioner to Eagen 5 December 1910). But it was too late.

Patrick's objective was to request an increase in the proposed size of individual land allotments from five to ten acres (the 1893 Agreement had specified five acres) and to obtain authority for the tribe to set up a "business committee or council and presiding officers to manage the affairs of the Indians in co-operation with the Agent" (Indians to commissioner 8 February 1911). Weeks passed, and by the following February even Patrick's supporters were growing restive in the absence of information from their delegate; they had not heard from him since he left the reservation. Furthermore, a letter sent from the Indian office to the Quechans in February 1911 did not relieve their agitation, because it implied that Patrick had not yet tried to contact anyone in Washington.

Patrick, they later learned, had been in Washington for only one day and had not been able to see the commissioner. Instead of waiting for an appointment, he traveled to Philadelphia to stay with friends and recuperate from a minor illness he had contracted during the trip. From Philadelphia, he wrote a letter to the commissioner (20 December 1910) in which he conveyed the requests of his tribe. The letter sounded distinctly unlike the bombastic Patrick of nine years earlier, as the following passages indicate:

> While here [in Philadelphia] I thought I would endeavor to get your decision on the request of the Yumas to be allowed to hold an election of a Chief and a council to co-operate with the Agent and Superintendent in handling the affairs of the Indians. The Yumas are badly in need of some simple form of government to guide and enable them to meet the new condition of life which is fast closing in on them. . . . We believe the old Indians should be taught, more by members of their own tribe, in a kindly way to see and adopt the white man's laws and it is to this end the more progressive members of the tribe request that they be allowed to have a council and presiding officer to pilot the ship of state of the Yumas [Miguel to commissioner 20 December 1910].

His letter made no reference to the increase in size of land allotments, and nothing in subsequent correspondence indicates that he broached the subject with the commissioner's office. The allotments were nonetheless increased to ten acres by Congress in 1911 (36 Stat. 1063), although the reason for the increase is not clear.[1]

True to administrative policy, the Indian office forwarded Patrick's letter to Agent Eagen at Fort Yuma for her comments. Miss Eagen concluded from it that Patrick was making his own bid for chieftaincy (Eagen to commissioner 21 April 1911). In her reply can also be seen the shifting criteria of progress that she and her predecessors, as well as Patrick himself, used to encourage official support. Obviously, the perspectives of the agent and Patrick did not coincide:

> There isn't any doubt but that the faction that Frank Pasqual governs is the progressive faction, whilst, on the other hand the faction that is led by old Simon Miguel [Patrick's father] is consistently opposed to every move that would be for the advancement of the tribe.

Only six years earlier, Frank Pasqual had been considered anti-progressive by Agent Spear! Eagen concluded, "It would be a calamity for this tribe to ever have to revert to the leadership of a Miguel, and I sincerely trust that such a thing will not happen while I am in charge . . . " (Eagen to commissioner 21 April 1911).

The reply to Agent Eagen from the Indian office made it clear that government policy on the appointment of chiefs had changed—apparently without the knowledge of the Quechans:

> . . . you are advised that the Office has given the matter careful consideration and cannot consistently grant the request of Patrick Miguel for the reason that the policy of the Department *has been and is,* not to recognize or create chiefs of Indian tribes, and to cause the Indians, as soon as possible, to break up their tribal relations and to assume their duties as citizens . . . you should advise the persons in interest to this effect [C. F. Hauke to Eagen 6 May 1911; italics added].

On the other hand, the alternative plan for a business committee or tribal council was not contrary to government policy, so Agent Eagen convened a mass meeting of all eligible voters (Quechan males over twenty-one years old) to elect a committee of eight members. She chose a ninth herself, the chairman, Gabriel Hammond, a well-educated Quechan who had worked in a Yuma newspaper office for many years. He was remembered in 1966 as "a wise man who could speak and the people would listen to him and believe what he said." He was also a vigorous opponent of Patrick Miguel, which probably explains why the agent selected him as chairman.

By then, the Miguel and Pasqual factions had broken their alliance (probably because of the dispute over Patrick's trip to Washington), and the Pasqual group had joined with a group of newcomers, the Escalantis, who had just moved onto the reservation from the Somerton homesteaders area. Four members of the business committee were Miguel men; the others were representatives of the new factional coalition. Patrick Miguel, back from Washington and present at the election, was chosen as secretary to the committee, "but with no voice or vote in any measure or business that may ever come before [it]" (minutes of meeting 25 June 1911).[2] This restriction was probably useless; Patrick obviously had influence with the four Miguel members of the committee, and, by being present at the meetings, he would not have to rely on secondhand information in plotting his next move.

The scope of the business committee was "to discuss questions of a business nature relative to the best interests of the tribe, and to decide on ways and means to dispose of such questions" (Eagen to commissioner 26 June 1911). Specifically, the agent had in mind the problems of providing irrigation for the forthcoming land allotments as the main concern for the new committee. Nothing was mentioned of the committee's role in school administration or other concerns of reservation government, and even within its limited range of decision-making it was to be carefully monitored and directed by the agent:

> I would suggest that [the organization of the committee be approved only] . . . with the distinct understanding that the meetings be opened at all times to the Superintendent of the reservation, and that no measure be adopted as final until it meets with the approval of the Superintendent. A brake of this sort should be applied to prevent such a committee from assuming too much power [Eagen to commissioner 26 June 1911].

There could no longer be any doubt in the Quechans' minds about how slightly the locus of power had shifted in their favor since Agent Spear's departure. What is more, the organization of the committee was tailor-made for continuing political disunity among the people. However democratic it may have been to have all factions represented, this single structural feature practically assured that the committee would never reach a unanimous decision on any important issue—not, of course, that any decision would be binding unless approved by the agent. Given the narrow range of committee concerns, most of the important issues confronting the Quechans would be beyond its jurisdiction anyway, even for mere discussion. Agent Eagen was well aware that factional representation would perpetuate factional disputes:

> My opinion, based upon long years of observation, is that factions are the greatest possible help towards progress on an Indian reservation; for whilst they are not conducive to the peace and happiness of an Indian Superintendent, they are the force which is destroying the old idea of following a leader in every thing [sic], and they are the cause of throwing many an Indian back upon his own resources where he soon learns to appreciate the privilege of being able to stand alone and to manage his own affairs [Eagen to commissioner 21 April 1911].

Factions certainly eliminated Indian consensus, perhaps ultimately leading each person to stand alone; but they also made it more possible for the Indian agent to rule without mass opposition.

The business committee struggled along as a hopelessly divided debating forum until 1913—less than three years. Its members were hailed as tribal leaders in official agency correspondence, but the only other mention of its activities indicated that the factional rifts had become more confused and intense. Walter Scott, for example, was ex-chief Miguel's lieutenant throughout the 1890s and went to jail with Miguel in 1893. In 1913, however, as a member of the committee, he was scorned by the Miguel faction as a "demented Indian" who lied to his people to curry the favor of the agency (Indians to commissioner 10 January 1913). The committee dissolved shortly thereafter.

Factional jealousies may also have been heightened by a seemingly contradictory practice of local Indian agents: between crises, they frequently appointed one or more faction leaders to paid positions on the agency staff. Ex-Chief Miguel, for example, was hired intermittently as a night watchman at the Catholic school under the regime of his enemy, Mary O'Neil. Walter Scott, his erstwhile associate, was hired as an interpreter. Patrick Miguel, just after his return from Washington, was appointed chief of the agency police, but, in a tiff with the agency in 1912, he resigned and was replaced by Walter Scott—hence the antagonistic assault on Scott by the Miguel faction in 1913. The fact that these positions were salaried made them attractive to anyone who needed cash (and many undoubtedly did). Too, for an active politician it was absolutely essential to have the ready access to the agency and its policies that these positions carried with them. Thus, there was competition for them in spite of the Quechans' declared abhorrence of working for the Indian agent.

The government was eager to have antagonistic Quechan politicos working for it. For one thing, there was the dim hope that some of the antagonism would be swallowed for the sake of keeping the position—that in this way the agent's opponents would be bought off. Then there was the jealousy among unsuccessful competitors for the job that kept factional schisms open, or the familiar colonial tactic of divide and rule. But perhaps the most important reason for hiring political dissidents was expressed by an agency clerk at Fort Yuma in 1913:

> If you will look over the records in your Office you will find that Patrick Miguel, from the time he was accused, along in the nineties, of burning a school building at this school, up to the present time, has figured as the chief actor in every trouble that has occurred with a superintendent here. For this reason it has been the aim of superintendents in the past, and was my reason when left in charge here for wanting to keep him as an employee—where he could be watched. . . . [K]nowing that it was just as natural for him to cause trouble as it is for sparks to fly upward, I preferred getting along without friction, if possible . . . [H. M. Carter to commissioner 10 February 1913].

So, putting Quechan political activists on the government payroll during peaceful periods was not at all contradictory. It was a worthwhile practice from which both the Quechans and the government profited—but in opposite ways. It was not a technique of reconciliation, but an alternative tactic in the continuing political warfare. The Quechans were not being inconsistent in their attitude toward the agent; they were merely being flexible in their antagonism.

After the failure of the business committee in late 1913, the Quechans must have become very frustrated. They were not permitted to have a principal spokesman to represent them, and any truly representative committee was rendered ineffective by internal dissension. In their disarray, some of them reverted to a much earlier but nonetheless unsuccessful tactic: they wrote to the commissioner to ask again that Frank Pasqual be formally designated as chief of the Quechans (Indians to commissioner June 1914). Six months passed without an answer from the government. The Indians wrote again in December and were finally told—once more—that the

Indian office had no authority to appoint chiefs (E. B. Meritt to Indians 31 December 1914). Ironically, the letter advised them that

> [It would be] more to your advantage to elect a tribal council, or something in the nature of a business committee, rather than to adhere to the primitive custom of electing a "chief," which is not in line with modern customs among civilized communities.

The Quechans found themselves on a bureaucratic treadmill.

Only once during the next twenty years did the Quechans again try to form a tribal council or business committee. This occurred in 1927–1928. As Patrick Miguel had done in his earlier, low-keyed bid for chieftaincy, the young proponents of this second council expressed the need for younger, more educated Quechans to take the initiative in leadership. (Patrick Miguel was a member of the group.) The end came when several older tribesmen challenged the voting procedures used in the selection of council members. Again the effort —after some initial optimism—collapsed from internal conflict.

Until 1936, the political scenario generally followed the patterns set during the years 1900 to 1914. The Indian agents wielded the political authority while powerless Quechan factions split, merged, then split again, making united fronts of opposition or support for any government program impossible. And Patrick Miguel was never far from the epicenter of dissension.

There were two discernable changes, however: political activists came increasingly from the younger, more educated tribal members —a shift from the traditional belief that the "real" leaders were the older men. And, the Quechans gave up the strategy of pitting their physical force against the agency personnel, having learned that ultimately this was a hopeless maneuver. (Actually, the closest they had ever come to a power standoff by using violence was in the several confrontations they had had with the unfortunate Agent Spear and his police in 1900–1905.)

Viewed retrospectively, the most successful strategy for Indian agents seemed to be the avoidance of head-on clashes with Quechan leaders. They accomplished this by agreeing to pass on Indian demands to higher authorities. The Indian office was then the villain if the demands went unmet, not the agent. At the same time, by encouraging the participation of all factions in councils or business committees, the agent could avoid being accused of partiality while assuring that there would be no consensus of Indian opinion. Spear seemed not to understand this approach; Anna Eagen employed it superbly. But in all cases, the agents' ultimate allegiance had to be to the Indian office, not to the Quechans.

THE PROCESS OF AMALGAMATION

Although the reservation's economic situation had not changed during the decade of political squabbling between 1900 and 1910, and there were no new government programs that offered alternatives to the earlier patterns of subsistence farming, small-scale marketing of produce and cut timber, or wage labor at menial jobs in Yuma, the people living in the several settlements off the reservation began to move onto it. The Fort Yuma agents had been warning them that if they moved within the reservation boundaries soon enough, they would be able to select good farmland for their allotments on a first-come, first-served basis; otherwise, the government would choose allotments for them later from the remaining, less desirable land. Aggressive Anglo settlers were also moving onto homesteads nearer the traditional territory of outlying Quechan settlements, providing additional pressure on the residents to relocate within the reservation.

Despite these pressures, however, in 1905 some members of both the Townsend and Somerton settlements decided not to become reservation dwellers, applying instead for homesteads north of the modern town of Somerton, Arizona.[3] Other families from these two settlements, together with the entire Sunflowerseed Eaters group that lived along the Gila, moved onto the reservation to choose individual plots in anticipation of the allotment. The Xuksíl^{y} group decided to remain where they were, south of the reservation, for the time being.

As long as regular flooding of the Colorado continued, basic farming patterns were not drastically affected by these movements. But were the flooding to end without other means of irrigation having been developed, or were the watering cycle to become more erratic, reservation farmlands away from the river's bank, as well as those of Xuksíl^{y} and of the Somerton homesteaders, would soon become worthless.

But while the floods were the Quechans' assurance of continuing livelihood, they were a source of distress to local Anglos. By 1909, the townspeople had convinced the government to build a dam across the Colorado, several miles upstream from the reservation and the town of Yuma. The construction meant jobs for many Quechan men; 150 of them were working on the dam in October 1909. This must have been a large portion of the adult male Quechan population at the time, because Agent Spear's 1905 census figures report a total reservation population of 675 (F. Mead to commissioner 18 May 1905; cf. Forbes 1965: 342). As it turned out, the Quechans were giving up the only natural source of fertility for their farmlands in exchange for perhaps a year's wages as common laborers, because, when the dam was completed, it reduced the incidence of flooding and thus reduced the deposit of rich river silt on the Quechans' land.

By 1910–1911, faced with the water problems created by the new dam and alarmed by increasing tensions along the border arising from the Mexican Revolution, the members of the Xuksíl^y settlement finally moved to new homes within reservation boundaries. From then on, truant children and their families could no longer flee across the border to escape school authorites, and dissident elements could no longer avoid conflict by moving to outlying settlements. Aside from the small group of homesteaders north of Somerton, the Quechan tribe was now living entirely on the reservation and waiting—none too eagerly—for the allotments to be made. The allotment system would destroy what was left of their unrestricted access to vital land and water.

ALLOTMENT

The assignment of allotments was the first step in what the government hoped would be a long-range program of agricultural development as the primary economic base for the Quechan community. The assignment process, however, took place under some bizarre and suspicious circumstances. The 819 Quechans were assigned to their allotments in 1912 (trust patents were approved in 1914). Yet, much of the good farmland in the northeastern portion of the reservation (later known as the Bard District) had already been sold to eager Anglos in a series of transactions that had been going on since 1910 (Eagen to commissioner 21 April 1911). According to the provisions of the 1893 Agreement, the Quechans were to have first choice of acreage within the reservation's boundaries; only after the allotments had been assigned was the excess land to be offered for public sale. Nevertheless, many Quechans who knew good land from poor had to take worthless semidesert tracts in the northwestern portion of the reservation, because much of the best land was already occupied by Anglos. From the Quechans' viewpoint, this was proof positive of Washington's treachery.

And, in fact, Congress was responsible for this apparent travesty. Without even mentioning the 1893 Agreement, it passed legislation in 1904 (33 Statute 189) that, under the provisions of a new reclamation program, declared all irrigable portions of the Quechan reservation to be public domain—except for a portion to be reserved for subsequent allotment to the Quechans. This meant there was no competitive bidding for the land. This was godsend to the Anglos, who paid a low, flat rate based on the appraised value before irrigation (knowing the land would soon be irrigated), and on an installment basis that cut the annual interest earned by the tribe from its land-sale capital in the U.S. treasury. It was a heavy financial blow to the Quechan tribe. Wrote one Washington official in 1970 ". . . it is obvious that irrespective of the harshness of the 1893 arrangement, the reclamation provision of the Act of 1904, as construed, was even more damaging to [the Quechans]" (W. H. Veeder to Phoenix area director 15 April 1970).

Why did the Quechans go along with such obvious chicanery? Some of them tried not to, which was precisely the reason why the government had insisted on establishing and maintaining absolute political dominance of the Quechans in the preceding decade. A protest sent to the secretary of interior in 1923 described the literal arm-twisting:

> In 1912 we were forced to accept allotment though we made our opposition to it. When they would not sign for allotment the Indians had their hands forced down by the Agent [perhaps the special allotting agent, Charles E. Roblin; Anna Eagen was the Indian agent at the time] to sign or make thumb marks. Nine of our old men who protest[ed] it were handcuffed and the Agent took them to Los Angeles and [had them] thrown into the jail [Indians to interior secretary May 1923; statement was signed by seventy-five individuals].

Through these actions, government representatives were preventing the reservation from ever fulfilling the ideals of the allotment system. In 1940, an estimated two thousand acres of alloted land—about one-quarter of all allotments—were still unusable according to the Bureau of Indian Affairs (Woehlke to commissioner 28 June 1940).

Again, the key to successful farming of any land in the area was an irrigation system. And the promise of free irrigation water had been the sole reason that some Indians were willing to cede their land in 1893; it was the basis for their bargaining. But the 1893 Agreement turned out to be a cruel sham on this vital issue as well, because no irrigation canal was built between 1893 and 1910. In fact, the Colorado River Irrigation Company's right to build a canal was revoked by the Interior Department in 1898, and the company was ordered off the reservation. This action should have nullified the entire 1893 Agreement (Veeder to Phoenix Area Director 15 April 1970), but Congress ignored such details, just as it ignored the agreement in the 1904 legislation.

The Quechans would eventually get their irrigation water, but it would hardly be free. They would pay for the reclamation service's construction not only on their own lands, but on those sold to Anglos within the old reservation boundaries as well. The costs of construction would be deducted from the proceeds from reservation land sales. Despite all the confusion and anger the 1893 Agreement generated, it was virtually worthless—but not yet null and void.

Shortly after the allotments were assigned in 1912, the United States Reclamation Service dug a series of irrigation laterals on the reservation, as well as in the surrounding area. Quechan men who had received prior permission from the agency were allowed to work as salaried laborers on the construction and maintenance of the main system of laterals. All smaller ditches running to individual allotments had to be dug and cleaned by the allottees themselves—without pay. The work on the main laterals would be another source of income for the Quechans for as long as the government was willing to pay them for their efforts (H. M. Carter to commissioner 10 February 1913). But this employment also turned out to be temporary; by 1915, the government had scaled down the irrigation maintenance system and no longer hired Quechan men for labor.

Some Quechans worked hard at digging their own ditches on usable land; then later, groups of men worked together to clean out the debris so the water would flow more freely. These men were considered good wage laborers and were very conscious of the distinction between volunteer and wage labor; occasionally an angry group would march up to the agency to complain that the volunteer work they were being asked to do on the irrigation laterals was not bringing them in wages (H. M. Carter to commissioner 10 February 1913; A. G. Pollock to commissioner 28 January 1913).

Confusion, anger, and frustration increased as those who could attempted to settle down and farm according to the allotment system. For one thing, the Indians recalled the government's agreement to provide for the "purchase of tools, farming implements, and seeds" from funds received from the sale of excess lands on the reservation (1893 Agreement, Art. IV). In January 1913, a few Quechans learned that a new shipment of farm tools had arrived at the agency, so they assembled for what they thought would be a free distribution. Instead, the agency informed them that they would either have to pay cash for the tools or earn them by working off the cost on public work projects arranged by the agency. The tribal business committee's Miguel faction dashed off an angry letter of protest to the commissioner. As usual, the Indian office returned the letter to the Fort Yuma agency for further explanation, but the agency's long report of justification made no mention of the provisions in the 1893 Agreement (Indians to commissioner 10 January 1913; A. G. Pollock to commissioner 28 January 1913). However conceived in the minds of administrators, this procedure of selling farm implements simply turned those Indians who could not afford to buy tools into debt peons, because the public works turned out to be labor on the school and agency farm tracts. How much time was required to reimburse the cost of the tools is not known; the point is that to receive the tools, a man had to be already successful as a farmer and have available cash, or else be working at wage labor (in which case he would not be working full time on his allotment), or he would have to work for the agency to pay off the cost of his tools, thus deflecting his energies from farming his allotment. In short, those who really needed the tools could get them only by spending less time at farming their own land.

In 1914, just over a year after the allotments had been issued, another paradoxical situation developed. Loson L. Odle, the agent who succeeded Anna Eagen at Fort Yuma, wrote the commissioner for permission to lease certain allotments to Anglo farmers. His request sounded reasonable enough:

> It will prove advantageous to the Indians in general to have all lands belonging to women and children, with exceptional cases, arbitrarily leased for a period of five years or less for improvements including clearing, leveling and placing in crops, fencing, etc. [Odle to commissioner 30 January 1914].

By arbitrary leasing, Odle meant that he as agent would arrange the leases; the Indian allottees would have no say in the matter. (Odle did have this power, granted him by the government's Omnibus Bill of 1910.) Many of these were to be improvement leases, whereby the lessee paid nothing for the first five years in return for his efforts to make the land usable. The Indian office approved the plan but reminded Odle that the aim of the allotment system was to induce the Indian to farm his own land. Odle calculated that of the 819 original allotments, 616 (or 6,160 acres of the 8,190 acres in control of Indian families) could be thrown open to Anglo lessees. If all this land were leased to non-Indians—those presumably with the capital and equipment to develop the land for farming—the reservation's economic base would certainly be improved. But common sense was sadly lacking in the plan. After spending time and capital to improve a tract, why would an Anglo lessee want to give it up after five years? And why would he leave the soil fertile enough for the Indian owner to be able to grow crops without having to fertilize it (at large expense) or let it lie fallow until it regenerated (which would necessitate its having to be cleared and prepared for farming all over again).

Odle's request implied that the Quechans, who had been clearing brush, planting, weeding, and harvesting in small cooperating groups of kinsmen for hundreds of years, were suddenly either unwilling or unable to perform these tasks in 1912–1913, at least on any more than a subsistence scale. Some Quechans probably were unwilling, particularly those with menial but secure employment in nearby Yuma. Others were probably unable to farm their allotments successfully because of the poorness of the soil and/or their lack of money for equipment, seed, and financial reserves to withstand the loss of a crop due to drought, flood, or other disaster. To turn the allotment system into a successful, cash-crop enterprise for most of the Indians would require more abundant aid than the Indian office was willing to give at that time. The Quechans could and did continue to grow crops for subsistence. But to grow them for more than mere survival, the Indians required cash, and most of them could not get it by farming their own lands.

The Quechans had another shock coming: they, not the lessees, had to pay "O and M" (operation and maintenance) charges on the irrigation water brought to their allotments. The charges were deducted from whatever lease money was received by the agency, on the grounds that because water charges arose from improvement of private lands, the Indian allottee and not the lessee or the tribe as a whole should bear the costs. Those Quechans wishing to farm their own land would, of course, be obliged to pay the charges whether the harvest was profitable or not. Again, none of the correspondence concerning this rather curious display of bureaucratic logic mentioned the provisions of the 1893 Agreement that had granted ten years of free water for one acre of each Indian's allotment.[4]

Anglo farmers were slow to take advantage of the leasing opportunity. And, for obvious reasons, the Indians' own farming efforts were sluggish. In 1916, only 2,000 acres of the reservation were under cultivation. Half of these were farms of Anglo lessees; Anglos had also leased another 400 acres but had not yet begun to improve the land (E. M. Sweet, Jr., Indian office inspector, 27 May 1916). But then much of the reservation away from the river was semidesert and could not be farmed easily by Indians or Anglos.

The thoroughly disillusioned Quechans could not understand why Agent Odle had the right to lease lands without their consent, and they felt the government had betrayed them badly by not furnishing them with free farm implements and water. Patrick Miguel was among the first to take retaliatory action. Acting in concert with an Anglo attorney in Yuma, Patrick placed a complaint about the agent and his staff before the Yuma County grand jury and asked for a complete investigation. At the same time, he and his faction urged Quechan parents not to send their children to the Fort Yuma school, a strategy that was not at all novel by then but still effective in arousing official attention. Agent Odle retaliated by issuing a warrant charging Patrick with burglary (correspondence describing the specifications of the charge is missing). The issue simmered down when the Anglo attorney agreed to drop the grand jury charges and help get the children into school in exchange for Odle's dropping the charges against Miguel and two other Indians (Odle to commissioner 28 October, 17 November 1914). Again, there was no change in the political imbalance.

All factions, acting separately, then flooded the Indian office with petitions of protest about the land administration (Indians to commissioner 30 March, 12 April, 2 May 1915). The office sent an inspector, whose subsequent report cleared the agent of any wrongdoing. This merely increased the Quechans' distress. By 1916, they were ready to try anything to change their predicament. Almost on cue, a dubious character calling himself Curley the Crow arrived on one of the incoming trains. He was, he confided to the impressed Quechans, the sole survivor of Custer's last stand. After listening to their complaints, he generously offered to take their case to Washington—if the Indians would take up a collection for his ticket. After pocketing the money, he left his hopeful benefactors and was never heard from again (Odle to commissioner 29 March 1916; Yuma *Daily Sun* 11 March 1916).

Three years later, in 1919, representatives of an organization known as the Mission Indian Federation convinced some Quechans that by joining the group, they could put greater pressure on the Indian office for a change in policy, particularly land policy. The federation was well-organized in southern California, with local officers on several reservations coordinating their activities and ideology with the overall director, an Anglo named Purl Willis. The Quechan branch's members came mostly from the Pasqual and Escalanti factions, along with some of the Somerton homesteaders who were kinsmen of the Escalanti group on the reservation. The federation provided two important services to the Quechans: it gave them news of the latest developments in government policy, and it offered them sophisticated advice on how to make protests to the government (primarily to congressmen or the secretary of interior rather than to the Indian office). Members of the federation quickly became another factional group on the reservation, bitterly opposed to Agent Odle and his allotment policies and openly hostile to Patrick Miguel and his group. "Patrick Miguel is a betrayer of his people," wrote the Quechans' federation captain, Henry Wilson, in 1923. Federation members began boycotting politically inspired meetings called by other factions and refused to have anything to do with measures sponsored by the Indian agency. But, although their petitions must have made Agent Odle and his superiors uncomfortable, they were no more successful than any of the other factions in altering the administrative status quo.

The leasing plan was not only a contradiction of the ultimate ideals of the allotment system, but it also denied the Quechans the full economic benefit of the only economic resource (besides their labor) that they possessed. It was plainly devised as an economic expedient for the Indian office. If everything went as planned, the primary cost of developing the land would be borne by Anglo farmers, and the Quechans would bear the money and labor costs involved in irrigation. The Indians could somehow survive for a few years until the land was improved; the development or improvement leases could then be cancelled; and the Indians could then farm their own allotments—or so it was reasoned far away from the scene in the Indian office.

Everything did not go as planned, however. Leasing for improvement was soon replaced by leasing for cash. These cash arrangements ran much longer than the "five years or less" mentioned by Odle, and leasing became a primary and permanent feature of the reservation's economic system. It, not allotment farming by Quechans themselves, was the basic source of the Indians' land-use income on the reservation from 1914 until 1974.

SOCIOCULTURAL IMPOSITIONS

While weathering the almost continuous assaults by Indians against his land administration practices, Agent Odle, more than any of his predecessors, attempted to manipulate the sociocultural patterns of the Quechans for the sake of their development. The Quechans' memory of Odle is not at all charitable. The memory is kept alive by the frequent retelling of personal experiences by those who knew him—stories of his deceit in land leasing, his monumental rages against Anglos who attempted to aid the Quechans, his favoritism in factional squabbles. These charges and others are preserved in National Archives documents, together with Odle's lengthy rebuttals. Nothing dispels the basic impression that, even when compared to other agents, Odle was a generally unsympathetic administrator who was much more attentive to the demands of the Indian office than to the interests of his Quechan wards. Compared to his predecessors, his administrative style had a greater impact on reservation life for two reasons: first, he was the Quechans' agent for an unusually long time—fourteen years—and during the period when the government's most concerted attack on traditional Indian life was under way; second, as the government's Indian policy crystallized, he was given more explicit instructions on prodding the Quechans toward civilization, instructions that were themselves unsympathetic to traditional Quechan values and lifeways. Odle's public personality was thus aided and abetted by an authoritarian hierarchy climbing above him all the way to the Indian office in Washington.

During Odle's administration, the Indian office pushed for two major educational changes. One was to transfer as many Indian students as possible to local public schools in Yuma. The plan had actually been proposed as early as 1911 but was shelved because of "adverse feelings" on the part of Yuma townspeople (H. Hall, Inspector, to commissioner 13 February 1911). In 1916, the Indian office again suggested that the plan be implemented. Agent Odle demurred, apparently to avoid offending Anglos; he reported that Indian students "would appear so dirty" if they were imposed on Yuma's public schools. Nevertheless, he sent five students to schools in Yuma that year and scheduled eight or ten more for 1917. The schools could have handled forty Indian students at that time (Odle to commissioner 7 June 1916). The plan had only token participation in the following twenty years.

The second change ordered by the Indian office was to place young Quechans in the homes of Anglos in Yuma, along the lines of the "outing system" developed by the government in the late nineteenth century. Those Indians who participated in the program (there were never many and most of those who did were girls) remembered some happy times in 1914 and the years following—trips to the ocean, holidays with the Anglos; but they remembered also, and emphasized, the physical labor involved—washing and housecleaning. The experience certainly provided the youngsters with firsthand knowledge of the Anglos' domestic life, but whatever practical skills they acquired only contributed to the increasing pool of local domestic help.

In brief, neither of these educational innovations had much impact on reservation development. The outing system merely provided a cheap source of domestic labor, and whatever assimilative benefits might have accrued from attendance at Anglo schools remained largely unknown because of Agent Odle's recalcitrance.

However, one educational feature at the boarding school did provide a model for Anglo-type organization that carried over to the reservation, and that was the voluntary association, or club. To stimulate a spirit of competitive achievement within the student body, the students were encouraged to join a series of clubs or teams. There was, for example, a Quechan football team that defeated the Yuma High School team in 1915. And the young girls were organized into clubs that gave exhibits of sewing and cooking at local fairs. The clubs were given names such as Musepaws (Bees) or the Nowadaha Club, and the accomplishments and prizes of some were held as goals to be emulated by others. Boys joined carpentry clubs, leatherwork clubs, and other vocational or agricultural groups. The clubs were thoroughly Anglo in conception, with elected officers, regular meetings, and other similar manifestations.

Although the school clubs may not have been the only stimulus, organizations like them soon sprang up on the reservation,—a tribal band that became famous throughout the southwest, a "Quechan Mothers' Club" whose members gathered with the agency's field matron to practice the techniques of Anglo homemaking, and a "Returned Students' Club" formed by those who had attended off-reservation government schools. (The latter became, briefly, a political pressure group in the 1920s.)

Unfortunately, the school's curriculum didn't change its graduates' prospects for obtaining any but menial employment, and reversion to the economic doldrums of the reservation was the only choice many of them had for years to come.

Agent Odle was also ordered to discourage the Quechans' traditional religious beliefs. He was aided in this by the presence of Christian missionaries on the reservation, as, by 1905, the reservation's exclusively Catholic domain had been penetrated by the Methodists, the Moravians, and a nonsectarian Christian group known as the National Indians' Association. Internecine struggles for Indian converts broke out immediately as Catholic officials protested the arrival of these other faiths to the Indian office (Bureau of Catholic Missions to commissioner 29 January 1907). It seems that the Methodists, and later the Nazarenes, were encouraged to gain a foothold on the reservation by Patrick Miguel. Perhaps partly for that reason, Agent Odle sent a series of complaints to his superiors about the Methodist missionary's "meddlesome interference" in his administrative functions (E. M. Sweet to commissioner 27 May 1916; Odle to commissioner 22 October 1921). In fact, after their arrival on the reservation, most of the mission groups served as sources of material aid for destitute Quechans. After 1905, Methodist missionaries in particular seemed eager to work in other than strictly religious realms of reservation affairs.

But Odle could not passively rely on the missions to stamp out traditional religious practices. Goaded by the Indian office, he intervened in the Quechans' mourning ceremonies. Of all the religious rituals, the practice of destroying or giving away the property of the deceased had been the most irksome to the government since the reservation was first established. The Indians were not yet protected by the federal Constitution, so the Indian office felt free to direct Odle:

> ... at once [to] take up the matter of the Indians giving away the personal property of deceased Indians and the

> supplementing of such property by purchases as reported by the Inspector. The Indians should be informed that the property left by deceased Indians must be distributed to the relatives of the deceased in accordance with the State laws of distribution. Please give this matter your immediate attention and submit a report at an early date as to the progress of your efforts in this direction. [E. B. Meritt to Odle 8 July 1916].

The Indian office memo to Odle was probably referring to the Quechan habit of providing new sets of clothes for the dead at funerals. The garments were carefully arranged near the body during the wake, then burned later in the funeral pyre. Bereaved Quechans again bought or made new clothing for the *karˀúk* mourning rituals; this, too, was consumed in memorial pyres. These traditions, of course, made no economic sense to the Indian office. To the Quechans, however, cremation was the only proper treatment of the dead; and their property had to be destroyed or given away, the spot where the charred remains were buried had to be carefully smoothed over, and no mention of the deceased's name in front of his kinsmen could thereafter be made—all for the purpose of erasing from kinsmen's minds the painful reminder of their loss.

To Odle, the memo meant that he should not only curtail the destruction of property, thus perpetuating painful memories, but that he should also end the all-important act of cremation itself. In direct response to the Indian office's instructions, he reported, "We have made some progress along this line since we have reduced the number of cremations from 53 in 1913 to 14 in 1915 and 14 in 1916" (Odle to commissioner 12 July 1916). It is questionable, however, whether this reduction was due to Odle's efforts, or to the fact that fewer people died during the latter two years. We have only Odle's figures to rely upon.

The Quechans were obliged to clear with Odle's office any plans for religious or convivial get-togethers on the reservation. The Indians had to plan well ahead, because Odle sent their requests to the Indian office for its comments before granting his own approval. In the following examples, the official government attitude toward traditional Indian lifeways is abundantly clear.

In 1915, the Quechans requested permission to hold a fair on the reservation. Odle sent the request to the Indian office, emphasizing that expressions of traditional Indianness would be soft-pedalled. The Indian office conveyed its delight that there would be no "Indian dances, horse races, or other harmful features of that character" to mar the essential rural Angloness of the whole thing (E. B. Meritt to Odle, 1915).

In 1922, a group of Quechans petitioned Agent Odle for permission to hold a *karˀúk* mourning ritual in memory of a tribal member who was killed in action in World War I. Again the agent forwarded the petition to the Indian office, and again the response held unswervingly to the assimilationist doctrine:

> Your desire to honor the memory of the Indian soldiers who lost their lives during the war is indeed praiseworthy and indicates a most commendable spirit of patriotism. However, I think one day should be sufficient for this celebration, and that the proper time for it is the day known as "Decoration Day" among the whites, which is May 30th each year. Under the circumstances, I cannot give my permission for the celebration October 15th to 18th, but will be very glad to have the Indians observe the next Decoration Day in some fitting manner similar to the way the white people celebrate it [E. B. Meritt to Indians 6 October 1922].

This apparently gave the Indians another idea: why not have two ceremonies—one, more or less clandestinely, on the order of the four-day *karˀúk*; the other, as the Indian office suggested, on the official Anglo Memorial Day? Since that time, the Indians have had annual Memorial Day services that are neatly split between Anglo Christian patterns (usually in the morning) and traditional Quechan patterns (late in the afternoon). The *karˀúk* has been staged less and less often, as the costs of the necessary food and materials have risen, but the traditions surrounding it and the cremation ritual could not be stamped out by the government completely. If anything, the added Memorial Day ritual increased the expense of the mourning process, because Quechan families not only felt obliged to make or buy new clothing for the Quechan ceremony, but also to provide large quantities of food for the Anglo ceremony. But in 1924, the government became legally powerless to continue intervening in traditional religious rituals because the Indians were made American citizens. Anthropologist Daryll Forde described a *karˀúk* held in 1929 (Forde 1931: 221 ff.), and I attended a truncated version in 1966.

Throughout the twentieth century, the rituals surrounding the death of tribal members have been sources of tribal cohesion—occasions when factions forgot their differences to mourn the loss of one of their members. In 1912, a group of Quechans, including Patrick Miguel, told an agency official that "on these festal occasions [i.e., mourning rituals] they forgot their differences and paid homage as one family to their dead, but that in the common affairs of every day [sic] life they were like white men—neither forgot or forgave an injury" (H. Carter to commissioner 10 February 1913). Quechans in 1966 used practically identical words to describe the tribe's feelings at funerals.

The rituals also gave frustrated political leaders, such as Patrick Miguel, a chance to play an important public role. Patrick and other factional leaders prided themselves on being ritual experts who planned the ceremonies and served as advisors when the people were unsure as to what ritual element should come next. The leaders were also careful at these times to give eloquent speeches, a perpetuation of the ideal qualities of the ancient *k^{w}axót̯*. These men on these occasions were doing something for the tribe as a whole and thus, whatever their other motivations may have been, were building up political support for use in confrontations with the government or among their own factions.

But, despite the government's incessant push for anglicization, there were some aspects of Anglo life that the Quechans were not expected to adopt. Agent Odle seemed particularly agitated about what he termed the "curse of whiskey" among his wards. His agitation was not entirely self-motivated. He had been ordered by the Indian office to cut off the liquor traffic among the Quechans. Earlier agents had indiscriminately labeled opposition within the tribe as antiprogressive. Odle seemed equally indiscriminate, but his opposition was billed as "the whisky element" in his letters to the commissioner: the Miguel faction represented the whiskey element; Anglo attorneys in Yuma who aided Patrick Miguel were members of the whiskey element; the Methodist missionary was "soft" on the whiskey element; and so on. The agent was also agitated about the growth of a small town on the reservation's southern border. Appropriately dubbed Winterhaven, the town was created as a gambling and drinking spa by its founders in 1917. According to Odle, it was the center of a trading network for illicit booze and, along with the small town of Algodones across the international boundary in Mexico, was the source of most of the liquor consumed by the Quechans. The interdiction of the Algodones trade was simple: Odle merely instructed customs officials not to allow Indians to pass unless they had the agent's written permission. The Winterhaven problem was more vexing, compelling Odle to play the role of sleuth. With an Indian office inspector and some Indian police, he hid for most of one night among the desert brush, hoping to intercept a whiskey shipment. Sure enough, just before dawn, his small force captured a Model-T Ford creaking along under a heavy load of bootleg alcohol. Odle promptly impounded the car and its cargo, then sent a very long report, complete with photographs of the booty, to the Indian office, telling of his role in the venture. This was perhaps his finest hour in the fight against the liquor trade, for soon the drinking problem among the Indians assumed major proportions and was still a problem in the mid-1960s. (Incidentally, the Quechans and other

Indians, unlike their fellow American citizens, were forbidden by law to buy or consume alcohol until 1953.)

Odle was also energetic, but only moderately successful, in his efforts to induce Quechan couples to marry legally rather than to live in the common-law bonds of Indian-style marriage. His motivation was probably based as much on economic as on moral grounds, because by 1921 yet another difficulty had surfaced to confound the allotment system: original allottees were dying, leaving their land to be divided according to the rules of the State of California (half to the surviving spouse, half divided among the living children). There were problems of deciding which spouse and which children from a series of consensual unions were legally entitled to a share of the land. More serious was the problem of dividing a single ten-acre tract among numerous children who were not themselves original allottees. None of them could make a profit from farming one acre, or even from cooperatively farming ten acres once they married and had children. Similarly, the lease money from a single ten-acre tract had to be divided among several relatives. This problem grew worse as time went on and more original allottees died.[5] There were a rapidly increasing number of Quechans who had no land of their own because of the effects of continual subdivision of the ten-acre plots. In yet another way, then, the formal mechanisms of the allotment system were subverting its idealistic intent.

It is unlikely that many composite family groups long remained on their allotments in the unfertile portions of the reservation—if they ever bothered to settle there at all. Whether they moved in from outlying settlements, or lived within the reservation's boundaries originally, Quechan families in the 1920s and 1930s were not evenly dispersed across the reservation. Most of them were concentrated in the central and southern portions of the area, along the main roads to Indian Hill, Yuma, and Winterhaven. This made it easier for them to get to town to shop or work, and also to socialize with each other. Many built their homes in family clusters close to the roads, each cluster consisting of three or four buildings and a ramada, separated from other clusters by approximately ten acres of open land. Those with enough cash built wooden frame houses, but at that time most of the homes were made of adobe walls with a wood and tarpaper roof. A few of the adobe structures had survived the harsh wind and sun of the desert climate as well as destruction by anguished, mourning Quechans and were still standing in the late 1960s.

Not all home units were composite families. There was probably a gradually increasing number of nuclear families (husband, wife, and children) who lived apart from close kinsmen. Individual wagework in all cultures seems to favor nuclear families, so most of those Quechans choosing to live apart from close kinsmen were probably wage earners in Yuma who would not or could not successfully farm their allotments. The nuclear family would not have been a viable unit in the traditional horticultural economy of the Quechans, but it was well-suited to Anglo lifeways. For reasons I will describe later, however, composite families have remained a significant feature of reservation social structure.

Gradually, too, the traditional clan divisions became blurred. Whatever their original importance (Bee 1963:217; Forde 1931:145), they were "just names" to many youngsters by 1928. Marriages between members of the same clan, earlier considered acts of incest, now evoked no more than a scolding from the old people. And traditional kinship terminology used by Quechans to refer to relatives, analogous to "mother" or "father" in our society, was yielding to English terms. Traditional Quechan kinship terms were very specific, distinguishing between relatives that in English would be lumped into a single term; the older Quechans distinguished between an older brother (*ancen*) and a younger brother (*aşúc*), for example (Halpern 1942:425–41; Bee 1963:214–215). Whatever significance such specific distinctions may have had was being undermined as the influence of Anglo language and culture became more pronounced.

One feature of traditional kinship behavior did endure, probably because of the persistence of the composite family, and that was the important role grandparents played in making household decisions. They were always present in the home to give advice, scold, or offer tender loving care. One older Quechan in the 1960s recalled that as a youngster she was reluctant to follow her mother's orders if they were contrary to those of her grandmother. Another tribal member declared that his ancient grandparents "tell me what to do no matter how old I am" (Bee 1963:219). Children in the 1920s and 1930s were still being taught to listen to the advice of grandparents and not to bother them with idle chatter. And, repeatedly, old people were referred to as "the real leaders of the tribe," although the actual patterns of political warfare did not seem to bear out such statements, at least in public leadership behavior.

For entertainment in the early 1900s, the people visited what Quechans described as gaming houses. The last one of these closed with the death of its owner in the 1920s. The gaming houses were places where the people could go to play cards, hoop-and-pole, *peón* (a variant of the traditional shell or moccasin game popular with other American Indian groups), or to listen to songs and dance. Allegedly there was another activity at the houses as well—changing blankets, or, as more candid Quechans termed it, changing wives. The houses were individually owned, and the owners provided food for those who attended. It was probably a rise in entertainment costs, together with increasing government pressure to obliterate expressions of Indianness, that ended the gaming houses as features of reservation life. While they existed, they served as centers of interaction among nonkinsmen, where reservation news could be disseminated and mulled over informally.[6]

Much to the chagrin of Agent Odle and his predecessors, Yuma and Winterhaven also lured Quechans having idle hours to while away. Some would go to get drunk on illicit liquor, panhandling to pay the price of a bottle. Others, particularly older men, gathered at the local pool hall for spirited games with each other or with Anglos.

But the Quechans' main recreation was visiting with each other in the coolness of desert evenings and, on Anglo holidays (such as July Fourth), gathering for reservation-wide "doings" that featured dancing, singing, and food.

LAND AND ECONOMICS ONCE MORE

Odle's long tenure as Indian agent at Fort Yuma ended in 1925.[7] During his term, little was done to promote the Quechans' own farming efforts, allotment farming being an economic venture they were increasingly eager to turn over to Anglos in exchange for lease money. Yet, at the policymaking level in Washington, the government still clung to its conviction that the answer to Indian development lay in the creation of small-scale Indian farmers. As the rest of the country was about to slide into economic depression, Odle's replacement at the agency announced to a mass meeting that the government was going to sponsor a "five-year industrial program" for those wanting to farm. In 1926 (the year the Meriam survey was commissioned), about eighty-five men met with the new agent, H. B. Jolley, to work out individualized plans to revive their farming efforts and improve their homes. The heart of the program was a loan fund that the Quechans could tap as needed for equipment, seed, and construction materials. They would repay the loans as soon as their ventures realized a profit.

In the next year and a half, the Indians added 250 acres to the total amount of land they farmed themselves. At the same time, the Indian agent reported, the amount of leased land decreased—although he did not give the amount of the decrease (Jolley to commissioner 1 December 1927). But some participants found fault with the plan. Among them was Patrick Miguel's brother, Joseph. According to Agent Jolley:

> This Indian said that the [program] . . . should have been accompanied by an order on one of the grocery stores to supply the Indians with plenty to eat and to support their families while the crops were growing. He claimed that one of the great needs of the Indians of this reservation was aid in support of their families while they were growing their crops; but I do not agree with him in his contention as the best of our Indian farmers take good care of their families and support themselves while their crops are maturing [Jolley to commissioner 1 December 1927].

Miguel's complaint should not have been dismissed so lightly. Many Indians agreed to the program because they were destitute; but if their loans were to be spent on equipment, building materials, and seed, how indeed were these Indians to survive while their crops were growing? As they had been surviving before the program was introduced, supposedly. But that could not continue, for the men would now have to devote their wage-earning time to farming their own land, receiving little or no income until their crops were harvested and sold—assuming no crop failure, and assuming there would be a net profit from the operation. The Indians who were most in need of an improvement program were therefore not able to take full advantage of this one; they could not afford to.

Still, it was possible to take the money, spend it on food or other items needed for survival, and not worry about repaying it. What, realistically, could the government do to collect the loan? Attach the land? It had already done that in a way, since the Indians could not sell their allotments. Attach lease income or wages? If the Indians were destitute in the first place, such action would only enhance their poverty—a responsibility the government agents were probably not anxious to assume. We can never be sure of the Indians' motives in this case, but the agent reported that the loans, even those incurred by successful farmers, were still unpaid almost two years after the program had begun (Jolley to commissioner 5 January 1929). By that time, too, only forty-five of the eighty-five Quechans in the program were actually engaged in farming. Some had stopped work and had destroyed their homes and equipment because of the death of a relative. Others had separated from their wives and had stopped trying to farm. Still others had gone back to leasing their farmland and had taken wage jobs in Yuma as a more profitable way of spending their time. One man used his loan money to hire a Mexican to farm his land, while the allottee continued his well-paying job with the railroad; but no others were in a position to try this gambit. There were still other destitute Quechans who were not allowed to sign up for the program because—from the agent's standpoint—eligibility rested on an Indian's attempt to imitate Anglo middle-class morality:

> Senator Wheeler: How about this fellow getting a reimbursible loan?
>
> [Agent] Jolley: When did I tell you I would not help you get a reimbursible loan?
>
> John Curran [a Quechan]: That was some time ago. I have been up here [to the agency] three times.
>
> Jolley: Why did I refuse your request?
>
> Curran: You refused me because I was not legally married; that is what you said.
>
> Jolley: Because you left your wife and took up with another woman.
>
> Curran: When I make an agreement to pay I got to pay just the same as anybody else.
>
> Senator Wheeler: There is just this about it, you cannot expect the Government to help you out unless you are going to behave yourself.
>
> Curran: That is right.
>
> Senator Wheeler: You have to behave yourself just like anybody else. If you do not behave yourself you cannot expect the Government to help you; at least so far as I am concerned I will not be in favor of it. If you have a wife you have to take care of her and not run around with some other woman.
>
> Curran: I do not run around; she is the one that runs around. Mr. Jolley knows all about it. I was not running around. [U.S. Senate 1931:8026–7].

Immediate economic aid, not merely long-term help, was what many Quechans needed. The reimbursible loans, if used in ways not intended by the government, met some of these immediate needs—for a few months at least. But this was not development; it was survival.

Most of those who remained in the program and were, in the agent's estimation, making a good living had two characteristics in common: they had at least twenty, and often thirty acres of good farmland planted in cash crops (mostly cotton, some alfalfa), and they had additional income from wages or land leasing. But even this partial success of the plan was soon to be stifled. By 1931, the effects of the depression had fallen upon the Quechans; farming was earning them practically nothing, and the sources of steady wage labor in Yuma had dried up.

Agent Jolley tried to get jobs for Quechan men on a local highway construction crew, but there were not enough jobs to go around. His efforts must have been somewhat motivated by urgings from his superiors, because, by then, the Indian office was feeling increasing pressure from Indian rights groups and from Congress, as a result of the Meriam survey. The office was on the defensive, pushing hard for Indian economic development at the worst possible time. But Congress had no intention of letting the matter depend on eleventh-hour tactics of Indian program administrators. It now demanded its own facts. In 1931, a senate fact-finding committee, part of the congressional team sent out to investigate the living situations of all Indian tribes on reservations, arrived at Fort Yuma to ask the agent some extremely probing questions and collect the statements of Quechans willing to testify about conditions in the community. For the first time, the Indians had an opportunity to discuss their grievances before a government body that was not affiliated with the Office of Indian Affairs.

Patrick Miguel had been an early participant in the five-year industrial plan. He took full advantage of the opportunity to talk to the senators, revealing in his statements the cynicism that must have been rampant in the community at the time:

> Senator Wheeler: These [Quechans] are pretty good workers, are they not?
> Mr. [Patrick] Miguel: Yes, sir.
> Senator Wheeler: They are all willing to work?
> Mr. Miguel: Yes, sir.
> Senator Frazier: Do you farm any of your own land?
> Mr. Miguel: I do not; now.
> Senator Frazier: What are you doing now?
> Mr. Miguel: I am working out here on the highway.
> Senator Wheeler: Do you actually work?
> Mr. Miguel: Sure.
> Senator Thomas: What kind of a job have you with the highway department?
> Mr. Miguel: Just as a laborer.
> Senator Thomas: What kind of work do you do?
> Mr. Miguel: Pick and shovel.
> Senator Thomas: A Carlisle graduate doing pick and shovel work? Did you graduate from Carlisle?
> Mr. Miguel: Yes, sir.
> Senator Thomas: How much time did you spend there?
> Mr. Miguel: About five years.

> Senator Thomas: Can you handle a pick and shovel better by having this education?
>
> Mr. Miguel: Yes, sir; more scientifically than the others.
>
> Senator Thomas: Tell the committee what became of your land.
>
> Mr. Miguel: I have got my land leased. I have got about 30 acres of it leased, and I have tried to get 30 more belonging to my immediate family leased, but on account of the financial depression all over the country I could not get anybody to take it [U.S. Senate 1931:7011–12].

The senate investigators found that another land problem had developed during Odle's tenure as agent and was smouldering on the reservation. Since the land allotments had been made, the Colorado's channel had moved steadily eastward, the progressive meandering reaching its climax during a flood in June 1920. When the muddy waters had receded, they left a 4,572-acre area of river bottomland between the reservation's old eastern border and the river's new channel. It became evident that this was a permanent change, and the Quechans clearly saw its potential. Arguing from a literal interpretation of the description of the original reservation boundaries, the Indians claimed this land as part of their community, thinking that it would provide additional fertile land to accommodate the growing number of people who had no reservation land of their own.

For a time the government hedged on the Indians' claim, then, much to their dismay, turned the new land over to the reclamation service for flood control purposes. Before long, opportunistic non-Indian farmers moved into the area and started farming the fertile soil. The Quechans watched this trespass helplessly, bitterly disappointed that the government would take no action to evict these newcomers. They protested to the senate investigators (U.S. Senate 1931:8030), asking that these lands become part of the reservation. Then later, they hired a lawyer to argue their case with the government. But the issue was never settled to the tribe's satisfaction and has remained a continuous source of agitation among the Quechans as well as a preoccupation of every Quechan tribal government since 1938.

POLITICS AND ECONOMIC DEVELOPMENT: 1900–1934

This was the heyday of the government's paternalism, of doing for the Indians self-righteously rather than doing with the help of their counsel. Leaders of powerless Quechan political factions vied with each other for community support. Their ideological positions veered wildly between conciliation and aggressive confrontation with each other and with government officials. Fleeting moments of factional solidarity (as in the election of the business committee, or in early protests against the land-allotment procedures) were always overwhelmed by the eruption of interfactional (or sometimes intra-factional) conflict that made any kind of mass political pressure against government policies impossible. Overtly, most of the agents and the Indian office lamented the factional rifts. Yet, unquestionably, the intracommunity strife made the administration of unpopular policy much easier, and factional rifts were kept alive in part by the bringing together of key members from the various groups in a so-called advisory committee that could not speak with a single voice, and thus could be largely ignored. The principle of democratic participation by the Indians was an illusion; by government design, no Indian was allowed to acquire a knowledge of the skills of orderly administration and civic planning. The order of the day was individual assimilation, not community viability.

To achieve economic development of the Quechans, the government was convinced it had to establish and maintain absolute political control of their reservation. It refused to give Indian leaders free rein over government resources without prior training (which they were not given), and, besides, it needed coercive force to impose economic programs (such as allotment) on the Indians, that it felt were necessary regardless of how the Indians felt about them. If the Indians wanted economic development, they had to accept government authority and work according to government guidelines. They could not improve their economic situation themselves because they could not get long-term credit from banks, and therefore could not prepare enough land to make cash cropping profitable. Without government protection of their land titles (by means of trust patents) they probably could not have even held their land base intact against the press of wheeler-dealer land speculators and Anglo farmers wanting more prime land.

But there was a series of paradoxes interacting also. From the Quechans' point of view their land base was being taken from them even with (and in part because of) government protection, specifically the land sold as public domain prior to the allotment and, later, the bottomland exposed by the Colorado's meanderings; it was the government, not Anglo settlers, that represented the greatest threat to their land base. In fact, Anglo farming interests after 1910 were better served by a leasing rather than outright purchase. The government appeared to be keeping "excess" former Indian land out of Quechan control without bothering to develop it in conjunction with Anglo commercial interests. And, while the government repeatedly asserted its political authority, it did practically nothing to provide for the long-term economic security of its wards. As in the preceding period, the local implementation of government policy and programs turned out to be a kind of antidevelopment. Why should the Quechans have become allotment farmers? The government offered them no source of capital until it was too late for them to make use of it. Meanwhile, they had to pay for implements and water; to put up with the arbitrary leasing procedures of their agent; and to face the constant prospect of economic ruin due to crop failures. Under such conditions, it only made sense to lease the land to outsiders, to settle for a small cash income that would keep them alive perhaps but would never make them prosperous. Even the lease income became insignificant as the heirs to original allotments grew more numerous. Through its efforts to reconvert the Quechans to self-sufficient small-scale farmers, the government forced them into positions of manipulated land leasers and menial wage laborers, who were preoccupied with day-to-day existence rather than long-term economic growth. As the depression settled over the country, even these economic alternatives were in very short supply.

Development was perceived by the policymakers as insuring the Indians' eventual emulation of the models Anglo society presented to them, hence their tireless efforts to impose such models on Indian community life. The models were often contradictory, yet Indian agents seemed to regard the Quechans as they would a courtroom jury—capable of striking from the record any evidence deemed inappropriate or improperly introduced. But the Quechans did not strike anything from the record and were thus fully aware of the contradictions confronting them: Agent Odle's preoccupation with championing law and order on the liquor question compared to his alleged involvement in illegal deals with Anglo lessees of Indian land (U.S. Senate 1931:8009–10); agents' mouthing the hope of eventual independent assimilation while keeping the Indians paternalistically protected from the means and experience necessary for assimilation; exposure to the good life of the Anglo middle class in the outing system that perpetuated a negative self-image due to those participating having to perform mundane and tiresome housework chores; the people being pressured to abandon traditional religious convictions in favor of a better way, the advantages of which could not have been clearly seen beyond the aggressive internecine competition for converts. The long administration of Agent Odle, in particular, seemed repressive, arbitrary, and exploitative to the Quechans, but the sad fact remains that in many of his tactics Odle was merely following orders from higher bureaucratic echelons.

"A Carlisle graduate doing pick and shovel work?" Senator Thomas seemed incredulous when he asked the question of Patrick

Miguel in 1931. The senator, for one, was finally acknowledging the clash between the idealistic intentions of national Indian policy and the realities of its local impact, specifically upon the Quechans. He should have asked his probing questions much earlier.

CHAPTER 4

The Policy Pendulum – A New Deal and Termination Threats: 1934-1961

THE DRIVE FOR INDIAN ASSIMILATION in the late nineteenth and early twentieth centuries began to slow down in the late 1920s, and was officially reversed by a group of President Roosevelt's New Dealers in the early 1930s. John Collier, outspoken Indian-rights critic of Indian office policies in the 1920s, became the new commissioner of Indian affairs in 1933 and promptly assembled a staff that shared his convictions and was willing to capitalize on the growing momentum toward policy change. Democratic group action within the various tribes, not the forced isolation-assimilation of the individual, was to become the new policy objective.

A revamped educational program was launched in April 1934 with the passage of the Johnson-O'Malley Act, a legislative result of the Meriam Report of 1928. The act empowered the secretary of interior to make contracts with individual states to cover their costs of educating Indian children in public schools and providing agricultural assistance, medical care, and other welfare benefits for Indians. This decentralized some of the power of the Indian bureau and, together with the Social Security Act of 1935, theoretically made it possible for Indians to enjoy the same quality and quantity of education and welfare programs as other residents of given states.

In 1934, Congress also passed the Wheeler-Howard Act, more popularly known as the Indian Reorganization Act (IRA). Hailed as the "Indian New Deal," it provided for immediate halts in the allotment system and in the piecemeal reduction of tribal land holdings; where possible, surplus public lands were to be returned to tribal domains and new lands were to be purchased by the government to add to existing land bases. It also directed that conservation of natural resources on Indian lands be ensured by plans coordinated with government technicians; established a revolving credit fund from which individuals or tribes could borrow capital to launch new economic ventures; provided means for Indians to get the best available college or vocational training; specified procedures to be followed by tribes wanting to form business corporations for economic development and outlined procedures through which tribes could draw up a constitution and organize politically; and waived civil service regulations so that more Indians could be integrated into the Indian office itself. Finally, in keeping with Colliers' insistence that all negotiations between the government and Indians be on a basis of mutual consent, each tribe was given the option of accepting or rejecting the IRA by popular vote.

Although 192 out of 263 tribes voting on the act accepted it, the IRA became a victim of world history. Congress was disturbed by the lack of improvement in Indian conditions in spite of the IRA, and apprehensive about continuing financial support in the face of the more urgent military demands of World War II. Money for the revolving loan fund was drastically reduced in the early forties, and there were practically no appropriations made for the purchase of additional lands. Politically conservative congressmen were further agitated by Collier's bent toward collectivism and pressed for his resignation, which he finally submitted in 1944. In 1946, Congress approved one last piece of IRA-inspired legislation: the creation of the Indian Claims Commission. This body was to simplify, and thus speed up, the process by which Indian tribes could sue the government for lands taken from them without just compensation. But the pace of settlement remained slow because of the heavy case load.

By the end of the war, the mood of Congress had once again become assimilationist. The thinking was much like that of the 1900–1934 period—that Indians should be assimilated by segregating them from sources of tribal identity—and in the early 1950s, the Indian bureau launched its relocation program, under which Indian families were voluntarily moved from reservations to urban areas and provided with jobs (or, later in the program, vocational training).

In 1953, Indians were legally permitted to purchase alcoholic beverages for the first time (67 Statute 586). That same year, both houses of Congress agreed to House Resolution 108, a call for the termination of government support to Indian communities as soon as possible. Two major tribes, the Klamaths and Menominis, as well as several smaller groups, were already considered economically and politically self-sufficient and were soon thereafter removed from federal jurisdiction. The results were disastrous (Shames 1972, e.g.). Once other Indian communities became aware of what was happening, they refused to consider termination. Community leaders became extremely suspicious of federal Indian legislation and combed through the legalistic jargon for any traces of the termination philosophy. The outcry against termination became so intense that Presidents Kennedy, Johnson, and Nixon publicly and explicitly repudiated its continued influence on official policy. Yet, by 1974, the resolution still had not been rescinded.

Congress turned out a bumper crop of Indian legislation in 1953. In addition to the alcohol and termination actions, the states of California, Minnesota, Nebraska, Oregon, and Washington were granted civil and criminal jurisdiction over all Indian lands within their boundaries (Public Law 280). This was another strike against community self-determination, and one made without the consent of the communities affected.[1] Indeed, the whole Collier-era emphasis on mutual consent between the government and Indians went by the boards in the 1950s. In a regional meeting in 1956, Commissioner Emmons observed that the principle of consent was "insidious" and too expensive (Zimmerman 1957:32).

When actual impact was compared retrospectively to expectation, it became obvious that neither swing of the policy pendulum during the 1930–1962 period did much to alter conditions on the Indian reservations. The Indian New Deal delivered little in the way of increased economic opportunity or political autonomy, and the dismal Indian march to assimilation as second-class citizens went on in spite of the good intentions of the Collier group. The pace was simply quickened by the postwar swing back to assimilation as an overt goal of national policy.

THE NEW DEAL AND EDUCATIONAL REFORM

On the Quechan reservation, the first thrust of the new Indian policy was aimed at the Fort Yuma boarding school, the focus of so much conflict in the past. In 1932, the government announced plans to convert it into a public day school as a means of upgrading the quality of Quechan education and thus promoting socioeconomic development. Some Quechans, including Patrick Miguel, had agreed just the year before that Quechan children should be placed in local public schools (U.S. Senate 1931:8007, 8009), so it looked as though the proposed change would be accepted without opposition.

But, despite the earlier opinions of Quechan spokesmen, the tribe's reaction to the proposal was thoroughly negative. Over a hundred Quechans met "regardless of factions" (as they put it) to draft a protest against the conversion of the school (Indians to commissioner 5 June 1932). Superficially, their argument was exactly that used by Agent Odle sixteen years earlier: their children were still too poor and unhealthy to benefit from contact with Anglos. But there were more basic material reasons for the resistance as well. While at the boarding school the children were assured of a good diet, health care, and sanitary surroundings. The Quechans feared these benefits would be lost if the school were to be placed under county supervision, and they were too costly for most Indian parents to provide, particularly during the economic doldrums of the depression. "Much as we want our children to acquaint themselves with the average white boy or girl, we are completely incapacitated" by the miserable domestic conditions, they wrote. These conditions were not really of their own making, because "no method of acquiring a decent domicile has ever been afforded our people." Otherwise, with regard to whatever other development schemes the government had to offer, "we can vouch with absolute certainty that the Yuma Indians will cooperate with the departments of the Government in every reasonable manner toward any constructive movement or toward any constructive ruling that would be beneficial to this tribe" (Indians to commissioner 5 June 1932). The hostile dependency relationship could not have been more clearly expressed. Once again factions had united briefly in the face of external threat.

The protest was to no avail, however, although it did delay the conversion for a few years. By 1935, as a result of the Johnson-O'Malley Act, the Fort Yuma boarding school was turned into a public day school in a district newly created from the reservation and its environs. The Quechans adjusted quickly and well. For the first time, Quechan parents could become participating members of the school administration, and for the next twenty-three years they held most of the elective positions on the local school board. Quechans seemed anxious to participate in the parents' organization and to perform voluntary tasks in such activities as room parties and assemblies. Quechan children were a large majority among the student population because of the way the school district boundaries had been drawn, but became an ethnic-racial minority when they completed the elementary grades and were bused to the public high school in Yuma.[2]

Despite their protest and petition against the school change in 1932, the Quechans agreed with the government that better education was a means for bettering the material conditions of Indian life.

By 1935 also, Quechan youngsters were able to take advantage of expanded vocational training at government schools in Phoenix and Riverside. But the same old problem still existed, made worse by the effects of the depression. In the absence of economic opportunity, particularly on the local scene, the education the Indian youths received simply developed them into better trained, unemployed adults.

INTRODUCING THE INDIAN REORGANIZATION ACT

Having resolved the education issue (with little input from the Quechans), the government turned to the task of persuading them to accept the more wide-ranging Indian Reorganization Act. It was to be a long and laborious process. The first step had to be the creation of a coordinating body among the Quechans, in keeping with the still untested policy of government-Indian consensus on policymaking. In 1934, the Indian office asked the tribe to select a committee to work with government experts in drafting a constitution and business charter. Younger activists eager to cooperate with the government were chosen for this task, a fact not at all to the liking of some Quechans. The cooperative committee was particularly unpopular with the federation faction, whose members had apparently learned of their central office's opposition to the IRA, and they lost no time in taking action to thwart work on the constitution. At their urging, "approximately 400 tribal members petitioned the [constitution] committee to defer action until general information could be had and considered by the tribal members of middle and advanced age" (R. C. Bennett to commissioner 28 February 1934).

If the figures are accurate, they indicate two things: that ignorance and distrust of the IRA were practically universal among Quechan voters; and that a coalition of factions had emerged to oppose any immediate or surreptitious action on the act. Undaunted, the committee continued its work on the plans for a tribal constitution. There really was nothing significant for the committee to do, however; as with IRA constitutions in other tribes, the Quechan document mostly followed a format and covered issues that had been worked out earlier by planners in Washington. The Quechan committeemen thus were glorified hucksters for a scheme that bore little of their own imprint. Aware of the tribe's agitation, their intentions were to keep their people informed on what was happening. A full ten months before the tribe was to vote on the proposed constitution, the committee ordered 300 copies to be circulated on the reservation. The response to it was not recorded but was dubious at best. The local agency staff members were also busily drumming up popular support for the constitution, only to be diverted at the most critical moment by orders to demote Fort Yuma to a subagency and transfer most of the important administrative functions to the agency at Parker, ninety miles to the north. A short time later, the tribe, after almost two years of careful preparation, voted by a margin of nine votes not to ratify the IRA constitution (*Yuma Daily Sun* 12 November 1935).

There was still no widespread enthusiasm for the constitution a year later when proponents of the IRA again put the matter to a community vote, but this time the people ratified the document by a margin of thirteen votes (129 for, 116 against). The number of those favoring ratification was virtually the same in both elections; the measure passed the second time because fewer of its opponents voted, not because the public relations work had been any more successful.

It was probably ignorance that made the people skeptical, since pamphleteering as a device for spreading information had never worked well in the community. Probably some were also convinced that acceptance of the constitution would be harmful to the tribal interest. At any rate, their doubts and misapprehensions created an extremely ambivalent atmosphere for the election of the first IRA tribal council in January 1937. Of the several proclaimed, elected, or appointed ad hoc councils of the past, none had enjoyed a lasting tenure. Now, for the first time, the community was to have a seven-member governing body, carrying with it the sanctions of both a written constitution and, more important, the endorsement of official government policy.

The new tribal government was immediately confronted with the task of preparing a tribal business charter, in the face of overwhelming odds against its becoming the executive base for corporate community action anytime in the near future. From Commissioner Collier's viewpoint, the ratification of the Quechan constitution and the election of the tribal council were "merely preliminary, as the [IRA] . . . will require the formation of a carefully worked out charter" (commissioner to R. C. Bennett 23 April 1934). The business charter, then, was essential for economic development under the government's new policy.

After ratification of the Quechan constitution, the staff at Parker agency immediately started their push for charter ratification. It was a replay of the three-year attempt to ratify the constitution. Late in 1936, the agency distributed 150 copies of the charter proposal among the Quechans and held several educational meetings to explain its provisions. The Quechans had had no significant input into the provisions of the charter; it was a stereotyped format drawn up in Washington, full of legalistic jargon that would have been incomprehensible to most Anglos. Again, the members of the federation faction balked, refusing to participate in any of the meetings. Five days before the vote on the charter's ratification, the group, claiming to speak for "the adult members of the Yuma Indians,"[3] wrote to their organization's president to complain that they did not understand the charter's provisions. They were joined in their opposition by others, including Patrick Miguel and a member of the new tribal council. It is not known why Patrick opposed the charter (he later came to favor it), but the combined opposition was effective, and the charter proposal was not ratified in the election. In fact, as of 1980 the tribe had still not approved a corporate business charter.

If ratified, the charter would have made the Quechan tribe a federal corporation composed of all tribal members. Among other things, it would have made it possible for the tribe to borrow money from the Indian credit fund established under the IRA; to enter into contracts and agreements with individuals, other corporations, the state, or the federal government; and to sue and be sued in courts (a critical provision, since potential private investors in enterprises involving the tribe would need some protection). It further provided the means by which the tribe could free itself from several important supervisory powers held by the secretary of interior; the tribe could, in effect, terminate itself if it so desired. By failing to approve the charter, the Quechans were unable to take full advantage of the economic potential offered by the IRA—at least in Commissioner Collier's opinion.

Actually, there were some reasons why the charter might not have been beneficial to tribal development. For one thing, the council, the tribe's governing body, would have also served as the board of directors of the corporation, resulting in a potentially dangerous combination of political and economic interests (see Brophy and Aberle 1966:31–32; Spicer 1962:562). Furthermore, unless the tribe voted to terminate the supervisory powers of the secretary of the interior, the authority in any major economic development scheme would have still been in the hands of the government, not the tribe. The most obvious incentive for accepting the charter therefore had to be the possibility of obtaining loans (Steward 1969:10). But by 1944, even that possibility had become remote, as the wartime Congress slashed more and more of the IRA's appropriations. So, in retrospect, it may have been just as well that the charter was not ratified.

Still, the tribe had adopted a constitution and had elected a governing body. Perhaps some Quechans thought this would be enough to secure them at least a partial share of the benefits of the new order. But if they did hold such hopes, they were to be disillusioned, because the creation of the council did little to increase the tribe's autonomy from the government.[4] Despite the ratification of the constitution, land leases were still subject to approval by the local subagency superintendent. The tribe's budget required agency approval before funds could be spent. Tribal funds were held at the Colorado River Agency and were issued only on written request from the council in conformance with agency rules and agency-approved budget items (although in the 1950s, a tribal checking acount was set up at the agency). True, these fiscal controls may have been justified during the early years of the IRA council system, when the Quechans were still learning the techniques of money management. But the federal government's regulations lingered on and on, giving the impression that its officials had no intention of even gradually turning economic control over to the tribe.

And repeatedly, the interaction between the Quechans and the administrators fell far short of the consensual decision-making scheme envisioned by the Collier staff. The government showed no increased willingness to act on development schemes proposed independently by the tribe. In 1940, the council drafted an eloquent and well-conceived statement of grievances against government handling of the IRA policy that was far more than just another faultfinding blast from angry petitioners, since its main body included a detailed proposal for community economic development. The primary architects of the plan were the council president Edmond Jackson, Sr., and Patrick Miguel, then serving as council secretary, an appointed position.[5]

The proposal called for a tribal farm that would concentrate on growing crops both for sale and seed. Some of the seed would be furnished free to those wishing to farm their own allotments, and the cash from sales would be spent for improvements on the farming operation. The tribal farm would need a tractor and accessories, but the cost of this equipment would be offset by renting it to individual allottees (Quechan Tribal Council 1940). It was a significant proposal —the first of its kind ever drawn up by the tribe—and it was thoroughly in the spirit of the Indian Reorganization Act. Its one major flaw may have been that it was drawn up on the assumption that small-scale farming was still economically lucrative, when, by that time, the tendency in the lower Colorado region was clearly in the direction of large, mechanized or heavily manned farming operations (Spicer 1962:350).

The council sent the document to Commissioner Collier and received a brief note acknowledging its receipt—then nothing more.

By February 1942, there had still been no response from the Indian office (K. Marmon to commissioner 15 February 1942). World War II probably deflected attention from the proposal, and the maze of federal bureaucracy also undoubtedly slowed down any decision. But there is no evidence that action of any sort was ever taken on the document. Although Patrick Miguel and Edmond Jackson, Sr., had operated according to the rules of the IRA—they had worked out an articulate statement on their own and sent it through official channels—they might just as well have saved their energy.

The consensual ideal was violated in yet another instance. In 1944, the council hired an Anglo attorney named Mathews to help with the still bothersome charter issue and give legal advice on other matters. This was, of course, a tactic that had been used off and on by tribal politicians since the late nineteenth century, to protect tribal interests from federal manipulation and make sure the tribe was receiving all to which it was legally entitled. But the government would have none of it. Attorney Mathews' services, it informed the council, would have to be terminated, because Mathews lacked an "approved" contract (Ladd to commissioner 15 January 1945). The rule may have been designed with the best of intentions, that is, to protect the Indians from unscrupulous legal entrepreneurs, but its result was to give the Indian office veto power over the fullest exercise of legal alternatives open to the tribe.

THE EMBATTLED COUNCIL

The defeats of these and other council efforts to establish tribal autonomy finally convinced the tribe's voters that their elected officials were useless. Confidence in the council was eroded even more by what was happening in tribal elections. Just as with the old business committee of 1910, the government under the IRA wanted "proportional representation" of all major factions on the council, with one voter voting for only one candidate—this appearing to be the democratic way of doing things. But it did not work out that way in actual practice (Venning to commisoner 9 January 1945). Ambitious council candidates who mustered the support of large numbers of relatives were reelected time after time, and candidates with fewer kinsmen-supporters became discouraged, as did other voters who disagreed with the political ideologies of the incumbents. Staunch federation members—all opponents of the IRA—would have nothing to do with council elections.

Furthermore, under the voting procedure of the IRA constitution, two potentially dangerous alternatives for tribal representation were possible. One was that factional representation might in fact become proportional. Just as in 1910, then, the council could become hopelessly divided on issues of importance, such as the allocation of scarce resources including property and money. This would blunt its effectiveness as an intermediary between the community and the government, leaving government agents to make their own decisions. The other alternative was even less acceptable: a council membership dominated by a single faction or coalition that pushed for its own interests at the expense of the tribal rank and file.

The biennial voting results over the years clearly reveal the tribe's declining confidence in the council. In the first election, there were seventeen candidates, the seven winners receiving a total of 121 votes (the total number of votes cast is not known). By 1945, after several years of decline, the election hit an all-time low with only eight candidates for the seven seats and a total of 76 votes cast. One candidate was elected that year with only a single vote (Cox to Ladd 18 January 1945). There was a brief resurgence of interest in the 1947 election, presumably sparked by the activism of returning veterans (thirteen candidates, 225 votes cast), but, by the next election, community interest had once again sagged. Even in times of high interest, only about half the eligible electorate bothered to go to the polls.[6]

It was a depressing cycle. Fewer and fewer people voted because it seemed useless to put candidates in the powerless offices; yet low voter turnouts assured continued reelection of the same council members, regardless of their popularity or effectiveness, and increased the frustration of the reservation's rank and file. An alarmed Indian office proposed a constitutional amendment that would allow each voter to vote for seven candidates, but it came too late and, predictably, failed for lack of support (it received only one favorable vote in the 1945 election).[7]

As sources of political support, kinsmen were as important under the IRA regime as they had been in the earlier days of factional combat, even though, by the mid-1940s, factional groupings had become smaller and more numerous. Why this factional change occurred is not altogether clear. It may have been the result of election procedures, the one-vote rule discouraging people from voting for other than the candidates most closely related to them. The tendency towards smaller, more tightly knit factions may also have been an adaptation to the growing complexity of issues facing the reservation. In order to cope with these issues and stay in office, council members needed flexible support—more flexible than the larger groups of the early 1900s were able to give—and enough kinsmen to ensure their reelection. (In years of low-voter turnout, a composite family was probably the only support necessary to keep a man in office.) With the unquestioning support of kinsmen behind them, council members could shift their positions to take advantage of changes in the political winds, carrying their support with them without having to devote time to political fence-mending.

The reduced size and increased numbers of kinship factions meant that intracommunity conflict had become much more complex by the 'forties and 'fifties. Frustration, jealousy, and suspicion focused on the IRA council but never generated enough community-wide motivation to bring on a recall referendum or pull voters together, even briefly, for the sake of election reform. People expressed displeasure by staying away from the polls, and, by so doing, ensured that their displeasure would be prolonged.

Why the conflict? Quarrels between council members themselves and between council and community could hardly have arisen from council decisions; the council's role was largely that of acting on alternatives offered by the government, not generating important new programs independently (cf. Basehart and Sasaki 1964). Nor could problems have come from the council members' salaries or their political patronage. The salaries were increased 100 percent in the late 1940s and early 1950s—from five to ten dollars per month; there were no patronage positions aside from the council secretary and treasurer, and these could only go to those with the required skills to fill them. In this poverty-stricken community, quarrels focused on the trifling monies council members did have access to, namely on those portions of the tribal budget reserved for emergency loans to tribesmen, and travel expenses for councilmen to go to the agency in Parker or area office in Phoenix. In this group where economic opportunities were severely limited, any signs of a council member spending excessively, such as the purchase of a new car or household applicance, immediately aroused suspicion. The money, the gossips reasoned, could only have been acquired illegally, that is, through misappropriation of tribal funds. Fear of gossip, in turn, forced council members to seek legitimate loans or reimbursement for travel expenses surreptitiously. This merely confirmed the worst suspicions of their opponents.

Much of the conflict among council members themselves was also generated by money problems. But beneath this surface issue, there was also a continuous effort on the part of the members to neutralize the authority of their political rivals. A particularly memorable battle broke out in the 1950s, perhaps the most serious to that point in the council's brief history. Patrick Miguel was at the center, as usual, charging some of his fellow council members with misusing tribal loan monies, among other acts. The defendants retaliated with a resolution calling for the "excommunication" of Patrick and one of his supporters from all tribal activities, citing their own charges against Patrick. Neither side prevailed, and the conflict continued in written and verbal exchanges until it ran out of momentum. But in subsequent quarrels, the incident was always dragged out to be added to the new series of charges and countercharges.

All this quarreling led nowhere, except to more conflict. In general, it had the effect of reinforcing the influence of government administrators on the reservation, as the people continued to go to the subagency superintendent, rather than the council, with their problems of land leasing, inheritance, or unemployment. Although there is no official correspondence to indicate it, the weakening effects of the conflict among council members must have reaffirmed the conviction of some government agents that the tribe was incapable of governing itself.

Relations between council members were not always contentious. Much depended on who was elected each biennium, as there was a fairly steady—if somewhat low—turnover of membership each election. Even the most conflict-ridden councils could, and frequently did, operate as a consensual unit on routine matters; that is, when money or authority were not involved. They could also put aside their differences when faced by external threat—the state or federal governments, usually—or when confronted with the prospect of federal assistance.

Quarreling over council membership and conduct was only one facet of the widespread friction on the reservation during the 1940s and 1950s. Regardless of specific issues, however, the conflict had a sameness to it, and its continuing presence meant that Commissioner Collier had been mistaken; in the mundane reality of reservation life, there was little spirit of community among the people. The success of the government's reorganization act depended on such spirit, even though, paradoxically, government policies of the past had been a vital force in destroying whatever spirit had existed.

MATERIAL IMPACT OF THE INDIAN NEW DEAL

The bleak economic outlook for Quechans on the brink of the national depression has already been described. This of course involved their material existence—their homes, sanitation, health, diet—as Indian parents protesting the closing down of the boarding school clearly recognized. How were the majority of tribesmen living in 1931? The agent at that time, H. B. Jolley, described conditions for the senate investigation team (U. S. Senate 1931:7978–79).

He noted that most of the people had no money to provide proper food and clothing for themselves. Allotment land, when lessees could be found, netted the Indians a monthly income of between $3.75 and $7.25 an acre after water charges ($4.75 an acre) were deducted by the agency. For the usual ten-acre tract, less the land for a home if any, this meant a total net income of between thirty and seventy dollars per year. Consequently, many families were dependent on government food rations for survival. The typical home on the reservation was a one- or two-room house with holes in the walls for windows, "sometimes with glass in and sometimes just burlap." The rooms were twelve to fifteen feet square with dried mud floors. Cooking and washing were done mostly outdoors, with irrigation canal water being used for both cooking and drinking. There was very little furniture: "Sometimes a few chairs, occasionally a bed, but more often a blanket on the floor, homemade tables, and very crude furniture."

The senators wanted to know why the home conditions were so poor. Incredibly (yet predictably for a loyal bureaucrat), Agent Jolley blamed it on the climate: "Good houses are not very much in demand in a climate like this, as they would be farther north." He completely ignored the failure of government development schemes as a contributing factor.

Except for the construction of a small hospital on Indian Hill in the late 1930s, material conditions in the Quechan community did not change dramatically with the passing of the Indian Reorganization Act. Some Indians continued to farm their own allotments; others tried to find lessees for their land. Some hired themselves out to Anglo lessees as farm labor on their own and others' allotments, working at picking cotton or harvesting lettuce—the major cash crops on the reservation. Citrus farming would soon pay handsome dividends in the area surrounding the reservation, but Anglo lessees of Indian land could not contemplate such an operation because of the short-term leasing regulations, and the tribe lacked the capital to start a grove. Anglo firms did work out long-term leasing arrangements that allowed them to build two cotton gins on the reservation, which provided some limited opportunity for Quechan laborers, but the profits went to the Anglos; the Quechans were merely wage earners.

The government stood ready to guarantee that the community would suffer no further land loss through the sale of alloted lands; with the ratification of the IRA, the trust period on the land was continued indefinitely. But these measures merely insured a continuance of the status quo; they didn't provide for any added government support of the Quechan farming operation. In 1934, some Quechans attempted to file a land claim against the government for the restoration of more acreage to tribal control. The Indian office apparently misplaced the claim (commissioner to H. B. Jolley 8 February 1935), then admonished the Indians not to submit another without first obtaining permission through proper channels.

By 1938, the government had completed a massive canal-building effort on the northern periphery of the reservation. Not only was it a dubious enterprise legally, but in time it would further hinder the Quechans' limited agricultural potential. The legal issue was complicated; the government took the position that, although the right-of-way for the canal lay squarely within the reservation boundaries as drawn in 1884, the 1893 Agreement had ceded this land to the government, and therefore the Quechans' consent for the construction was not required, nor would they receive compensation for the land (Department of Interior Solicitor's Opinion M–28198, 1936). A more accurate interpretation of relevant statutes, including both the suspicious 1893 Agreement and the earlier Dawes Act of 1887, suggests that reservation land was to remain under tribal jurisdiction until it was sold to settlers and the proceeds were deposited to the credit of the Quechan tribe. The land had never been sold. The solicitor's opinion in 1936 thus illegally deprived the Quechans of their rights to consent to the canal construction and receive compensation for the lands taken. The tribe had to wait almost forty years before the injustice was finally acknowledged by the Interior Department.

The All-American Canal, as it was christened, was designed to irrigate land in the lower Colorado River area but had quite a different effect on those lands lying along its banks. Indian landowners in these areas soon noted a drastic increase in the alkalai content of their soil, caused by canal seepage that pushed buried alkalai up close to the soil's surface. Much of this land had been unusable because of its distance from irrigation laterals; now the excess alkalai made it even more difficult to develop. This unanticipated effect of the new canal was one more source of frustration for those Quechans who still hoped to eventually farm their own land.

Although the prospects for Quechan farming enterprises remained dismal, the government did provide other sources of financial aid. Under 1935 social security legislation, Quechans were hired on Works Progress Administration (WPA) projects in the reservation area. Others became eligible for old-age payments and aid to dependent children provided by the state, unprecedented sources of income. (But such financial aids merely allowed the Quechans to subsist and were by no means the basis for any long-term economic development, but only strengthened the community's dependence on the whims of federal and state generosity.) Being on welfare was not embarrassing to the Quechans, nor was it regarded as a temporary arrangement; it was another source of much needed money to be milked for all it was worth.

World War II brought a brief respite from the reservation's economic stagnation. Whatever the rigors of military service, the absence of Quechan draftees and volunteers provided economic relief for their family groups. In addition, Yuma proved to be geographically ideal for a military air base, supply depot, and proving ground, and many Quechan civilians, some of whom had taken advantage of the government's vocational programs, found well-paying jobs at the installations or with businesses generated by the influx of people to the area. Older Quechans continued to survive with the help of lease money and state aid.

But after the war, Quechan veterans, welcomed by their people as returning heroes regardless of action, soon discovered that economic conditions on the reservation had returned to their prewar depressed state. Many veterans in 1961 recalled that for this and other reasons, readjustment to reservation life had been difficult. Drinking was a means of avoiding the reality of their predicament, just as it had been for their fathers during the 1920s, some of whom had died in the brush from a steady diet of canned heat strained through tattered pieces of cloth (U.S. Senate 1931:8040–41).

The Yuma region settled into a postwar pattern of scaled-down military operations with severe cutbacks in related civilian jobs; continuing growth of cotton, lettuce, melon, and fruit farming; and a tourist industry that flourished in the winter months but went into suspension during the blistering summers. As before, the Quechans could compete for low-paying, unskilled jobs in town, working as construction laborers, warehousemen, or domestics. There were two businesses, a laundry and a garment manufacturing company, that were willing to hire Indian labor and, at one time or another, employed many of the Quechan women. And the government also offered several jobs at the subagency office and small hospital on Indian Hill; some were skilled (such as the assistant to the subagency's agricultural specialist) but most were unskilled janitorial, maintenance, or grounds keeping positions.

For reliable Quechans, some of these jobs had the potential of becoming long-term, with limited increases in pay. Aside from civil service positions, however, most of them lacked guarantees of permanence and were often terminated with changes in the firm's economic situation, or even with changes in management. One Quechan man, who had worked many years as a warehouseman, was summarily laid off by a new supervisor who had new ideas about how things should be run. The Quechan, in his mid-fifties at the time, had no pension plan to fall back on.

Anglo employers in Yuma, like those in other towns located close to Indian reservations, were skeptical about hiring Indians. While most of them could claim acquaintance with "several good Indians," Indians in general were considered unreliable, drinking up their paychecks and staying away from their jobs until the money and liquor ran out. But Anglo firms were not skeptical of taking on Indian debtors, most of whom were tied to long-term, high-interest payment plans that would probably outlast the products they purchased. Salesmen would descend on Indians whose debts were about to be paid off, tempting them with other products of Anglo technology and thus keeping them perpetually in debt.

In spite of a postwar farming boom in the Yuma area, Indians became more and more reluctant to work as laborers in the local fields. The wages, by Anglo standards, were very low compared to the effort involved; unemployment compensation (if available) or welfare paid almost as well and with much less physical effort. Besides, groups of Mexican *braceros* flooded the local farm-labor market, working hard for low wages during the height of cultivation and harvest seasons, then moving back across the border during slack periods. After years of sputtering decline, farm work for the Quechans—on their own allotments or those of Anglo lessees—petered out entirely by the late 1940s. It died for lack of capital, lack of technical assistance, and because of a flooded labor market.

The best opportunities for economic security still lay in urban areas away from the reservation, provided an individual had the necessary skill and capital to make settling into an urban environment possible. Some veterans, for example, chose relocation as a means of meeting their economic needs. Other Quechans made do by turning the composite family into a unit of production and consumption, with members pooling their economic resources. Grandparents would contribute old-age pension checks; others would contribute welfare payments; employed members would add their paychecks; and everyone breathed easier for a time after the land-lease payments came in.

Whatever the economic opportunities available to the Quechans between 1934 and 1950, none was the direct result of government programs for long-term Indian economic development. To be sure, government funded vocational training enhanced the employment potential of some young adults, but job opportunities—even for this group—arose from antidepression measures aimed merely at survival or from the industrial demands of World War II, rather than from the government's development strategies.

MATERIAL IMPACTS OF THE RENEWED DRIVE FOR ASSIMILATION

In the early 1950s, a new relocation policy made the prospect of leaving the reservation more attractive to the Quechans. Younger families (and, a few years later, single individuals)[8] would apply to the Indian bureau for permission to relocate in an urban area (usually Los Angeles or San Francisco-Oakland) and, after a short waiting period, would be notified to be ready to leave for the city by a given date. The government paid transportation costs, located housing and employment, provided one year's free medical insurance, and extended credit for the purchase of home furnishings, clothing, and food until the wage earner's first paycheck came in.

It all sounded very appealing. What is more, the Quechans were able to adapt to city life because they had grown up near Yuma and had learned such skills as how to shop for low prices. The few hours from Los Angeles to Fort Yuma was also an easy drive, making it convenient for urban dwellers to visit the reservation, particularly on holidays.

But the new alternative did not incite a sudden exodus from the reservation; a few Quechans, averaging seven small families and fifteen individuals, left each year, but a third usually returned before they had a chance to adjust to the new life (unofficial Indian bureau estimates, 1966). Some came back convinced that the Indian bureau had deceived them about the advantages of the program. Hoping for permanent employment, they had discovered that a number of the jobs they had received were short-term in an employment environment already flooded with unskilled labor. They felt the government should have been obligated to find them employment again and again when such temporary jobs evaporated. Yet, in keeping with the pattern of hostile dependency, they complained about the amount of control the bureau exercised over their city lives in such matters as vocational school curricula, medical payments, and the purchase of food and clothing during jobless intervals. And they complained about the treatment they received from bureau personnel, such as being made to feel inferior or like beggars for the benefits that were theirs by law. A disenchanted Quechan brought these problems into greater focus during a conversation 1966:

> A fellow met us [when we arrived in Los Angeles] and . . . he took us to a motel. The house we were going to live in hadn't been cleaned up yet. We stayed in the motel two weeks, then ran short on cash. We got support money all right. Everything was all right until we got a house. The

> BIA [Bureau of Indian Affairs] man said he would buy the necessary things we needed. He bought us sheets, pillows, pillowcases, work clothes, school clothes; he went and got us second-hand furniture. There was a dispute over clothes and the BIA man wouldn't believe my husband when he said the clothes he [the BIA man] was going to buy for my husband were the wrong size.
>
> My husband went to work and we were told that when he got his first paycheck they would discontinue our support allowance. They did. My husband got laid off his job shortly because an expected government contract didn't come through. He got another job. We were told it [the job] was strictly seasonal and would last only about five months.
>
> In the meantime, all allowances [from the government] had ceased. I had asked if there was a set amount to the allowances so I could budget my spending, but they won't tell how much allowance you're going to get.
>
> My husband had to go wait in the BIA office for job leads. Those [BIA] employees don't make us feel like we're entitled to anything. They make us beg for every crumb. Then I got to talking to an acquaintance working at the BIA office and got a date to talk with the top man. He said he was sorry, but that was all that could be done. He could give us tickets to get back home on, but that was all. Those relocation people went ahead and did everything and wouldn't explain much of anything.
>
> We left for relocation in September, and by January we were cut off voluntarily.

Another Quechan left with his family to enroll in college, under the vocational training program. He dropped out before graduating. In an interview he recalled that "as far as the Indian students went, out of five or six there, only two stayed in town. The others went back home. One of the Sioux boys tried like heck. He was a neighbor. He had only part time jobs, and the pressure got too much—pressure from lack of money." Added another, "That's the reason why a lot of them give up, because they don't have enough money to get along on."

Thus, a number of Quechans, particularly those with families, discovered that the financial disadvantages of relocation outweighed the advantages. Others who had hoped that relocation would help them break the pattern of temporary employment and problem drinking that had come to characterize their reservation existence were also disappointed. Periods of idleness on relocation made it impossible for them to stay away from alcohol, which in turn spoiled their chances for employment in Los Angeles or Oakland as much as it did on the reservation.

Relocation as an economic strategy favored those with job skills and/or younger, unmarried members of the tribe without heavy financial obligations who settled well away from the reservation area. The program did not alter economic conditions in the Yuma vicinity, as too few people left to relieve the pressure on the local labor pool, and the program, by design, did nothing to increase local economic resources. It was a strategy of individual rather than community development—its intention was to get the Quechans away from their community—but was more successful than pre-IRA attempts at individual assimilation because the government provided the necessary operating funds. If the recollections of those Quechans who withdrew from the program are accurate, it might have been very successful had there been even more funding and more flexible administration at the grass-roots level.

Between 1945 and 1962, the single most important material development on the reservation was the arrival of government surplus housing. The deplorable housing conditions had changed very little since the senate investigations of 1931. Finally, in the mid-1950s, the government offered the Quechans a chance to obtain prefabricated plywood houses that had been built for shipyard workers in San Diego during the war. Quechan crews were hired to disassemble the houses, transport them to the reservation, and reassemble them for those wanting them.

The prefab structures soon became the most prevalent house type in the community. They had obvious advantages over the older, dirt-floored adobes, but in the heat of summer were much less comfortable than the older dwellings because they lacked the insulation of the thick mud-and-lath walls.

Many of the prefabs went up in clusters to house a composite family, occasionally surrounding an older adobe house where elderly members of the group still wished to live. Besides houses of either type, the homesites included a privy, a ramada shading collections of steel bedsprings and chairs, one or two washing machines, and an assortment of old cars, some of which had not run for years. The families could not afford grass or other landscaping, so the yards were mainly bare, sun-dried earth that swirled up in clouds of dust when a car passed or a strong wind blew. Water for washing and cooking still came from the irrigation canals or shallow wells (the water table being less than twenty feet below the surface on most portions of the reservation). Most families in densely settled areas had television sets, refrigerators, and electric or gas stoves, but only a few living in remote areas had invested in electricity for their houses.

The surplus housing was as significant an improvement in reservation material life as any under the earlier IRA, even though it came at a time when assimilation was once again the policy.

But, as with welfare payments and rations, it was a device to ease the harshness of reservation conditions rather than a program of economic development. And it was fortuitous; it was not a systematic long-range plan of the Indian bureau, but was an ingenious, ad hoc way of solving a major logistical problem for the Department of Defense.

SOCIAL INTERACTION IN THE COMMUNITY

John Collier, commissioner of Indian affairs during the IRA period, correctly perceived that any scheme for community development depended in large measure on relations within the community —how and when people organized into groups to perform particular tasks, for example, or how they did or did not get along at such times. Community development schemes in the case of the Quechans also depended on communication, on getting word of impending meetings or events to individual tribal members. As in most small communities, this information was exchanged informally for the most part, during evening visits with each other, ceremonial gatherings, and the club meetings that comprised so much of the community's interaction.

Word of one recurrent event spread throughout the community more quickly than others, and that was the death of one of its members. The news flashed from a small circle closely related to the deceased outward to increasingly widening circles of more distant kinsmen and friends. Quechans felt it extremely important to get word to relatives as soon as possible and were particularly upset if they did not receive news of a death until after the funeral ceremonies had begun.

Announcements of mass meetings were spread more formally by a modern day runner, dispatched by the tribal council and reimbursed by the tribe for his gasoline expenses. Mass meetings were usually informal hearings on intratribal friction or federal administration of Quechan interests, including land. Inevitably, they were billed as efforts to "get the facts to the people," but, almost as inevitably, they simply added to the prevailing confusion. An elderly Quechan, veteran of many mass meetings, asserted:

> The only way to get to the people is for the council to go to each home on the reservation, talk to them, tell them. Even then some of them won't understand. . . . I know one time we went to a [mass] meeting and some man from Washington got up. The way I understood him was one way, but another [Quechan], who was so well educated, had a different idea [about what was said].

The confusion was occasionally due to the Quechans' difficulty in understanding formalized English rhetoric used sometimes by lawyers and bureaucrats. But matters also became distorted because very few people attended the meetings, relying on friends' and relatives' accounts of what took place; and the opinions expressed by those who did attend were not necessarily representative of the majority of the tribe. Furthermore, participants in the communications network allowed their preconceptions about individuals and issues to color the information they passed on, so that the more often the accounts were repeated, the more likely they were to become distorted. (Small wonder that the attempts to introduce the Indian Reorganization Act through mass meetings met with so much skepticism.) Nevertheless, the government considered the mass meeting to be the most effective way of getting information to the people, and government administrators were convinced that by holding such meetings the issues were being properly aired before the people.

Members of the community had both radio and television sets, and many subscribed to the *Yuma Daily Sun;* but none of these media covered reservation issues unless they affected surrounding Anglo communities as well. Beginning in the 1940s, the tribal council mimeographed a community news sheet—the *Quechan News.* This monthly paper had administrative items, editorials by council members on important issues, vital statistics, and brief notes on the activities of both individuals and groups. It went out of print in 1963 for lack of funds.

Because many Indian families lacked telephones, the spread of information was also affected by reservation geography. Families living "in the brush" (that is, well away from major hard-surfaced roads) were last to be informed. In fact, among some isolated family groups, there seemed to be a direct correlation between their location and their conservative approach to reservation life. These groups were more reticent than other Quechans in their interaction with outsiders and were sometimes referred to as "uneducated," "ignorant," or "hard to get along with" by their fellows. But whether they were conservative because they lived in the brush, or lived in the brush because they were conservative, was an open question, as not all conservatives lived in brush areas.

Most people remained where they had been in the late 1920s and 1930s, clustered in the east-central and southern portions of the reservation along the major roads leading to Indian Hill, Winterhaven, and Yuma. In the late 1950s, many were still grouped into composite families, a persistent feature of reservation social structure (Bee 1963:213). In addition to the economic influences mentioned earlier, other factors contributed to this behavioral pattern.

Young adults, for example, tended to marry before they had the income to support a family or the land to build a home, and therefore they had little choice but to move in with relatives, although many hoped someday to have a place of their own.

But in spite of economic, political, and other conditions that favored the persistence of the composite family as a social structure, many families were unstable, with members vacillating between low-paying temporary employment and periods of idleness with nothing but lease money or welfare to support them. People would move in or out according to their economic condition, their potential for finding other housing, or their inclination to visit Los Angeles (which could turn into a stay of several months). Quechans felt that breaks in the families were usually the result of conflicts among members. Frequently the blame was laid on "meddling in-laws," and an irate young husband or wife would storm out of the house after a row with in-laws about money or how to treat a child's illness. Sometimes the conflict and eventual breakup were results of lengthy drinking binges.

In 1961, older Quechans believed that marriages (both Indian style and legal) were becoming less and less stable, but then they also felt the younger people on the reservation were going to hell generally. An estimated two-thirds of the marriages on the reservation at that time were second (or third or fourth) unions for one or both spouses, but it is not clear that this represented any change from previous years (Bee 1963:225).

Beyond the composite families, Quechans interacted with each other as members of a surprisingly large number of clubs and associations for such a small community. Since 1900, the people had demonstrated a distinct tendency to hyperorganize. More accurately, they had had a large number of associations created for them by outsiders, another product of Anglo supervisors, organizers, and instigators.

These associations could be grouped into several categories. There were tribal government associations, including the tribal councils; various community development associations that sprang up during the antipoverty efforts of the mid-1960s; several youth-oriented groups such as the Boy Scouts, 4-H, and parent-teachers' associations; and five associations organized under the larger structure of Christian mission groups, such as the Methodist Women's Society for Christian Service and the Mormon Relief Society. There was a host of baseball and softball teams, two nativistic ritual associations, and, on weekends, a number of cliques that usually got together for parties or visits. Many of the associations were not exclusively Quechan in membership.

The distinct "Angloness" of Quechan organizations was due also to the fact that the people had few traditional associational groupings of their own—no warriors' societies or curers' societies, for example—upon which to model organizations of the early reservation period (Forde 1931:145, 161, 199). More influential, however, was the feeling of Anglo agents that the path to eventual "civilization" of the Quechans was best traveled by their emulating as many attributes of Anglo middle-class associations as possible—the let's-get-organized syndrome, including elections for presidents, vice-presidents, secretaries, treasurers, and at least the appearance of operating according to *Robert's Rules of Order* during formal meetings. Most of the Christian mission groups operated in this fashion, and the pattern was also apparent in the formation of the IRA council. In some associations, sanction from sponsors was withheld or promised benefits delayed until appropriate Anglo-type order had been established. Many Quechans were therefore motivated to emulate the Anglos in forming associations, because they realized that such behavior was sometimes a means to lucrative ends. The group of older, tradition-oriented planners of *karˀúk* ceremonies, however, spurned such features as formal elections, bylaws, rosters of named officials, and the like.

In many associations, clusters of relatives were the important sub-elements. Christian religious groups were made up of clusters of kinsmen, for example, supporting some Quechans' observations that religious affiliation seemed to "run according to families." One woman's kinship cluster in the Methodist Women's Society of Christian Service group included her two daughters, an aunt, two nieces, and a nephew's wife. The Quechan Women's Community Club featured several mother-daughter pairs. In its heyday, the Mission Indian Federation comprised several kinship clusters, and the tribal council of the late 1930s and early 1940s was dominated by members of two large families.

These kinship clusters provided ready-made task forces and thus helped to make the association as a whole more efficient. But they could also become ready-made units of conflict. One of the factors in the demise of the Quechan women's club was that interpersonal conflict rapidly became interfamilial conflict when relatives rallied around their own in a dispute.

Conflict both within and between associations was a constant feature of reservation life. "There's no cooperation among the people any more," the Quechans complained in 1961. "People just can't seem to get along." Older tribal members talked about a romanticized and probably distorted past when everyone got along with everyone else in farming, warfare, ceremonies, and other more routine activities.

None of the Quechans liked to express hostility face-to-face if he could avoid it. Indeed, friction between two people first became apparent when they stopped speaking to each other. Each tended to air his grievances to his own supporters, who then repeated them to others. Inevitably, the facts became distorted and the controversy became more bitter through added misunderstanding. If the issue was not too serious, the antagonism was eventually resolved by mutual agreement. In such cases, not speaking as a means of expressing hostility tended to reduce it by providing a cooling-off period. But some disputes, such as that pitting Patrick Miguel against other council members in the early 1950s, never have been resolved. They become temporarily latent, only to be revived and added to other grievances in later battles.

Quechans within the same association most often quarreled over two issues. One concerned the prerogatives of leadership. Members incessantly accused their leaders of "trying to run the whole show" (that is, of trying to assume unwarranted power to make decisions in the name of the group); of being "dumb Indians"; of "working against the rest of the group." "We don't like to see people make something of themselves," they declared. "Seems like we no sooner get someone in to head up something than we're trying to get them right out again!" Patrick Miguel was typical of association leaders. They were usually more articulate and extroverted than others in the community and tended to be extremely knowledgeable about reservation affairs. They were also in the public eye and therefore likely to be criticized.

It was clear that the definitive values of traditional leadership, both political and apolitical, were no longer relevant in the late 1950s. Aside from a general consensus that tribal council members should "fight for the people," no consistent, community-wide ideals of leadership had surfaced to replace the traditional ones, and the acceptable limits of modern leadership behavior were largely undefined. (Actually, a narrow notion of leadership responsibility would have been a disadvantage in a situation where the thrust of outside factors—such as government policy, or, more likely, new agency administrators—shifted radically and quickly.) Instead, several conceptions of the "good and proper leader" emerged, which were used at whim to evaluate leaders in the associations.

The idea of becoming a public personality, who could interact easily with strangers and live with unremitting criticism and gossip, did not appeal to most association members. This meant that ambitious Quechans could simultaneously hold leadership in several different groups; Patrick Miguel was such a person, for example. Sometimes these leaders mustered the votes to be elected time and again. Others holding important positions (such as tribal council president) simply proclaimed themselves officers in other associations also. In community-wide activities, this overlap in community leadership resulted in a concentration of leadership tasks and discouraged the emergence and specification of separate responsibilities.

The second major source of contention was again money. In those associations that required funds to stay alive, there were frequent problems over finances. As with the tribal council, members of the various other associations were keenly interested in the management of association funds, watchful lest other members help themselves to much needed personal income (however measly) at the expense of fellow members. Here, too, the gossips considered any observable monetary gain as illicit, sometimes in spite of the owner's conscientious efforts to give a proper accounting. The tribal band was always pressed for money and was frequently criticized for how it handled what little it did receive. In at least three cases (an athletic club of the late 1930s, the American Legion Post, and the Quechan Women's Club of the early 1960s), financial difficulties brought about major alterations or even termination of the association.

Conflicts between associations erupted when ideologies or activities either competed with, or were unacceptable to, other associations or the community at large. For example, the ideology of the Nazarene mission group favored burial rather than cremation of the dead. There was a good deal of tongue clucking and occasionally a more intense display of hostility when a Nazarene funeral became the focus of community attention. The Mission Indian Federation, whose members stood squarely against the Indian office and tribal council, was another association that often deviated from community ideology. Until the 1960s, federation members convened their own mass meetings on important issues to "ask questions and find out the *truth.*" This manifestation of deep, biased, and aggressive interest in current reservation affairs first unsettled, then infuriated, tribal council members and others not sharing the federation's convictions. Christian mission groups competed too, for members, in fund-raising activities at pow-wows and other events, and in making decorative wreaths for Memorial Day ceremonies (the people viewed this as competition in spite of the public assertion that it was interdenominational cooperation).

But the most pervasive conflict was between kinship clusters, not between associations as wholes. Some of the disputes which seemed to be between associations themselves, on closer analysis turned out to be between kinship clusters within the associations. Divisions between associations were incidental to the quarrels or, occasionally, merely fronts to conceal other issues. Thus, much of the intermittent conflict between "Catholics" and "Methodists" on the reservation was, some Quechans reported, really a dispute between two large kinship clusters on opposite sides of the factional fence.[9]

The associations were not rigidly organized, well-coordinated, smoothly functioning aggregates. For one thing, almost all groups claimed more members than actually participated in their activities. This was particularly true of the various mission associations and the veterans' group, and at tribal band rehearsals, barely enough players would be on hand to carry the melody (but, somehow, the band was almost always at full strength for public performances). Each of the several concession stands at tribal events, designed as a money-making enterprise for entire associations, was usually operated by the same four or five active members, often from a single kinship cluster.[10] There was a wide tolerance of behavior within most associations. Membership was never cancelled for nonparticipation or other flagrant deviations. Leaders complained frequently about lack of cooperation, but didn't impose penalties on noncooperators, and members could either help with the inevitable dirty work connected with major functions, or remain away, content to let others make the effort. Unquestionably, there was also cooperation within and among associations, but of a very special nature. For the annual Memorial Day ceremonies, for instance, a number of associations cooperated with each other, providing a good example of the way they worked together. In the 1950s and 1960s, the tribe had still not discarded its traditional preoccupation with death and ritual mourning for deceased relatives, so the ceremonies were considered very important by the people and one of the most positive expressions of community spirit. Associations responsible for the ceremonies included the tribal band, the tribal council, the veterans' association, the mission groups, and a clique of elderly ritual specialists known to the community as "the old men." However, except for the band and council, the areas of responsibility of the different associations were somewhat blurred. The Methodist women's group, for instance, made paper wreaths, but the women were usually joined by nonmember friends or relatives who merely wanted to pass time or help out. Similar activities also went on at other missions on the reservation. Still other individuals made wreaths on their own, often while watching television soap operas in their homes. The veterans and old men were supposed to be responsible for cleaning up the cremation grounds, but only a few ever showed up for work. Sometimes they were joined by nonmembers who would work awhile, leave to do something else, then return for more work and conversation. Everyone seemed to know what had to be done because it had been done so many times before, and, as a result, the leaders were very low-key; in fact, they were usually absent from the work site, busily making arrangements with various civic groups in Yuma or the Indian subagency office. There was no shouting of orders on the Quechan reservation, nor strident calling for volunteers.

To the outsider, the culmination of all these preparations—the Memorial Day service itself—seemed destined for failure. No one had rehearsed the flower girls bearing the paper wreaths. For some reason (nobody seemed to know why), a large number of choir members from the combined mission groups failed to show up. A public address system announcer had to be recruited at the last minute. And so on. But the Quechans never seemed disturbed. They made ad hoc arrangements to overcome the problems, and, usually after a brief delay, the ceremonies unfolded in an orderly and impressive way.

There was a basic contradiction in much of the Quechans' community activity. On the one hand, there was an expressed ideal of formal structure, elected officers, and rules of order; on the other, there was the actual pattern of informality so characteristic of traditional community interaction. The persistence of this extempore activity pattern into the 1950s and 1960s meant that, despite Anglo influence, the tribe still performed community tasks (effectively if somewhat chaotically) in much the same way as it always had. References to faultfinding, to the apparent lack of participation by a majority of members, and to flaws in the ceremonial scenario should not mask the fact that cooperative tasks were still being performed successfully. However, it is also important to note that none of the community-wide efforts required the long-term cooperation of large numbers of people, such as weeks or months of collaboration. In any given year, there were few activities that required cooperation (aside from attendance) from the community and, when it was called for, it involved short-term events that had clear precedents, with leaders acting as planners and coordinators rather than as supervisors.

Understanding the interaction of the community's social elements is important for understanding the Quechans' reaction to the War on Poverty in the 1960s. The government would repeatedly emphasize that community-wide, long-term cooperative involvement was required for the poverty program's success, much as champions of the Indian New Deal had extolled the virtues of Indian communalism thirty years before. But the Fort Yuma community was not predisposed to such cooperation; indeed, insofar as the reconstruction of traditional Quechan life can be trusted, the community may never have had such qualities, and government policy would only have squelched them if and when they had existed.

THE ROAD BLOCKADE OF 1960

The tribal council had tried since it was created to assert its autonomy and authority under federal wardship, but nothing had changed the frustrating status quo. In fact, the State of California had added its authority to that of the federal government in the affairs of tribal life. Public Law 280, passed by Congress in 1953, made the Quechan tribal court and police force superfluous, causing these small loci of the community's judicial system to disappear as the state assumed its responsibilities. Not only was California responsible for law enforcement, but for various forms of welfare payments, and education as well.

Tribal leaders soon came to view the state administration as a threat to tribal autonomy when they learned what had happened to other tribes that, as a consequence of the federal government's termination policy, had fallen prey to state government jurisdiction. As they saw it, their mandate to "fight for the people" included keeping a wary watch on state attempts to influence tribal life,[11] while insisting that the largest possible amount of state aid be furnished to the tribe. Friendly cooperation with state agencies, according to the tribal leaders of the late 1950s, would only have resulted in greater loss of tribal autonomy.

The road blockade of 1960 was a calculated, unilateral attempt to wrest Quechan political autonomy from state and federal control. It was also one more of the Quechans' many futile attempts to augment the community land base.

The issue that sparked the confrontation had been festering for years. The government had repeatedly refused to turn over to the tribe the rich bottomland in the area known as the Island, the 4,572-acre tract that had been exposed years earlier by the Colorado's eastward meandering, declaring that much of it was needed for flood control and could not legally be inhabited. As mentioned before, non-Indians had steadily infiltrated this area, much to the chagrin of the Quechans; and the government had made no significant move to evict them. Over the years, some of these trespassers had managed to create substantial farming operations.

Early in 1960, the council hired Joseph W. Hough, Ph.D., an Anglo who had recently come to Yuma from Los Angeles with claimed expertise in business administration. He was designated as the tribal business manager by the council, and became the Indians' major advisor and spokesman in ensuing events.

About the same time, the council again demanded action on the land issue from the Colorado River Agency of the Bureau of Indian Affairs. As usual, the agency's response was not satisfactory to council members, revealing, they felt, the same old disinclination to take action on the Island or its inhabitants. This time the council would not abide what it considered another bureaucratic stalling operation. At its April 1960 meeting, Lee Emerson, the council president, decided that precipitous action was called for:

> So I told the council we were on our own . . . The council met and decided that a letter or resolution doesn't help. I've seen what unions do, so I suggested, "Let's do this strike, a good old American custom!"

On 22 April, the council, with the help of its Anglo business manager, wrote a news release for the Yuma newspaper, outlining the Quechans' intention to blockade all access roads into the Island area. The members served notice that the council had withdrawn the land from the government and would lease it to interested farmers. Ignoring the provisions of Public Law 280, they appointed a judge, chief of police, and twenty-nine deputies to man the roadblocks. They also passed an ordinance calling for non-Indian residents of the Island either to sign new leases with the tribe or leave the area.

On 25 April, the Quechan deputies set up four roadblocks, all of which were on reservation, not state, roads. One was prominently erected on a road leading past the cremation grounds, where trespassers had been an irksome problem to tribal members. And the press releases kept coming. In one, the tribal president made a statement that would have excited even the most passive participant in reservation life:

> When our sacred, hallow Kerook ceremonial ground has been invaded by trespassers, the Tribe is aroused in anger and is deeply concerned for the bit of ground that our ancestors valiantly fought for. Therefore it is the intention of the Tribal Council, with the support of the Quechan tribe, to stop the trespassers by using this effective means of closing all entrances to the reservation [*Yuma Daily Sun* 25 April 1960].

Some of the older tribesmen were not convinced at first that the blockade was a good idea. Eventually, however, they threw their support behind the effort, making the blockade one of few important issues on which the tribe as a whole reached nearly complete agreement. From the Quechans' standpoint, they were being threatened by external forces that were trespassing not only geographical boundaries of the community but cultural ones as well.

On the first day of the blockade, the deputies armed themselves with rifles, pistols, shotguns, and at least one bow and arrow. The intent was not, however, to prevent vehicles from passing, contrary to the implication of earlier tribal news releases. Rather, the idea was to demand tolls from all those passing through. The deputies made no overt attempt to force individuals to pay the tolls, especially those who displayed anger, but the mere presence of weapons was enough to cause tempers to flare on both sides. At a meeting of the council that night, it was decided to disarm the deputies to avoid the possibility of serious injury.

On the second day, the district attorney of California's Imperial County stated that his officers could take no action because the blockaded roads were under the jurisdiction of the federal government. The sheriff of Yuma County, Arizona, likewise disclaimed jurisdiction over the area. The council was fully aware of this quandry, and Dr. Hough used the standoff as proof that the council had acted wisely:

> "You have a letter from the Indian Bureau which passes the buck to Imperial County. District Attorney [James E.] Marabel [of Imperial County] has said that he isn't going to do anything for you. That only leaves your tribal laws" [quoted in *Yuma Daily Sun* 28 April 1960].

That same evening, the council decided to wire some senators and congressmen in Washington to inform them of the blockade and solicit their help in pressing for legislation that would return the land to tribal control.

On the fourth day, the blockaders concentrated their attention on the road beyond the cremation grounds, where they had built a log barricade. The men were fed in shifts, with food prepared by the women's club and other volunteers. Other tribal members stopped by the area to offer encouragement, along with cigarettes, candy, and other articles of comfort.

At least one Anglo farmer in the Island area concluded that the whole affair was a communist plot and trumpeted his conviction to the local press.

On the sixth day, the deputies abandoned the blockades entirely. Council President Lee Emerson declared publicly that Imperial County was not providing adequate protection for the Quechan deputies, but, privately, he felt the effort had received ample publicity, and the cost was becoming burdensome while the net receipts from the tolls only amounted to $5.70. Also, Anglo resistance to the blockade had become more forceful. An organization called the Associated Farmers had issued a statement listing the reasons why the Quechans' blockade was illegal and advising Anglo farmers not to pay tolls.

On the last day of the blockade, the Colorado River Agency finally issued a statement, observing that the Quechans' action was unjustified and ill-considered because "a bill is before Congress for the purpose of settling the title question to the land [and] the Department [of Interior] has instituted suits along the river course for the purpose of seeking solution to the so-called squatter problem. . . ." The statement also reminded its readers that the Indian bureau had advised the tribe to adhere to the provisions of Public Law 280, but that "they have been proceeding in apparent disregard of the same" (*Yuma Daily Sun* 1 May 1960). With that, the incident was over.

The council had very little to lose and a great deal to gain by their action. Farmers who leased reservation land would not take sides, and the tribe's relations with the others had already deteriorated over issues such as irrigation system management, school bonds, and local taxes. Finally, the council members were clearly "fighting for the tribe" and thus risked no loss of tribal support.

However, the council's disregard for the provisions of Public Law 280 was selective, not total. The councilmen wanted, and claimed, greater political autonomy vis-à-vis outside agencies, but they also demanded, and expected, protection from these same authorities when the tribe's actions sparked hostile confrontations. The federal Indian bureau and state governments of California and Arizona may have been thrown off balance temporarily by the council's maneuver, but, as far as authority was concerned, they held the upper hand and always would as long as the tribe depended on them for services. Consequently, once the roadblock was removed, they didn't make the slightest move to give the tribe additional political authority. So, Quechan political autonomy, after a brief flash, burned down to the level of the preblockade period, where it was to remain for approximately two years more.

The tribe did slightly better in the land issue. The blockade succeeded in directing legislative attention to the problem, and the Quechans were on the verge of a qualified victory when, shortly thereafter, the government offered to return a portion of the disputed territory to tribal ownership. But, as their opening bid in what they probably assumed would be a negotiated settlement, the tribal council rejected the government's offer and demanded a return of all the disputed land. The government abruptly withdrew its offer and made no further effort to negotiate. In bitter hindsight, tribesmen in 1966 laid the blame for the council's faux pas on bad advice from its Anglo business manager. Whether true or not, the Quechans themselves were not aware of the possible consequences of their intransigence on the government's offer, and the potential victory turned quickly into defeat. In 1961, less than a year after the blockade incident, the government signed long-term leases with the non-Indian inhabitants of the island, and none of the proceeds went to the tribe. Fourteen years later, in 1974, the Quechan claim to this territory was still unsettled.[12]

All in all, the affair followed the pattern of disputes of half a century earlier. Patrick Miguel would doubtless have been in the middle of the confrontation, had he lived long enough to participate (he had died less than a year before), as political authority and land were his favorite issues. Enlistment of Anglo advice, whether from lawyers or other experts, was a tactic both he and his ex-chief father had used, and public intransigence in negotiations was also a familiar Miguel trademark. Whatever council members felt in 1960 about Patrick's work and public personality, there was no denying that they were adhering to a set of precedents that he and others had established years earlier.

The blockade was a community-wide cooperative effort and followed the pattern of task performance already well established on the reservation. Those who were willing to help did so, regardless of associational membership. Some members of the women's club and veterans group were the most active, but so were others who had no connections with either group. There was community enthusiasm and cohesion for the blockade, just as there was for the Memorial Day activities; but neither this nor the active cooperation of tribal members lasted for long. Shortly after the blockade ended, the council became embroiled in a factional dispute over whether Quechans living on disputed land could hold council membership. Public confidence in council effectiveness waned once again.

THE CONTRADICTIONS OF POLICY AND PRACTICE IN DEVELOPMENT: 1934–1961

Neither the idealistic, foisted "communalism" of the Indian New Deal nor the insidious "freedom" touted during the termination era had a major effect on the basic political and socioeconomic structure of the Fort Yuma reservation. The new tribal council of the late 1930s eagerly assumed the greater autonomy and authority it thought it possessed, only to learn that in spite of public declarations of policy change and collaborative groundwork laid between local and national administrators, the government had actually increased its control over tribal administration. Limited council authority, election procedures that favored those with many voting relatives, a general willingness to believe the worst about council activities, and continual factional haggling, soon sapped the community's confidence in its leadership. Once created, community apathy and suspicion then defeated any efforts to reform the election procedures or convert the tribe into an incorporated business enterprise.

Lack of tribal confidence in the council's effectiveness only perpetuated the government's pervasive influence. Council members, already aware of community attitude, became even more prickly and sometimes downright belligerent in their continuing efforts to hammer out an autonomous yet productive relationship with Indian bureau officials.

For the first time, the state government became a factor in the community's development, being both benefactor and villain, ready to seize land and personal possessions of those unable to pay property taxes should the federal government ever terminate the Quechans. The relationship between the council and the state was as contradictory as that between the council and the Indian bureau. As in their relations with the federal government, the council, in interacting with state authorities, was constantly torn between cooperation that only strengthened tribal dependence, and confrontation that underscored the tribe's independence from state government. The council's ambivalence in this situation surfaced clearly during the road blockade of 1960.

The threat of termination was extremely effective in keeping the tribe dependent on the federal government. As much as council members chafed at bureau supervision of their activities, they were fearful of a sudden removal of that supervision and the disastrous consequences that could result. As long as alternatives for tribal development were understood in terms of polar opposites of termination or dependence, dependence remained the only possible option.

Between 1934 and 1961, the federal government did nothing to develop the reservation's economic potential. State welfare and pension payments provided additional income for some, especially the composite families, but hardly enough to launch them into anything recognizable as economic growth. The surplus housing made living conditions more bearable for the Quechans, but produced no capital for them. It was the same with food rations distributed by the government from time to time.

The opportunities, as always before, lay off the reservation. Economic development was still an individual or family affair, demanding at least a partial breaking away from community life. Yet off-reservation employment, even that available under federal relocation programs, offered no guaranteed income. Much of it tended to be short-term, seasonal work for those with no specialized skills. For such individuals, it was safer to return to the reservation, where they could face economic instability in the company (and often with the aid) of their own people. Yet in the 1950s and early 1960s there were federal vocational training programs available to those willing to leave the reservation. If lack of specialized skills was the only factor bringing them back after a sojourn in the city, the Quechans' response to these training opportunities should have been greater. But the fact that it was lukewarm suggests that reservation life was not only economically safer, but socially more satisfying than a potentially wealthier existence in places like Los Angeles or Denver.

Such as it was, development of the reservation's land base was accomplished piecemeal and privately, as in earlier periods. The gains were individual gains, with the largest share still going to Anglo farmer-investors, and only a small share going to Quechan landholders. Furthermore, the individual Quechan's share was becoming increasingly smaller as inheritance problems and fractionated land ownership spread the profits over larger and larger groups.

As one would expect in a small, economically deprived yet ethnically distinctive community, the irregularly constituted, kinship cluster was a vitally important political, economic, and social group. A wage-based economic system and the federal government's efforts at acculturation had not changed this structural feature that had presumably existed since prereservation times. It was not that the political, economic, and social conditions of reservation life had remained unchanged under the intensive Anglo contact; rather, the nature of the changes favored a persistence of kin-based interaction and cooperation.

The matter of community-wide interaction and cooperation would become pivotal during the subsequent War on Poverty. Community cooperation would be demanded by a government that had been trying to subvert cooperative effort for the previous one hundred years. In view of the high incidence of community conflict during the 1950s and early 1960s, there was scant reason to assume that effective, long-lasting, community-wide cooperation on development projects would suddenly or easily emerge in response to unprecedented opportunities for community benefit.

CHAPTER 5

The Politics and Problems of Self-Help: 1961-1974

JOHN F. KENNEDY'S ADMINISTRATION IN 1961 brought another change, reminiscent of the Indian New Deal, to federal Indian policy. In 1961, for example, a special task force of investigators was dispatched by Kennedy's secretary of interior, Stewart Udall, to visit Indian communities and determine their economic and social needs, as a prelude to a new series of development programs. As in the Collier era, talented academicians were recruited as both builders and implementers of the emerging policy changes; for example, Philleo Nash, a politically active anthropologist specializing in American Indian studies, was made the new commissioner of Indian Affairs. (He served from 1961–1966.) In the developing policy, there was a familiar Collier-like concern for the maintenance of reservation communities—a welcome relief from the anxiety created by threats of termination in the 1950s. And it continued the trend—only beginning in the mid-1930s but well under way by the late 1950s—of spreading financial and administrative responsibility for Indian development among different federal and state agencies, rather than giving the entire responsibility to the Indian bureau.

The New Frontier and its successor, the War on Poverty, not only returned to the Indian New Deal philosophy of developing Indian communities as wholes, but also continued, and even expanded, off-reservation vocational and employment programs for individuals and families. But what really made the Indian policy of the 1960s different from Roosevelt's mid-depression New Deal was its munificence. The country was coming out of a minor recession when Kennedy took office, and the national economic picture remained bright for much of the decade (Dowd 1974:85). Millions were funnelled into programs to improve the lot of the impoverished—Indians as well as others—with the conviction that the national economy would sustain their long-term development. Daniel Moynihan would later write, "It can be said of the War on Poverty that it began not because it was necessary, but because it was possible" (1969:29). Indians were still confronted with their two long-standing alternatives: to leave the reservation, taking advantage of the Indian bureau's employment assistance programs, or to stay on the reservation and avail themselves of the new community development programs. But, for the first time, it looked as if these alternatives would be adequately funded and administered to meet the need for economic development.

The reservation-based programs were launched in 1961 when the Department of Commerce implemented the Area Redevelopment Act. Under the terms of this legislation, Indian tribes were asked to submit long-range plans for economic development to the Area Redevelopment Administration (later redesignated the Economic Development Administration, or EDA). These plans were reviewed and, where appropriate, were funded in whole or part in the form of federal grants. Indian response was so enthusiastic that a special Indian office was created in the EDA to coordinate the various programs (Officer 1971:51–52).

That same year, the federal government's Public Housing Administration (later renamed the Housing Assistance Administration, or HAA) made Indian communities eligible to receive assistance in the construction of low-cost housing; these projects were administered locally by housing authorities made up of Indian residents and non-Indian administrators. In time, the Department of Housing and Urban Development (HUD) also provided funds for reservation housing as well as community centers and small industrial buildings.

Hoping to brighten the economic picture still more, the federal government embarked on a campaign to attract private industry to reservation areas to utilize Indian labor. Tax incentives were offered, and the fact that Indian labor was cheap was held out as added inducement. But new plants, new community centers, and new homes were the physical trappings of progress; human resources had to be developed as well. Perhaps no single legislative action was more crucial to this end than the Economic Opportunity

Act of 1964, creating the Office of Economic Opportunity (OEO) to act as coordinator of federal appropriations for vocational training, preschool enrichment programs (Head Start), and small-scale experimental projects for community economic development. In fact, in the 1960s, the Bureau of Indian Affairs was rivaled as an administrative agency for community development by the burgeoning bureaucracy of OEO; Indian demand for OEO programs was so heavy that a special Indian desk had to be created in OEO's Washington headquarters. The BIA's activities were not drastically cut, however, as there were still annually increasing appropriations for the bureau's various administrative functions, including the extremely important one of land management.

Community participation was the watchword of the New Frontier-War on Poverty effort. In 1964, the Department of Interior outlined the spirit of the Economic Opportunity Act for Indian readers:

> The legislation is premised on the assumption that people want to help themselves, and will help themselves if they are given the financial means to take the first step. It stresses community action and relies for its success upon community initiative.
>
> "... government aid can build a floor of programs to alleviate poverty and the other human miseries that poverty engenders. But the people must develop enough faith in themselves to see themselves as creators as well as beneficiaries of their environment" [Department of Interior 1964:2, quoting John Carver, assistant secretary of interior].

The Indian War on Poverty was unquestionably the most ambitious assault on the problems of Indian community and individual development in the history of Indian-Anglo relations, and, besides being the most munificent, was probably also the most humane of the several federal policies. It endured for a decade before inflation and unemployment in the early 1970s caused severe cutbacks in federal funding and jeopardized what economic strides had been made.

But conditions in 1974 were not as bleak as they were in the twilight of the Indian New Deal. For one thing, many reservations had more capital, coming in large part from land-claims settlements. Some, including the Quechan community, had put much of their poverty funding into the beginnings of reservation-based economic ventures. Indian leadership was more sophisticated than it had been four decades earlier. And Indian families, while still poverty-stricken, had better homes and sanitation facilities. In short, the poverty programs may have lasted long enough to have generated some limited economic growth.

The most critical questions still remained unanswered, however. In competition with local and regional interests, and in the midst of a deteriorating national economic situation, could this small-scale growth endure? And would it ever reach sufficient magnitude to bring true prosperity to tribal governments as well as to their constituents?

THE NEW FRONTIER REACHES FORT YUMA

Eight months after the blockade incident of 1960, both the Quechan and national governments changed hands. Three of those who served on the blockade council were reelected, along with some newcomers who were members of the community's most politically active families. It was a young group with all but one member in their thirties; but then youth had been a prominent feature of the councils elected under the Indian Reorganization Act.

The youthful aura of the council was matched on the national level by the spirit of John F. Kennedy's new administration. It was at the American Indian Chicago Conference in June 1961, during discussions of reservation housing and economic development, that council members got their first indication that federal Indian policy was in for another change.

Uppermost in the minds of the council, however, was still the unsettled issue of the Island area. So, two tribesmen flew on to Washington from Chicago to discuss the matter with the new administration of the Interior Department. Again the Indians were impressed with the change in federal attitude. Secretary Udall promised to look into the dispute and told the Quechan envoys that if their claims were valid, he, as secretary of interior, had the authority to return the land to the tribe without lengthy legislative action by Congress. After a tour of key congressmen's offices to publicize the land issue, the envoys returned to the reservation expecting "to have good results from this trip" and wondering why no one had thought to send knowledgeable tribesmen to Washington years earlier to discuss the matter (*Quechan News,* Summer 1961). Direct dealings with high officials were infinitely more satisfying than the plodding, frustrating alternative of working through the maze of bureaucratic channels.

Signals of change from Washington were still positive five months later when the council, together with other leaders of southwestern tribes, met the new Commissioner of Indian Affairs in Tempe, Arizona. The gist of Commissioner Nash's message was that the Kennedy administration was reviving the push for economic development of the reservations. Termination, the Indians understood him to say, would no longer be the immediate goal of federal policy. Instead he issued a call for tribes to formulate their own development plans and to push hard for improving the education of their members. The Quechans had heard much the same proposal thirty years before, but this time they were off to a flying start. They had been working on an overall development plan since their return from the Chicago conference, but, because it depended on the vagaries of federal highway construction, its details and timetable were hazy at best.[1]

From the council's perspective, then, the Kennedy administration's "New Frontier" offered another Collieresque chance for tribal development. The government seemed more willing than ever to help solve the economic problems on the reservation, and this time with what was promised to be significant input from tribal members. True, most of the government action in 1961 was just talk, but the council was neither impatient nor demoralized. The *Quechan News* proclaimed:

> The Tribal Council is doing their very best to keep in line with the "New Indian Frontier Program" recommended by President Kennedy. The Council realizes that the Quechan Tribe can no longer remain stagnant but must progress with the new era for the advancement of the American Indian. Progress can be made and [we can] still retain our Tribal culture that we hold sacred [Winter 1961].

Yet nothing definitive came from Washington the following year either. The council's plan for overall development, forwarded to Washington in 1962, seemed to be in some sort of bureaucratic limbo —reminiscent of the tribe's 1940 proposal.

The Island issue was also stalled someplace, presumably locked into the ponderous process of "further study." The Quechans' two major land claims had been submitted to the Claims Commission in the 1950s, but there, too, definitive action was withheld.[2] The 1961–62 council ended their term, still looking for some visible government movement toward the New Frontier.

In the 1963 council election, five members were reelected, including those who had taken part in the economic planning and coordination with the government agencies. Within a few months of the election, things finally began to happen. By August 1963, the council had approved the final version of a plan to build low-cost housing for the large number of Quechans living at the poverty level. Tied in with nationwide mutual-help housing programs, the plan called for the construction of 130 new homes on the reservation over the next several years. It was to be administered through the BIA in cooperation with a local housing authority, but the funding would come from the Federal Public Housing Authority and the Federal Housing Administration.

In June 1964, the council signed a formal agreement with the Public Health Service (PHS) for installation of a water and sanitation system that would eventually bring running water and indoor bathrooms to those Quechans willing to pay a small monthly charge for the benefits (see 73 Statute 267). That same summer the council was urged by the BIA to submit still another overall economic development plan to be projected over the next ten years. The council did so, only to learn that the newly passed Economic Opportunity Act made their own plan obsolete. (The "New Frontier" had by then become the "War on Poverty" under Kennedy's successor, Lyndon Johnson.) After more planning and negotiations, the council in 1965 inked the final agreements for a Community Action Program (CAP), funded by the new Office of Economic Opportunity (OEO), and for a Neighborhood Youth Corps (NYC), under the auspices of the Department of Labor. The NYC provided part-time wages for students who needed money to stay in school. The CAP was more diverse in its aims, but in general offered specialized advice, technical training, and preschool preparation programs.

All these programs to some extent involved the Quechans in the planning stages, but none originated with the tribe. Not one of the three economic development plans drawn up by the council between 1940 and 1964 had received meaningful attention from the government. In 1966, the council did ask BIA Superintendent Homer Gilliland from Parker Agency what had become of the council's ten-year development plan drawn up in 1964. The superintendent had no idea. He said it was probably pigeonholed because it duplicated the CAP program, and the matter ended there. However, none of the government programs were really replacements for the plans the tribe had been working on during the 1960–1964 period. None mentioned a tribally-owned roadside business, for instance, or any other long-term economic plans for that matter.

The tribe's future was still being determined by the government, not the tribe; the tribe could launch its development only when the government was ready, and the procedures would be the government's, not the tribe's. But no one, least of all the tribal council, wanted to make an issue of this fact in this unprecedented era of federal benefits.

Then, in August 1965, the tribe was informed that one of their two pending land claims had been settled for $520,000, payable after the deduction of attorney's fees and provided that the tribe and BIA developed a workable plan for distribution of the money. The council was jubilant. Through the years, council members had tried to file land claims several times but had always been rebuffed by the government, until it established the Indian Claims Commission in 1946.

These varied windfalls were noteworthy on one account in particular; they came from a number of funding sources. The Bureau of Indian Affairs was no longer the monolithic source of all tribal benefits, as a result of the policy of diversification that had gained popularity in the late 1950s.

THE COUNCIL'S ROLE

The War on Poverty programs involved a certain amount of coordination between government representatives and tribal members. Initially, the council was treated as the public voice of the tribe; members sat in on all planning sessions and signed the formal agreements of acceptance for each program. There were some minor difficulties in writing up proposals for the CAP and NYC programs, since the tribal council had never written a formal grant proposal before and the proposals had to come from the community involved. But with the help of local Anglo educators and civil servants, the proposals were eventually put into approvable form.[3]

The council was also a ready-made coordinating committee and for this reason became the official sponsoring agency for both the CAP and NYC programs. Both council members and government administrators were optimistic about this new status, as it would give the group much needed experience in coping with problems of administration. Among other things, council members were responsible for seeing that the tribe fulfilled its part of the agreements. Of greater concern to the members, they were to have the authority to hire and fire personnel for both programs, even though directors and key supervisors could be hired only with a favorable recommendation from a Community Action Advisory Committee. That committee, made up of both Anglos and Quechans, was beyond tribal council political control.

The council was not involved as a supervising or sponsoring agent in any of the other programs, but it did appoint some of its members to both the water program and claims monies planning committees, and the chairpersons of both were council members. The housing authority also included a council member as vice-chairman; he and a former councilman were the only two Indians on the five-member board, chaired by an Anglo woman. There was therefore a good deal of overlapping leadership on the committees, as in other community organizations, but in this case it had the advantage of keeping the council constantly in touch with committee actions. It also had a disadvantage: feuding among council members carried over to the coordinating committees and interfered with their effectiveness.

Throughout 1965, council members cooperated with government administrators and technical experts. They lacked sophistication in administrative techniques, and some of the details in the program procedures caused problems; but overall the programs moved along smoothly. As the community at large was drawn into active participation, however, the people turned more and more to the council, rather than to outside experts, with their questions and complaints about the programs. Council members listened to complaints, conducted inquiries, and in general saw to it that both they and the tribe were getting all the benefits and considerations to which they were entitled. As a result, the council members became as much watchdogs for the programs as advisers, planners, and beneficiaries; in acting out these contradictory roles, their stance of cooperation with the government gradually turned into one of confrontation.

By early 1966, council members had become openly hostile and suspicious toward program administrators who, they felt, were not informing them of significant program developments, or were doing so after they had already become known by the community at large. The only exception was the members' relationship with the new CAP director, William Gray, an Anglo experienced as an educator and civil servant who gave timely reports at council meetings and made sure the council approved of his proposals. His conduct gave meaning to the council's status as sponsoring agency of the program and kept occasional tension within manageable limits. But smooth relationships were rapidly deteriorating between the council and the administrators of the other programs.

In the summer of 1966, for example, the Anglo chairwoman of the housing authority cancelled a meeting at the last minute because, the council charged, she wanted to avoid answering a growing list of complaints about how the work was proceeding. Later, two Quechan applicants for a supervisory position in the program were turned down, even though the position remained vacant. Whether either applicant was qualified for the job became a side issue for some Quechans, who viewed the chairman's action as blatant discrimination.

For another example, a running feud developed between Public Health Service technicians and the council over work on the water mains. The council continually demanded to be brought up to date on construction developments in the program. The PHS technicians replied that they were quite willing to pass on the information, but to the water program committee. Privately, one Anglo technician accused the council of meddlesome interference: "They're playing a game of pretense; they act like they're running the whole show!" The council members, of course, felt the same way about the PHS technicians.

The feud became much more intense after a clash in the spring of 1966 that at first had little to do with the water program. The crisis centered around Louise Tannheimer, a councilwoman who held a number of leadership positions in community organizations, including that of NYC director and chairwoman of the water committee. (The council had earlier hired her as NYC director on the recommendation of the Community Action Advisory Committee.) Mrs. Tannheimer had not had an easy time as NYC director. Because of frequent shifts in NYC funding and procedures at higher echelons, her reports to the council were sometimes delayed and often contradicted earlier ones. However, a public meeting called to inquire into her management effectiveness collapsed when (in the Quechan pattern of waging conflict) her most outspoken critics refused to come into the meeting to make their allegations publicly. They stood outside the open entrance, quietly talking and smoking.

In May 1966, Mrs. Tannheimer and her husband moved to a home just beyond the reservation's eastern boundary. The council immediately passed a resolution calling for her resignation as councilwoman, in keeping with the tribe's IRA constitution that required council members to live on the reservation. Mrs. Tannheimer chose to fight this resolution. Not only would she not step down, she declared, but if pressed, she would report to government authorities that the residence rule had not been strictly enforced in the past. Thoroughly angered by what they regarded as her contempt for their authority, the council members drafted another resolution, this time calling for her removal as director of the NYC. To their chagrin, they learned that this action was useless, because the local NYC had been taken out of their control and put under the auspices of Imperial County, California. (They had been apprised of this possibility some weeks before, but did not know when or if it would occur.) The San Francisco regional office of the NYC told Mrs. Tannheimer to ignore the council's second resolution.

But Mrs. Tannheimer was not content to have external authorities provide her only support. She enlisted the aid of close kinsmen to publicly condemn the council's tactics. Utilizing the political network forged by her father, Edmond Jackson, Sr., and his activist kinsmen years before, she packed the next council meeting with tribal members sympathetic to her position. In a particularly dramatic ploy, her mother prevailed upon Pete Cachora, the tribe's prominent elderly ritualist and funeral orator, to stand up in the meeting and denounce the council. Softly but effectively, in native Quechan, he chastised the councilmen for practically ensuring Anglo domination of the poverty programs by taking such aggressive action against one of their own people. He ended his monologue on a more personal note: he declared that, as far as he was concerned, Mrs. Tannheimer's claims to Quechan ancestry were less dubious than some of her fellow council members. (Her mixed-tribal ancestry, marriage to an Anglo, and inability to speak Quechan fluently had been used against her by political rivals.) The council listened to his and other critics' statements impassively, but the words cut deeply. The council president, for one, felt that his political strength lay with the tribe's elderly traditionalists, who were now being such outspoken opponents of the council's action.

Without recognition of their authority by Neighborhood Youth Corps administrators or community support for their actions, there was little more the council could do. Mrs. Tannheimer did resign from the council, but remained as NYC director. For a time following this incident, she also maintained her office in the Fort Yuma commandant's former quarters on Indian Hill, while the council temporarily yielded its own office to the burgeoning Community Action Program and set up operations in the entryway of the Bureau of Indian Affairs subagency office.

Because of the narrow distribution of leadership among politically active tribesmen, the effects of the dispute diffused into the water program, where Mrs. Tannheimer was serving as chairwoman. Earlier, she had agreed to prepare copies of the proposed articles of association of a new water corporation for the council to study. (For weeks the PHS had been prodding the council to approve the articles, but the members kept asking for more time to study the issue.) After her resignation, Mrs. Tannheimer informed the council that the copies had been made and that it was the council's job to distribute them. The council did nothing, feeling it was her responsibility to make the distribution. The impasse continued for several weeks. Finally, an NYC enrollee simply picked up the copies from Mrs. Tannheimer's office, carried them across the old Fort Yuma parade ground, and laid them on the president's desk.

The PHS needed council approval for the corporation proposal before it could move ahead on billing procedures for individual users of the system (some Quechans had already begun using the water). The continued delay could not have made PHS functionaries too optimistic about the council's administrative competence, but members had no alternative but to delay until they were sure the proposal was in the tribe's best interest, particularly since it relied on cash payments from some very impoverished tribal members. (Actually, the water corporation issue was something of an anticlimax. It never became operational, and the entire water system was replaced in 1974 by a more efficient and voluminous one.)

Council members felt threatened again with erosion of their authority when some of the Anglos serving as CAP specialists proposed that state experts be called in to provide technical advice and equipment to control mosquitoes and flies around reservation homes. Fritz Brown, the tribal president, flatly opposed the suggestion. He feared that state involvement would only pave the way for more pervasive state interference in tribal administration, for more conflicts over state and county zoning ordinances and building codes, and, most threatening of all, for more energetic efforts to collect state property taxes from reservation dwellers. (The state had already made a number of unsuccessful attempts to levy property taxes on reservation homes, in violation of existing federal laws.) State intervention, Brown declared, would be allowed only in the form of advice given to the CAP on public health matters.

By late summer 1966, then, the ambiguity of the tribal council's role in the several development programs was clearly causing difficulties. The situation was complicated by the suddenness with which the council was thrust into its administrative role after its long history of factionalism and powerlessness, and by the contradictory demands on council members as both supervisors and beneficiaries. However, despite the heated declarations at the height of the NYC crisis, there was never a serious doubt in any council member's mind about continuing the programs. As in the disputes with the school authorities in the 1890s, the issues were still how and by whom the development effort was being managed. These issues were largely out of the council's control, despite the members' increasing involvement in administrative decisions. But the council members were not giving up yet.

THE PATRONAGE ISSUE

In a community as small and poverty ridden as Fort Yuma, it might be expected that political patronage would surface in any scheme involving desirable benefits. The council's critics were well aware of this possibility and pounced on any indication that a political pay-off might be lurking behind a council decision. Because of this eternal suspicion, the War on Poverty programs were relatively free of political plum-picking. To be sure, six of the first ten new homes were built for council members or their close relatives, but these Quechans were just as qualified as others to receive the homes, and their applications had been among the earliest handed in to the housing authority. Council members and their families were not the first in the community to get running water from the new system. The priorities were set according to the most efficient routes of pipeline construction, not by membership in the tribal government.

Aside from the new houses and the prestige of being a leader on one of the coordinating committees, the most immediate program benefits for the council and their kinsmen were the wages paid to aides and trainees. In March 1966, a councilman was working as an aide in the CAP, along with two wives and a daughter of other council members. The principal of CAP's Head Start program was the council president's half brother, and the assistant director of the CAP was a councilman's brother. None of this escaped the notice of the council's outspoken critics even though the latter two cases did not involve political patronage or nepotism, because both men were adults with families of their own and were well-qualified for their respective jobs.

Nonetheless, the paid participation of councilmen and their families in the OEO programs was questionable, despite financial needs and other qualifications. In April 1966, the council was warned by the Anglo CAP director that it had better follow some newly promulgated OEO guidelines by dismissing the councilman and family members of other councilmen from the CAP. Otherwise, the director observed, funds for the program might be held up and the entire Fort Yuma administration might end up with a bad record in Washington. The council agreed and drafted a resolution of dismissal that this time was effective.

Individual council members, as CAP and NYC sponsoring agents, still could try to influence the selection of applicants for the various jobs in the CAP and NYC so as to pay off friends and distant kinsmen for political support. Those wanting a job with one of the programs would submit a formal application to the program director. The director then handed a list of all qualified applicants to the council, who made the final choice (usually in terms of need and reliability). Council members could speak in behalf of constituents whose names appeared on the list, but the small-town familiarity that made council members aware of individual needs in granting personal loans in the past, operated in this case to prevent flagrant political patronage. A council member's favorite applicant may have been less qualified than others on the list, and this would be pointed out by other members who, themselves, might be pushing for their own favorites. As a result, during the hiring process in 1966, the most qualified applicants generally ended up with the jobs, due to this informal system of checks and balances.

A combination of federal guidelines, community vigilance, tribal politics, and skillful management made the Fort Yuma CAP operation more successful than CAPs elsewhere, particularly those in urban areas where nepotism and flagrant exploitation are matters of public record. In fact, in Fort Yuma the council later passed an even more restrictive ordinance preventing council members or their immediate families from holding employment in any government programs on the reservation.

THE PROGRAMS AND THE COMMUNITY: MEANS AND ENDS

The programs started out very well. In the fall of 1965, the first group of self-help homeowners, along with a few others who wanted to learn basic construction skills, poured concrete floors as BIA photographers stood by to record the undertaking. But soon things started to go wrong. Within six months, the homeowners' participation began to sag. Part of the difficulty stemmed from confusion about work schedules, which frequently had to be changed at the last minute by the Anglo construction foreman. The attitude became even more uncooperative when several homeowners failed to show up for work even after the schedule changes. Why, they reasoned, should they exert themselves when others stayed away but were still getting their homes built? Their complaints soon included the BIA subagency superintendent and the construction foreman, as well as Anglo technical experts hired to instruct and supervise. The superintendent, the Quechans declared, was far too worried about orderliness and had unjustifiably halted work until bits of dried mortar had been cleaned up off the floor. The construction foreman was not decisive enough in his instructions and enlistment of workers. The technical experts (several were hired and fired between January and August 1966) did not know their jobs. Eventually, their criticism extended all the way to the government, for the poor quality of the materials being used in the homes. One Quechan observed disgustedly, "Mister Indian is getting what no white man would want."

Nothing seemed to bolster the flagging cooperation.[4] Pep talks at housing authority meetings and attempts to shame the laggards into more work by publicizing their poor attendance were ignored. Council members exhorted each other in meetings to "drop by and see how the boys are doing, maybe say a few words to them to show we're interested." There was still no improvement. Yet, the houses were getting built. Two of the ten homeowners established good work records and were helped by the BIA subagency superintendent and the construction foreman (whose civil service job efficiency ratings depended on the completion of the homes), and also by a Mexican-American who wanted to learn carpentry, and by trainees in other community poverty programs who were being paid for their time.

Other homeowners could pinpoint no single cause for their doldrums. When asked, they simply repeated the list of criticisms. The Anglo supervisors were stymied. The relationship among the workers had seemed good during the early stages of construction. The work had offered them a chance to exchange jokes and gossip in an all-male setting, away from their families. Most of the work was done in the evenings, after the heat of the day had passed. There was the opportunity to learn valuable construction skills (although it was debatable whether they would gain enough experience to land jobs on the outside). And there was the stimulation of intertribal competition, as, during the first few months of the operation, the Quechans proudly pointed out that they were well ahead of their Mohave counterparts to the north (although the Mohaves eventually completed their project ahead of the Quechans). But perhaps most confounding for the Anglos was the Quechans' lack of interest in doing everything they could to get themselves and their families into brand-new homes. The twelve-month timetable for completion was revised, then revised again. It was not until early fall of 1967, some twenty-three months after the project had begun, that the first ten Quechan self-help homes were ready for occupancy.

The course of events in the water system project followed a similar pattern. The community responded very well to the request for voluntary labor on the construction crew; then came the drastic ebb of willing workers.

Mrs. Tannheimer and her brother, Edmond Jackson, Jr., who was serving as tribal business manager, finally suggested a scheme they had heard about from Indians on another reservation, and that was to bring in convict labor from the Imperial County Jail to do the work on the water line. The sheriff was agreeable if the tribe would feed the workers at noon. The tribal council also agreed, although it would be hard pressed to find the funds and cooks to feed the prisoners, and hired a Quechan man as labor foreman and truck driver. The prisoners were not consulted, but they needed no convincing because the ones selected were Indians themselves, serving brief sentences for public intoxication or disturbing the peace, and to them it would be like getting an early reprieve.

Again, Anglo experts called in for advice were astounded at the community's recalcitrance. No Anglo suburbanite would behave in such a way. The people, however, were not Anglos, they were Indians. They were products of their history of dependence on the government, a history that had made neither cooperation nor voluntary effort on federal programs viable alternatives, at least not until other possibilities had been tested.[5]

Not that there was no cooperation among tribal members. The annual Memorial Day service was an excellent example of the cooperative patterns, but it made different demands: it was not long term; it involved organic cooperation in the sense that different community segments—the voluntary associations—performed different functions, rather than everyone doing the same thing at the same time; and it was Quechan-directed without much Anglo involvement. Also, there was selective participation by individual Quechans, who could participate in the activities as much or as little as they wished without risking much more than short-lived, whispered criticism.

Furthermore, the Quechans had developed a cash-oriented response to federal development schemes. In 1913, for example, they had demanded pay for working on the maintenance of the reservation's irrigation system (H. M. Carter to commissioner 10 February 1913), and in the 1950s, they were paid for work on the prefab housing project. By 1966, economic conditions on the reservation made it essential for the Quechans to convert their time and skills into cash. (CAP planners estimated that, in 1965, the per capita income of all but ten of the community's 180 families was below $4,000 per year.) In the midst of such conditions, it was naive to assume (as the government apparently did) that the Quechans would suddenly reorient their priorities, ignore historical precedent, and cooperate wholeheartedly in unpaid labor in the hot sun. Once the mutual commitment had been made, however, the government was not anxious to cancel it, in part because too many civil servants' efficiency records rested on the completion of the programs. The Quechans were thus free to change the rules (in the form of withdrawal of voluntary labor) to their own advantage, and collectively they developed a "wait and see" posture while the government pondered its response.

Instead of terminating the programs when the Quechans withdrew their cooperation, thus forcing closer adherence to the official rules, the government kept the benefits coming in by seeking to circumvent the (cooperation) problems. This is not to suggest that there was a central body of Quechan string-pullers who were deviously directing the tactics of their followers. As far as the Quechans were concerned, the housing and water programs were not all that different from government development programs of the past. To be sure, the scale of benefits was larger, but it was nonetheless the same government with the same built-in, ponderous, bureaucratic, operating procedures. Also, the Quechans did not look on their withdrawal action as devious or as even a breach of contract. They refused to work because others were not fulfilling their part of the agreement, whether they were fellow tribesmen or government administrators; once broken, they did not consider the labor requirement in the contract as any longer binding.

The Quechans, then, responded to the housing and water programs according to precedents established in earlier government development programs. These historical precedents did not cause the Quechan's reaction to the new programs; they were simply there for everyone to know and apply, in his own way. Clear for all to see, the houses were being built and the water was beginning to flow. The withdrawal strategy by any measure other than the ethics of Anglo protestantism made downright good sense. The Quechans were not Anglos, nor were they brimming with the protestant ethic in spite of the missionaries' earnest efforts.

COMMUNITY ACTION PROGRAM AND NEIGHBORHOOD YOUTH CORPS

To the Quechans, the CAP and NYC were different from the water and housing programs. The people were paid for their time so that some of the benefits were immediate. The government viewed the wages as means to the ends of vocational training, staying in school, or otherwise mobilizing community talents in a self-perpetuating development effort, but for the Indians, the wages were the most important ends.[6]

The Quechans responded enthusiastically to the call for applicants for the various positions, particularly in the CAP where age and student status were not as important as in the NYC. Bill Gray, the Anglo CAP director, and his talented Quechan assistant, Felix Montague, moved quickly to create a healthy morale among employees. They held "gripe sessions" each payday when employees met with the director to air their criticisms. The going was slow at first, as employees were reticent and unwilling to make their complaints publicly. But within a few weeks, the sessions became more freewheeling, and the employees were even contributing small donations from their checks for monthly dinners or group junkets to the local dog races. By mid-1966, the Fort Yuma CAP had become a model program in the eyes of area administrators, and Gray was selected as regional "Director of the Month" for March. He continued to stay on the good side of the community by offering construction materials to those wanting to build bathroom additions and by sending CAP vehicles to haul wood and other supplies for the annual pow-wow.

Still, the CAP suffered through its share of squabbles that could not be resolved in the gripe sessions. The Quechan serving as Head Start principal clashed with Gray over the operation of the school, eventually resigned, and left the reservation; his position was filled by an Anglo. Quechan aides in some of the other projects balked at having to perform menial cleanup chores at the end of the day. They understood that they were to receive wages and vocational training; they did not understand why the vocational training included wiping off tables and sweeping floors in the home-enrichment room. Some complained that the Anglo supervisors were "too bossy" for insisting that the typewriters be covered at the end of the day, or that coffee breaks be kept within time limits. Gray rearranged the clean-up responsibilities so that everyone was involved—supervisors and aides—and in time, the gripe sessions mediated flare-ups between the aides and Anglo specialists, some of whom were obviously not suited for their positions and eventually resigned.

The director was lenient in dealing with drunkenness and absenteeism, letting employees know they would be given three warnings for showing up drunk for work, malingering, or absenteeism before they would be permanently dismissed. The program could not accomplish its goals, he felt, with a get-tough policy toward employees who had not had good working experiences on the outside. The council, as sponsoring agency, also offered advice and support to employees with drinking problems, its members wanting to keep the good reputation of the program intact and not wishing it harmed by unusually high numbers of malingerers.

The CAP staff was bothered by continual hints from higher echelons that their appropriations were about to be cut. But, as the council had earlier discovered, direct contact with the government in CAP negotiations was most effective. Gray and Felix Montague worked hard to create direct links between themselves and key personnel at the OEO Indian Desk in Washington. They found that long-distance calls and flights to Washington not only avoided long delays while proposals and recommendations filtered up through the various channels, but also gave the local staff up-to-the-minute information on the prospects for further funding and kept the Fort Yuma program constantly in the attention of the administration. The local CAP staff was soon on a first-name basis with the Indian desk director, reminding him also of the progress being made at Fort Yuma. This relationship and the program's good reputation were to pay handsome dividends over the next few years.

The administration of the NYC presented more problems. For one thing, it was a smaller program than the CAP, with funds available only for the director, Louise Tannheimer, and for the youths hired as enrollees. At first there had been money for an administrative assistant, a position held (while it lasted) by Mrs. Tannheimer's sister. This bothered Mrs. Tannheimer's political rivals. Another Quechan woman volunteered her help as the program was getting under way and became an unofficial counselor for the young enrollees. She was forced to quit when rumors were spread that she was secretly receiving pay for her work. How else, the gossip reasoned, could she afford the new car she was driving? (Actually her Mexican-American husband and she had saved up money for the car from other earnings.)

Wages were the primary benefit of the NYC program for the youthful enrollees, but because of the financial and administrative muddle at the higher NYC administrative levels, some enrollees claimed they did not know whether they were still employed by the program or not. Furthermore, Mrs. Tannheimer had so many obligations that, without help, she could not adequately supervise the work of the enrollees. Without supervision, the young people evaded their work responsibilities. "Just put in your eight hours," the volunteer counselor told them early on. "You don't even have to work hard—just keep working!" Months later she lamented that many of the enrollees "weren't even doing that much." The community critics (including some of the enrollees' parents) agreed. But Mrs. Tannheimer continued to keep even the most notorious malingerers on the payroll, in the hope that they might eventually become productive. In spite of this deviation from the spirit of the program, however, the NYC may well have had the desired effect: between 1966 and 1969, only nine of the fifty-three Quechans enrolled at one time or another in the program dropped out of high school—a very low rate compared to the national average for Indian pupils at that time.[7]

The participation required in the CAP and NYC programs was more congruent with the community's social and economic conditions than either the water or housing schemes. Since the benefits (wages) were immediate, withdrawal would not work as a strategy for getting the greatest payoff for the least amount of time and effort. There was the familiar criticism of others who were "not doing their fair share" or were being "too bossy," and antipathy between those holding CAP positions and those who had been turned down. But there was also competition for the jobs and a relatively small employee turnover rate in most of the projects. The Quechans continued to participate in these programs either for wages or for the various technical services they provided, such as home enrichment, public sanitation, or education for preschool-age youngsters.

THE CLAIMS PROGRAM

In contrast to the relative speed with which the poverty programs were launched, the first of two major claims settlements was a long time in coming. The government, through the BIA, was not about to turn $520,000 over to the tribe to do with as it pleased. First, a comprehensive and detailed plan had to be drawn up by the tribe, showing how the money would be spent. It furthermore had to be an approvable plan—the secretary of interior had to approve it—which, in the operational procedures of the Washington bureaucracy, meant that it would have to follow precedents set with other tribes. Innovation was therefore stifled from the outset, even though the official record of the planning process repeatedly mentioned "important" input from the tribe itself.

In mid-summer 1965, the council learned that a Claims Commission decision was close at hand, and Fritz Brown as council president was authorized to appoint fourteen members of a claims planning committee to draw up a program for spending the money. In addition, BIA officials from the Fort Yuma Subagency and the Colorado River Agency were to serve also. Brown put the entire council on the committee, and, in contrast to the youthful appointees on the various poverty program committees, chose the rest of the members from a much older, predominantly male group, some of whom spoke no English. This was only fair, the president felt: "They're the ones who've been fighting for years for this money; they should be the ones to decide how it's going to be spent." It was a shrewd political move on Brown's part, because his support had come in large part from the old people. Lee Emerson, a council member who had for years diligently collected information on the 1893 Agreement and other land expropriations, was made chairman of the committee. As one of the leaders in the blockade effort of 1960, he had shown no inclination to knuckle under to government schemes that would give less than a full measure of restitution to the Quechans.

A tentative program was drafted during July and August 1965, in which the various budget categories were essentially those worked out in the claims programs of other Indian tribes.[8] By late August, after the Claims Commission decision was made official, the committee scheduled a series of seven tribal meetings. Although the meetings were convened to gather suggestions as well as to inform, most of the active discussion was carried on by the BIA representatives and members of the tribal council. Attendance at the meetings was sparse, given the high interest in the claims issue; records show that there were never more than ten tribal members in the audience, other than those serving on the planning committee itself. Although solicited time after time, the few suggestions and questions from the floor focused mainly on the so-called family plan. Most of the Quechans wanted cash grants to go to each family on a per capita basis. Instead, according to the plan, each family would merely be issued shares on this basis. The shares could be pooled to buy such items as new refrigerators or stoves, but only after the tribal council had approved the purchase. The Indian families would never see cash in the transactions; the shares were in effect promissory notes that would be paid by the government from the tribe's award. Tribal members asked repeatedly why this plan was proposed instead of per capita cash payments. Government officials replied that a plan for cash payments would probably not be approved by the government, because of past instances in which Indian recipients had "squandered" the money on "useless" activities and items. Of course, the officials concluded, the tribe could go ahead and push for cash payment if it wanted to, but such a proposal would delay or even block eventual approval of the program. Under these circumstances, the tribal members agreed to the family plan. They were numbed anyway after learning that the shares would only amount to about fifty dollars each.

The older members of the claims committee were generally reticent during the planning sessions. When asked for their ideas, they rose to express in Quechan their confidence in the younger members of the committee to act in the best interests of the tribe. And the tribe's best interests, as its members saw them, were incorporated into the plan, regardless of its similarity to other plans. Education, tribal administration, and land purchase provisions were the main concerns, even if the allocations for each would be subject to later adjustment. As for the family plan, all that waiting for only fifty dollars struck some as simply another low in reservation life under the government. "Fifty dollars!" bitterly laughed one old man, living alone after fighting for years with Patrick Miguel and others on the land issue. "Now what the hell am I supposed to do with fifty dollars? What kind of refrigerator or stove or TV can I get for fifty dollars?"

As the series of public meetings dragged on, the committee developed an urgency about getting the program submitted. Once again, as in the various poverty program committees, the attitude was one of "let's get this thing approved and get the money; we can sort out the problems later." Almost a year after the Claims

Commission decision was announced, the tribal plan was finally ready to go to Washington.

CONDITIONS OF DEVELOPMENT IN 1969

Previous to the development programs, Indian Hill, the administrative hub of the community, was badly deteriorated and covered with dust. Old, tumbledown, boarding school buildings had threatened to collapse with the first strong wind, and trash had blown across the old fort's parade ground, a sand and rock square bordered by brown patches of grass and scraggly, untrimmed palm trees. By May 1969, however, the hill had changed radically. The rickety buildings had been replaced, using salvaged lumber, by a new, low-profile, tribal administration building and library. There was no more blowing trash. The old fort's officers' quarters had been refurbished inside and out. The grass was green, the trees were trimmed, and small groups of Quechan men continued to work on building, watering, or more trimming. There were yet more transformations. Just to the north below the hill, where as late as 1966 the tribal dancing ground had been bounded by thick brush and roads strewn with beer cans, a large new trailer court and shopping plaza was awaiting tenants and proprietors. And three-quarters of a mile further north, vocational trainees were building the framework of a new youth center. The first ten self-help houses were finished, and work on a second group of twenty had begun. In all, it was a sight to impress even the staunchest critics of the War on Poverty.

Unquestionably the decision-making responsibilities in these efforts lay with several council members who had been in on the development plans since the early 1960s, as well as with William Gray (the CAP director) and two of his Quechan associates. In its first three years, much of the CAP effort had shifted from what Gray called "soft" programs, such as remedial reading, guidance counseling, and public health instruction, to an emphasis on construction by paid vocational trainees. Gray, together with a new tribal council president, Henry Montague, and Gray's former assistant, Felix Montague (Henry's younger brother), who was now the local representative of a new development organization known as IDDA (Indian Development District of Arizona), used their close ties with the Washington bureaucracy to gather funds from a number of federal agencies.[9] It was a circular process: new funds boosted the CAP's apparent productivity (in the form of new buildings) and reputation, and this helped to ensure the receipt of still more funds.

Besides the manifestations of community development—new buildings, green grass, and so forth—individuals also appeared to be better off economically. Late in the summer of 1966, the CAP had seventy people on its payroll, fifty-six of whom were Indians. Three years later, 132 people were working in the program, 102 of them Indians. Most of the employees were construction workers on the short-term vocational training projects.[10] The burgeoning construction programs meant more cash for more families, even though the wages were ridiculously low compared to those earned for similar work off the reservation. By 1969, the government had also implemented a surplus food program that issued large quantities of free food to those living at the poverty level (as many Quechans were). Six hundred people living on or near the reservation received free food through the program each month, over two-thirds of them Indians.[11] A family might subsist solely on the commodities, but the people usually bought sweets or fresh fruit and vegetables to enrich the canned and dehydrated fare.

But despite the mini-boom of 1969, the reservation's economic structure was like a house of cards waiting for a breeze. Very little of the money being pumped into the community went for long-term growth projects. The trailer park and shopping plaza were money-making enterprises, but these benefitted only a small maintenance staff and the several Quechans who were able to raise the capital to start a business in one of the plaza's sections. Most of the funds went for wages and construction, with the government acting as super-employer: members of approximately 130 of the reservation's 180 families received full or part-time wages from government programs between 1966 and 1969. The wage structure was designed to be temporary. Federal money would keep flowing only as long as the various training programs lasted.

The people realized full well that lasting economic security would depend on the effectiveness of their training and the availability of jobs in nearby areas. They also realized that the outlook was bleak for both these requirements. The trainees were receiving good experience, such as it was, but it was hardly extensive enough to equip them for skilled or semiskilled jobs off the reservation. Between 1966 and 1969, only two Quechans left the training programs for better paying construction jobs in town, and both had had extensive experience in construction work before the training programs began. Furthermore, even when jobs were available that the Quechans could handle, they did not necessarily get them. According to tribal leaders in 1968, there was still a good deal of local aversion to hiring Indians.

Younger tribal members were confident that "something would turn up" after the training ended, but had no idea what it would be. "We joke about what will happen when the training ends; we say we will go hungry. But that probably won't happen. We've always got the food commodities to tide us over." Older Quechans, many with physical disabilities that would make it impossible for them to get jobs elsewhere, believed their training was a waste of time, although they were glad to get the money and have something to do each day.

The tribe's only major asset was, as always, land, and land improvement continued, but still according to patterns that had been laid down at the beginning of the century. The tribe leased the less fertile portions of the reservation to Anglo developers for very low prices (all of which usually went to pay operation and maintenance charges).[12] In this way, most of the useless seepage areas west and south along the All-American canal were transformed into productive plots during the 1950s and 1960s.[13] But the lease income from a ten-acre plot, even after the plot was improved, would not support an individual for a year. In addition, the BIA still controlled the leasing arrangements, and there were complaints during the 1960s that the subagency superintendent was stifling competitive bidding for Indian land leases by giving options to lessees to lease the same tract year after year. Without government pressure to raise rental fees, Indian land remained a bargain for Anglo developers, leasing for about thirty-five dollars per acre per year in 1969–70. Several lessees had become wealthy from reservation farming. The tribal leaders knew this and resented it, but no one in the tribe had the capital or equipment to farm on a scale even approaching that of the wealthy Anglos.

While the CAP flourished, the NYC by 1969 had withered away to the point that it had no effect on the reservation's economic pattern. Mrs. Tannheimer had resigned as director in 1967 and the NYC administration was transferred to officials of the local San Pasqual High School, built just east of the reservation in 1954. The total number of enrollee positions had shrunk to only nine; and in the high school, where Indians made up roughly forty percent of the student body, only two or three of the available positions were assigned each year to Indians.

The premise of the mutual-help housing program was changed by the growth of the vocational training programs. Vocational trainees did the work. When necessary, directors contracted highly-skilled jobs out to Anglo companies on a competitive bidding basis. Homeowners were still encouraged to help, but only two or three of the new group of twenty appeared regularly at the sites. The Anglo builders did not have to fill an Indian quota in hiring workers but they agreed to give first consideration to eligible Indians when there were job vacancies. As a result of this new strategy, the housing effort moved rapidly toward its goal of 130 new homes.

Tribal politicians were either enthusiastic or disappointed at the impact of the programs, depending on factional alignment. The programs were still arenas for political struggles, and by 1969 the CAP had finally become the primary cause of contention. As usual, the basic issue was authority, that of both outsiders and political rivals within the tribe.

Two changes had occurred to make the issue hotter. Bill Gray, the Anglo CAP director, had become very influential in tribal council decision-making. And the job of tribal council president—thanks to the claims monies—had become full-time and salaried, with the use of a tribal car for official business. There were those who thought Gray had acquired too much power and that he should be replaced by a Quechan. This was, they reasoned, in keeping with the general scenario of the CAP when it was first inaugurated. And some felt that the council's ideal of a consensual pattern of decision-making was being ignored, that there was now too much "one man rule."

Henry Montague was treading the same thin line as his predecessor, Fritz Brown, and those before him: to retain his political support, he had to make effective decisions that would benefit the tribe; but by so doing, he left himself open to criticism for not keeping to the consensual pattern of decision-making—even though the Quechans had repeatedly been forced out of that pattern ever since Major Heintzelman had designated Pasqual as chief in the 1850s.

Actually, the fluid funding situation and complex operating procedures probably demanded the kind of quick, flexible, small group, decision-making strategy that had made some council members irate. In 1966, when Fritz Brown was president, they had hailed the same strategy as being necessary to cut through the red tape to get the programs going; by 1969, it had become a source of conflict between tribal politicians seeking the new perquisites of the tribal presidency.

None of the persistent haggling produced any formal attempts to change program management, however, and the disenchanted critics on the council bided their time while Gray and his staff continued their quest for more funds. Within a short time, Gray and the council president began face-to-face negotiations with the Office of Economic Opportunity on a plan that—at last—held some hope for long-term economic development for the tribal community as a whole.

But up to that point, the War on Poverty had generated some self-defeating contradictions. The best job opportunities were still off-reservation, and even outside the greater Yuma area. Presumably most of the vocational training programs were designed to train people for such jobs and therefore were a means of getting the

Indians to leave the community. At the same time, other programs were moving rapidly to make the reservation itself a more attractive place to stay—new homes, new water system, technical advice on public health and home management, and so on. Lasting economic security—the victory over poverty—lay off-reservation and could be had only by taking a considerable risk with a better than even chance of ultimate failure. The obvious adaptive strategy for unskilled Quechan workers confronting these alternatives was to stay put on the reservation and to keep applying for low-paying and temporary training positions.

DEVELOPMENTS IN 1974

In the summer of 1974, after almost a decade of antipoverty programs, the physical changes in the community were even more dramatic. The CAP had been redesignated the CAA (Community Action Agency) and had taken over all the buildings on Indian Hill except the Public Health Service hospital. The tribal council and its staff, together with the BIA subagency staff, had moved out onto the reservation into a new air-conditioned community center, complete with a well-equipped gymnasium. A few hundred yards to the east, next to the youth center of 1969 vintage, was a large complex of greenhouses and an administration building—the new hydroponic tomato farm. North and west, near the All-American Canal, two new pumping stations had been installed to provide water for the brand-new reservation water system. This was not another fragile plastic pipe affair such as had been put up in 1966, but an extensive system of large-diameter mains that would eventually provide water and also a sewerage system for both the reservation and Winterhaven. To the east of Indian Hill, columns of smoke rose from piles of brush being burned off of 600 acres of farmland in the Island area, leased by the tribe from the government pending a final settlement of tribal claims to the tract. Just below Indian Hill, the trailer park had been expanded to 170 spaces, and, nearby, a small apartment complex for disabled elderly Quechans was going up. Across the road from the trailer park and shopping plaza, a new, modern "big house" or mourning shelter had been built, facing east toward the reservation's funeral grounds. And everywhere there were new homes—153 of them, built mainly through the misnomered mutual-help housing program. Most of the new construction was the result of federal monies; and some of it was a meaningful start on the community's economic development. But, after more than ten years of intensive antipoverty effort, it was still only a start.

The federal government remained the primary source of the Quechans' earned income. Out of 160 Quechans listed as employed in 1973 (Memo, Fort Yuma Subagency to Phoenix Area Office 20 September 1973), 87 had full-time positions in the federally funded development operations, and another 41 worked in BIA, PHS, or tribal government jobs (Bee). In other words, 128 of the approximately 160 job holders were financed by federal funds or funds allocated to the tribe by the government. Neither figure includes the 50 NYC enrollees who were earning part-time wages (two dollars an hour) in the summer of 1974, under a revived program administered by the Indian Development District of Arizona (IDDA).

The figures indicate that federal funds had turned the Quechan community into a small job-generating enterprise. It was not, and never had been, a training area for off-reservation employment. In 1974, only eight of all the poverty program vocational trainees from the 1966–1969 period were working on outside jobs related to their training.[14] Others had been absorbed into reservation projects (such as the tomato farm), were still in training, had off-reservation jobs unrelated to their vocational training, were unemployed, or were deceased. Many Quechans had simply become professional trainees; that was how they made their living. The vocational training was not wasted on the Quechans, however. Rather, its objectives had been redirected, and on-reservation government or tribally sponsored projects kept much of the labor force from leaving the community. Dave Pasqual, Gray's Quechan successor as CAA director, recognized this and noted that community action goals had changed accordingly. "Now we want to train people to take part in reservation development because we need their talents," he said. "We don't want to lose them to off-reservation jobs."

FARMING AS AN ADAPTIVE STRATEGY

In the mid-1960s, tribal councilmen determined that the difference in income between the Quechan allottees and their Anglo lessees had amounted to roughly three million dollars over the preceding few years.[15] At that time, they suggested that individual allottees pool their lands into a cooperative and either farm them or have them farmed for a percentage of the harvest rather than for a flat lease rate. But the tribe lacked capital, and individual allottees couldn't afford to give up the security of the flat-rate leases (or the emergency advances on lease monies from the Anglo lessees). The Quechans, including members of the council, concluded that the co-op would be too difficult to implement.

After he was hired as CAP director in 1965, Bill Gray had also pushed for a cooperative, or something like it. The government had shown its willingness to support poverty programs, and therefore it was a good time, he had felt, to approach OEO and other agencies for a grant to get the plan under way. The council remained skeptical, however, and the issue was shelved.

Then in 1969, during a conference in Phoenix, the tribal council president, Henry Montague, who had worked for twenty years in local farming operations, and Gray met with the director of OEO's Indian desk and another OEO official for an informal chat in a motel room. By that time, a friendly personal relationship had grown up among these men, and OEO had demonstrated its confidence in the Quechan programs by granting funds for the various construction projects. The Indian desk director had in fact declared that no other Indian program in the nation was receiving more financial help relative to the community's population size than the Quechans'. The conversation turned to farming and the Quechans' traditional attachment to their land. The focus then became more specific: with the help of OEO funds, what could be done to make farming a lucrative business for them? It would have to be a limited operation, because OEO could fund only small-scale, innovative efforts. Gray remembered a greenhouse farming operation being built in Glendale, Arizona, and also knew of similar work being done by the Environmental Research Laboratory at the University of Arizona in Tucson. Why couldn't something like that be done on the Quechan reservation? Clearly enthused, Montague and Gray then pressed the OEO men to find out how much funding might be available. Dr. James Wilson, the Indian desk director, pressed back: how much would such a project cost? Interpreting this as "go ahead and submit a proposal," Montague and Gray returned to the reservation to convince the rest of the council to go along with the idea and draw up the plans. This would be a farming operation with a source of outside funding from the beginning. No allottees would be displaced because the greenhouse would be built on tribal land. It would provide tribal income as well as wages for Indian employees. And it could be the first step in a much larger agricultural operation.

After some persuasion, the council members accepted the idea. The Indian desk director also liked the proposal, but he wanted another federal agency, EDA (Economic Development Agency), to share in the construction funding. This, he felt, would make more money available and would be more in accord with the federal policy of diversifying funding sources.

The initial cost of constructing the plant came to over half a million dollars. The EDA and OEO funded the entire amount—in the form of grants, not reimbursible loans. The BIA, not wanting to be left out of the picture, later financed the necessary training program for the plant's employees.

The tribal council thus became the sponsors of a new agribusiness. But, to keep politics out of the plant operations as much as possible, administrative decisions and procedures were turned over to a farm board, made up of several Quechans not on the council and three non-Indians. The council appointed Bill Gray to serve as the plant's managing director, and the CAA directorship went to Dave Pasqual, who had replaced Felix Montague as Gray's Quechan CAA assistant.

Twenty-two Quechans, men and women, were on the plant payroll by July 1974, and another fifteen were added as part-time employees when the second of the two yearly crops was ready for harvest. If crops and markets were good, the plant was expected to bring in $375,000 a year in sales, with a payroll amounting to over $200,000—before expansion.[16] By mid-1974, however, Gray and his staff had submitted a second proposal to EDA for a $710,600 addition that would mean jobs for still another fifteen Quechans.

Heartened by the success of the tomato farm venture, the council by 1974 was ready to reconsider the notion of farming the entire reservation. Although the tribe's claim to the Island area had still not been settled, the government had earlier leased 600 acres of it to the council, ostensibly for the creation of an industrial park and small airstrip. But soon after the lease was finalized, federal money had tightened up. The bonanza of the late sixties was over as the government, intimidated by economic problems, slashed poverty program appropriations and practically gutted the Office of Economic Opportunity. So, the industrial park had not materialized, but the land was still there and, with a little improvement, would make good farmland. The council, Gray, and the farm board decided to try to raise the necessary capital to convert the land into a tribal open-air farming operation.

This was a real test of the tribe's resourcefulness as fund raisers, because the sympathetic OEO Indian desk director familiar with past Quechan programs had left office to work with a Plains tribe, and funds for OEO-ONAP programs had become scarce indeed. During the decade of the poverty programs, however, the Quechans had become extremely sophisticated in ferreting out funding sources. For example, Harold Chaipos, one of those who had worked on the first of the poverty program proposals in the 1960s, later attended a host of workshops and other conclaves on fundraising. His solution for the current problem was to solicit funds from well-endowed Christian denominations that had money available for Indian development. His approach was personal, focusing on face-to-face discussions that included a succinct statement of what it was the tribe intended to accomplish on the 600-acre tract. He used no form letters or other blanket appeals for aid. And his efforts worked. Two churches agreed to contribute a total of $300,000 to the experiment, and, encouraged by the tribe's ability to raise funds on its own, the Office of Native American Programs agreed to contribute an additional $150,000. The government was also persuaded to provide some of the heavy equipment for clearing and leveling the land.

The open-air farm was to be another experiment-demonstration, to investigate first-hand the contingencies of large-scale farming and convince Quechan allottees that a tribally-operated farming operation could be profitable. Soon, the council and other planners hoped, the tribe itself would become the lessee for the already developed allotments on the reservation; in fact, the council had already begun negotiating a lease for 400 acres of allotted land to be farmed beginning in January 1975. The allottees would receive not only the going lease price for their acreage, but a percentage of the profits of the harvest.

If everything worked as planned, the reservation would eventually become a giant, multimillion-dollar farming operation, with tribal members benefitting from both the wages paid to workers and the money paid to allottees. Theoretically at least, they would no longer have to depend on government munificence or the availability of off-reservation employment. Yet, there were also drawbacks to the large-scale scheme. Farming was hardly the most reliable way of making a living because of the vagaries of the weather and the fluctuating market. Unless it was started gradually, with cash reserve available for emergencies, the enterprise could fold with one poor season. This would be a gamble that few poverty-stricken Quechans would want to take. Operating capital, as distinct from construction capital, would still be the major problem.

The individual allottees would be a tough lot to convince as well. They had come to depend on cash advances from lessees, something that might not be available to them under the new plan. Too, leasing to non-Indians had become more lucrative for them by 1974, as a result of another change in government handling of Quechan affairs. In the early 1970s, the Anglo BIA subagency superintendent was replaced by Lorraine White, an Indian woman with over twenty years of bureau experience. What is more, she was a Quechan—the sister of Elmer Savilla, the tribal council president who took office in 1973. And the Quechans themselves, for the first time in the history of their dependence on the BIA, had been allowed to select her from a list of candidates proposed by higher BIA officials. Mrs. White focused her attention immediately on the leasing situation. She called an abrupt halt to the practice of extending options to lessees from one year to the next, and opened a series of meetings between lessees and allottees that were in effect competitive bidding sessions for lessees. In the three years between 1971 and 1974, the lease rate for reservation land jumped from $35 per acre to between $125 and $135 an acre, with lessees paying the water charges. Of course, the galloping national inflation wiped out some of the gain, but it was still a great improvement over the leasing procedures that had been followed before her arrival, and a factor to be considered by allottees before deciding to lease their land to the tribe.

Some felt that the demand for operating capital could be met by starting slowly and tapping local banks for farm loans. Now that the tribe had a remunerative project in process, banks were no longer the reluctant creditors they once had been. Gray reflected on the about-face in 1974:

> There's no problem with banks any more. It sure wasn't always that way though. When I first signed on here years ago, I once called up a bank and asked about getting a loan for some of the programs. They asked what the tribal assets were. I told them, "about seven hundred dollars." Shoot, they just laughed and hung up on me.

Others, including government officials, were not as optimistic about the tribe's chances for finding the kind of capital the project would demand.

Whether or not the large pool of unemployed or underemployed labor in the community would want to work in the farming enterprise was another question. Some Quechan leaders were dubious. "A lot of the youngsters feel that farming's not their line of work," they said. "Years ago, when farming was still kind of profitable for the small farmer, there were only two Quechans who worked at farm labor. And another thing—the going wages for farm labor in the area are low, and it's not easy work at all." In 1966, however, the wages of the CAP trainees had been low and the work hard, but there was a steady demand for available jobs. Gray was more optimistic about the labor potential. His experience as director of the tomato farm had convinced him that good leadership could wipe out absenteeism and high turnover rates. "The guy in charge of the farming operation has to be compassionate. Can't be 'holier than thou.' Get the people oriented, give them responsibility, give them authority—they'll do the job." To the extent that the community's high unemployment rate was due to lack of jobs, the field farming operation, by providing more jobs, could probably count on a good labor supply.

Overall, there was general enthusiasm for the still immature farming scheme in 1974, tempered with the misgivings about money and manpower. Meanwhile, the 600-acre demonstration farm would provide a critical test at practically no cost to the tribe or its members who were allottees.

THE LAND ISSUE—STILL

In the early 1970s it looked as though the government was finally ready to take some definitive action on the Quechans' remaining and largest claim against expropriated land. (Leasing a portion of the Island simply delayed a final decision.) Once again, the government was motivated by continual and increasingly sophisticated pressure from the tribe and its allies rather than self-generated humanitarianism at high levels in the Departments of Interior and Justice. This time, however, the tribe's allies included the BIA area office, since John Artichoker, an Indian who formerly served as superintendent of the Colorado River agency, had assumed the position of area director.

Using archival research, provided by a trust protection unit set up by the new area director, along with the legal advice of the tribal claims attorney, the tribal council decided in the early 1970s to make a radical tactical shift. Rather than to ask for cash compensation in their pending Claims Commission case, they pressured for a return of all land within the boundaries of the original 1884 reservation that was still under federal control. They were reminded that Secretary of Interior Udall had told tribal envoys in 1961 that this was possible, and their research and the opinion of knowledgeable Washington officials had convinced them that they were legally entitled to a return of this land.

The Quechans waited for the Washington bureaucracy to digest this change in their claim, but finally concluded that the government, as usual, was taking far too long to make a final decision. The council needed an issue to publicize its frustration and apply more pressure. With near perfect timing, Imperial County provided the necessary spark by subleasing a portion of the original reservation land being claimed by the tribe without getting the approval of tribal officials. On 3 October 1973, an angry group of Quechans left the reservation and marched southward behind a large yellow road grader. They had decided to blockade the disputed portion from trespassers, including the county developers. Once there, the road grader dug a shallow trench around the tract, while Council President Elmer Savilla delivered a prepared statement to the press. The words were practically identical to those written by Lee Emerson, another council president, thirteen years earlier.

> Basically ... we're fed up with Federal bureaucracy and unwillingness to help us with our land claims....
>
> We Quechans have reached that point of frustration where we will do whatever is necessary to protect our lands.
>
> We want no violence.... If there is violence it will be initiated by Imperial County [Quoted in *Wassaja,* November 1973].

Again, as in the road blockade of 1960, one Quechan showed up at the site with a bow and arrow.

The tribe's 1973 blockade effort was more limited than the earlier one, but was no less effective. Within two days, President Nixon's special counsel, Leonard Garment, called the council president to assure him that "some favorable action is imminent for the Quechan controversy" (*Wassaja,* November 1973:6). By the following summer, the government was finally ready to make a concrete proposal.

In a momentous but sparsely attended public meeting in July 1974, representatives from the Interior Department's solicitor's office met with the council to outline the negotiated settlement. It included a return of approximately 25,000 acres of land to tribal control—a parcel three times larger than tribal holdings at that time but still smaller than the original 1884 reservation domain. The tribe could also submit a claim for damages stemming from the All-American Canal, because it was tentatively agreed that the land taken in the canal's right of way had, in fact, been tribal land (Solicitor J. J. Clear, memorandum to secretary of interior 2/4/74 [087]). During a quick trip to Washington a few days later, the council president and the tribal claims attorney decided to ask for two and a half million dollars in canal damages. The proposal for returning the land and launching the revised claim was on Secretary of Interior Rogers Morton's desk waiting to be signed when the crisis of President Nixon's resignation descended on Washington and forced yet another frustrating delay.

Much of the land to be returned to tribal control was rugged desert. What to do with it would be a problem for the tribe to solve later; what mattered at the moment was getting it back. Council members and their supporters were elated at the prospect of the new settlement, in part because they would reap the political benefits for finally calling the government to account. Meanwhile, the council's political rivals—and there were still many in 1974—wanted to hold out for a larger settlement that would come only from a clear-cut nullification of the 1893 Agreement. They wanted to demand compensation not only for the All-American Canal, but for the large and fertile Bard District and other valuable tracts that were taken from tribal control by the agreement and other means. The return of some of the land was fine, they conceded, but should hardly be a final settlement since the Bard District had been taken by legislation that was now probably null and void.

ADAPTIVE STRATEGY FOR DEVELOPMENT: 1961–1974

In 1974, the tentative steps being taken toward true development were due to a combination of conditions that had been missing—by design in some instances—during the previous century of Quechan-government contact. The most obvious of the unprecedented conditions was the availability of money—lots of it. Not even the Indian Reorganization Act, the most ambitious of the pre-1960 schemes of Indian development, could match the munificence of the federal government in the mid-1960s. A second condition without historical precedent was that Quechan leadership was being allowed to assume an increasingly important decision-making role at crucial junctures in the series of emerging programs. And, finally, the Indian Bureau, through both the area and subagency offices, was offering the tribe increasingly sympathetic and pervasive technical help.

To see the emergence of these conditions as solely the result of action at the federal level would be grossly misleading, for the continuing funding, the limited increase of local decision-making authority, and the added input by the BIA were also the results of action taken by the tribe and its leaders. The leaders had not only to tap available financial resources but constantly had to seek new ones; they had to keep pressing for more authority; and they had to insist repeatedly that the BIA provide enlightened assistance. A crucial aspect, in short, was the shrewd strategy employed by the tribe's leaders.

To be effective, the strategy had to include realistic ideas coupled with increasingly sophisticated administrative and negotiating skill. Long denied a chance to hone such skill, the tribal leaders had persistently sought the help of sympathetic outsiders to feed them information and advise them on tactics. Not that the tribe had lacked good ideas; rather, they had been forced to depend on outsiders for the kind of administrative and negotiating know-how needed to bring the ideas closer to reality. Bill Gray brought administrative knowledge to the tribe at a time when the government was willing to provide material support, and by 1974 his efforts had served as examples for four different councils and their presidents. However, had he not shared the tribe's enthusiasm for expanding local programs, or had tribal politics and jealousy short-circuited his efforts, or had there been no funds to hire him in the first place, his role could not have been as significant.

The leaders' efforts to keep themselves involved in the programs gave them opportunities to refine their administrative and negotiating skills on a trial-and-error basis—to put their accumulated knowledge to the test and thus to increase it. An example was their person-to-person approach in dealing with high-level government officials. This approach, like other features of the strategy, was not altogether unprecedented: whenever possible in the past, the Quechans had attempted to avoid bureaucratic entanglements by appealing to the top echelons—the commissioner, the president, senators and congressmen. For decades, however, they had had to be content with letters because they lacked funds for travel to Washington (Patrick Miguel's mission being the exception). But the vastly improved tribal financial status in the 1960s and 1970s made trips to Washington feasible.

By 1974, the Quechans had refined what they called a "business approach" in their negotiations: a frank, concise statement of the tribe's position delivered personally to high-ranking officials; an openness about negotiating specified issues; and a certain toughness that combined a conviction that they had been mistreated in the past with a keen sensitivity to attempts to delay, confuse, or deny for arbitrary reasons. ("We are not going to sit still while the government pushes us around," they declared repeatedly.) The fine points of the business approach may have been new; but the attitude underlying it had not substantially changed for three-quarters of a century.

The marked increase in the BIA's technical advice, the result of increased personnel at the Fort Yuma subagency through enlightened action at the Phoenix area office, contributed also to the tribe's increasing administrative and negotiating knowledge. For years the subagency had included only the superintendent, a secretary, an agricultural expert, and a Quechan agricultural assistant. By 1974 there were four specialists (one a Quechan) plus the Quechan superintendent, a secretary, and several clerks, in spite of a trend to diffuse the bureau's former responsibilities to other federal agencies. (By 1975, the subagency had been reelevated to the status of agency.)

One measure of the tribe's increasing administrative and negotiating maturity was the way it was responding to the rapidly diminishing supply of federal money in the summer of 1974. Another measure was the surprising influence—relative to the size of the Quechan community—that Quechan leaders had assumed in regional Indian organizations. During the early 1970s Quechans held high-level administrative posts in the Affiliated Indian Tribes of Arizona, the Phoenix Office of the Indian Community Action Program, and the California Intertribal Council. A former Quechan council president was executive director of IDDA in 1974, while the 1974 council president was also serving as chairman of the Arizona Intertribal Council.

Administrative and negotiating know-how are of course virtually worthless unless there is something to be administered and unless the negotiating is done from a position of some leverage. By 1974, the Quechans and their allies in their administrative struggles had managed to create a modest negotiating leverage that they clearly lacked in 1964, and had certainly lacked in the preceding decades. This leverage was gained—or better, won—by the way the Quechans used their growing administrative sophistication to exploit the various funding opportunities.

Specifically, the tribe was wise to concentrate OEO and other money on construction projects rather than to pour it all into "soft" programs such as home enrichment or remedial reading. This concentration made the fullest possible use of the federal policy to diversify funds by dovetailing CAP management with monies and materials from OEO, Department of Labor, and other federal agencies. The construction projects not only provided wages and vocational training for a large number of community members, but produced physical evidence, in the form of new buildings, that the money was being used for development. This was evidence that OEO and Department of Labor officials could appreciate much more readily than they could a vague set of statistics about how many hours had been spent in remedial reading training or in teaching techniques of sewing and cooking. Here, then, was the source of the leverage: the successful construction created confidence in the tribe's potential and attracted new funds for still more building and consequently, wages.

The planning strategy—to concentrate development money on projects offering both wages and tangible results—was working as well in the "mutual help" housing program, although the tribal council was less directly involved. Housing and Urban Development officials were reportedly impressed with the Quechan and Cocopa projects in 1974, largely because (according to one local administrator), "We don't just let the money sit in the bank while we iron out this or that little problem; we get the houses built! That volunteer labor plan wasn't working [in 1966], so we got something else going."

The something else, of course, involved a reallocation of funds into a contracting system that offered limited wagework for some Quechans and produced new homes quickly and efficiently. And, since the emerging wages-with-construction plan blended well with the prevailing patterns of cooperative interaction among Quechan community members, its success was not likely to be compromised by the same kind of community nonsupport that had developed in the water and housing projects during the mid-1960s.

In marked contrast to tribal leadership and nascent economic development, the brutal fact remained, however, that the economic woes of most Quechans still remained unsolved. BIA subagency figures showed an increase in the number of welfare cases during the 1970–1974 period and no significant change in the ratio of employed to unemployed adults. Even with the new housing boom, exactly one-third of the community's 201 housing units still included composite families—a condition probably due largely to the continuing necessity of pooling financial resources among small groups of kinsmen (cf. Jorgensen 1971).[17] And local economic conditions promised to deteriorate still further as inflation threatened the economic health of the country as a whole. For significant development in the upcoming years, the tribal members would have to move against the ebbing tide of the national economy.

Nor had increasing administrative sophistication and improved negotiating postures vis-à-vis outside agencies displaced the persistence of intratribal struggles for political power. Ambivalence about Gray's role in the various programs was still present in 1974, as it had been in 1969. There were those who believed his usefulness to the tribe had passed, but there was no well-orchestrated action against his continued involvement (although there was a good deal of hinting that managerial changes might be made if one of the contending factions were to regain council control in the December 1974 elections).[18] There was also opposition, running along factional lines, to both the 1974 council president and his sister, the BIA subagency superintendent. Their rivals complained that neither of them could understand the community's problems because both had lived away from the reservation for most of their adult lives. Furthermore, some were unhappy that both individuals had married outside of the tribe and that neither spoke Quechan fluently—the same sorts of charges levelled years before at Mrs. Tannheimer when she assumed positions of leadership in the community. The charges were manifestations of a deep-rooted concern for tribal identity in the face of change. But they were also in keeping with a persistent tendency (noted by the Quechans themselves) to be hypercritical toward tribal leaders—whoever they might be.

Unquestionably, the crucial political maneuvering had come to center on the competition for the tribal council presidency. Since 1961, the office had become not only more remunerative but extremely important, because critical decisions had to be made ever more quickly—often with no time for the council as a whole to meet and deliberate the issues. In fact, the president's obligations had become so heavy by 1974 that he asked the BIA to send an expert to formulate a plan for streamlining tribal administration. The plan included provisions for a tribal administrative manager to coordinate the administration of the various development programs, the tribal staff, and all fiscal matters. The council president would then be free to deal with loftier issues such as coordination with federal agencies (EDA, HUD, BIA, PHS, ONAP, and so on) and various private groups (IDDA and the California and Arizona Intertribal Councils, for example).

Ideally, the reorganization would also prevent the possible use of the development programs for political patronage by making the administrative manager an appointed position whose occupant could be removed only for cause and only after an extensive review by a grievance committee. The plan therefore served as a reminder of the persistent, contradictory role the council was playing in the development effort, and of the still limited degree to which their decision-making leverage had been enhanced. They were expected to use their collective leverage to obtain additional funding or seek structural or procedural reform in existing programs; they were not, as individuals, to use their leverage to gain special benefits for themselves or their kinsmen-constituents. The plan, if it worked, could only reinforce the persistent and troublesome cleavage between the roles of council members as entrepreneurial overseers of the people's interests on the one hand, and their roles as individual beneficiaries of the programs on the other. While continuing the struggle against the nemesis of political domination by the federal government, the Quechans were still confronted by the threat that politically they would become their own worst enemies.

The crucial question also remained whether the Quechan planners would ever be able to compete with local non-Indian farming interests, various Yuma County and Imperial County development interests, Colorado River water management groups, and other state and federal agencies in the ultimate determination of what would be done with tribal resources. The record shows that for decades, the thrust of federal intervention had been primarily determined by interests outside the Quechan community. In 1974, the prognosis was not very hopeful that this historical trend would be broken. There had been plenty of skirmishing among various interests over resources being claimed by the Quechans; but the hard decisions—about continuing support for the reservation-wide farming cooperative, the ownership of the Island, and about the return of the thousands of acres of former reservation domain—were still being put off by the Washington bureaucracy. Whether the Quechans had been able to free themselves from a legacy of internal-colonial manipulation was yet to be determined in the gigantic arena extending from the lower Colorado River to Washington, D.C.

CHAPTER 6

The Quechan Community as a Product of Internal Colonialism

WITH MINOR VARIATIONS, COLONIALISM—wherever it exists—results in a political and economic subordination and exploitation of the colonized by the colonizers. Local native leaders are recast into the role of administrators of colonial policy, or are removed altogether from legitimate positions of leadership. The economic livelihood of the colonized—control of local resources including both labor and material—passes into the hands of the colonizers. A cultural subordination is also usually involved, with chauvinism among the colonizers leading to conscious attempts to shred the fabric of the colonized people's way of life. And always a profound discrepancy exists between the declared humanism of national policy and the actual impact of that policy at the local level.

During the nineteenth century, one of the endlessly repeated national goals was the eventual economic assimilation of American Indians, ostensibly with the same rights, opportunities, and obligations as other American citizens. Scholars critical of federal policy have pointed out, however, that the local effect of the various assimilationist schemes simply created a pool of unskilled, cheap Indian labor to be exploited by industrial sectors of the economy (e.g., Jorgensen 1971). There is no doubt about the existence of such a labor pool among the Quechans between the 1870s and 1970s, or about the role of federal administration in its creation. But their labor was exploited sketchily and indifferently—well short of the systematic utilization of cheap labor characteristic of mining regions of modern Africa, for example. In fact, some federal programs actually discouraged a mass exodus of the unemployed from the reservation to feed the labor appetites of Los Angeles, San Francisco, Phoenix, or Denver, even during periods of maximum pressure for Quechan economic assimilation. The Indians could not become prosperous by staying on the reservation; but then, with welfare, food rations, medical care, education, and housing benefits, their existence under conditions of poverty and job insecurity was relatively happier there than it probably would have been in urban centers.

Furthermore, if the design was to create exploitable labor pools, the government's timing was incredibly bad. Except during the brief bonanza of the 1960s, federal efforts to offer marginal vocational training came precisely at times when national and local labor markets were glutted, either because of depression or economic slowdowns prompted by inflation or recession. And it was during the bonanza of the 1960s that financial incentives for staying on the reservation and working in community programs were most lucrative.

In contrast to federal attempts to develop labor pools, the efforts to assimilate the Quechans into the local agrarian economy as small-scale farmers were remarkably consistent: consistently antidevelopment and exploitative. The most flagrant and shameful colonialistic exploitation of the Quechans' economic resources has historically centered not on their labor, but on their land base and the water to irrigate it. It began with the creation of a reservation that dramatically reduced the amount of usable land available to the tribe, and it continued with the deceitful 1893 Agreement; the sale of the Bard district; the allotment and further withdrawal from tribal control of the majority of the original reservation; the building of the All-American Canal through tribal territory without compensation; bureaucratic waffling on issues of disputed ownership of fertile lands exposed by the river's meanderings; and with a persistent reluctance on the part of the Fort Yuma superintendents to look after the Quechans' best interests in land-leasing and water-rent negotiations.

For much of their history there was in operation an insidious local development strategy that attempted to keep the Quechans minimally appeased in their material wants, and thus hopefully docile, while at the same time keeping enough federal economic and political control on their activities to keep them out of direct involvement in major attempts to develop their land. Their minimal material needs were satisfied in one of two ways: by helping the Indians move away from the reservation and into low-paying jobs; or by pumping funds into the community for projects that were simply ramifications of a basic welfare program.

To be sure, the Quechans' economic nondevelopment was nourished partly by factors that were beyond the control of the Indian bureau, the most obvious one being the lack of a stable source of lucrative employment in the greater Yuma area. Inadvertent mismanagement was also partly to blame at times. The bureaucratic entanglements of the BIA and other involved federal agencies generated plenty of confusion and oversight, as did sudden shifts in personnel and procedures. But, as with the 1893 Agreement, the allotment procedures, the leasing management, and the irrigation charges, many important actions were clearly aimed at gaining and exercising economic control over Quechan resources for non-Quechan profits. To conclude that federal incompetence was always to blame would be too charitable; a more objective conclusion would be that federal efforts fell short because they were never intended to succeed.

This apparent internal-colonial strategy needed no continuous, conscious conspiracy to perpetuate it—although conspiracy at crucial times seemed pretty evident. Decent, altruistic Anglo civil servants, merely following precedents without protest and then moving on to other posts, kept the inherently exploitative situation alive and well. Meanwhile, local farmers were able to avail themselves of cheap leased land; Yuma and Imperial County developers moved ahead with their own plans for land being claimed by the tribe; construction companies took large quantities of gravel from disputed land—as they were still doing in the 1970s—without compensating the Quechans; and powerful interests pondered ways of diverting still more of the Colorado's water to arid areas of the southwest without serious, sympathetic consideration of the rights of Quechans and other Indian groups affected.

Another federal policy goal was the cultural assimilation of the Quechans and other Indians into a middle class Christian version of the American life-style. Ultimately, this policy too only succeeded in creating havoc with their distinctive lifeways without offering a consistent and dignified substitute, and cannot, in retrospect, be distinguished from the policy of economic assimilation. To the extent that much of the sociocultural assimilation effort focused on vocational training (in its broadest interpretation, to include instruction in the traditional three "R's"), it was indeed a part of the strategy for economic assimilation. The assault upon traditional Quechan culture went beyond vocational training in an attempt to eradicate native religious beliefs as a source of community identity. This, too, could be seen as part of a strategy for economic manipulation of

Quechan resources insofar as it was aimed at undermining any community solidarity that stemmed from common belief and ritual—solidarity that could (and did at times) become a troublesome obstacle for outside manipulators. It was a feature of the colonial ploy of divide and rule; yet it never quite succeeded in a complete eradication of native religious beliefs and rituals.

Political manipulation, again with the apparent end of ensuring continued economic manipulation, also affected traditional social relations within the community, exacerbating the divisiveness of factional combat over positions of powerlessness. If community solidarity was intermittent at best in prereservation Quechan life, then the combined effect of direct assaults on traditional patterns of Quechan behavior, coupled with the effects of colonialistic economic and political manipulation, did nothing to make it more prevalent after the reservation was created.

In fact, economic manipulation of the Quechans and their resources had a greater impact on traditional behavior patterns than did federal policies aimed explicitly at cultural assimilation. The amalgamation of the outlying settlements, the land allotment, the emergence of a cash-and-wage-based economic system, the leasing strategy—all of these moves had a profound effect on preexisting features of Quechan society and culture.[1] The net result was economic poverty and some of the social maladies that accompany it: alcoholism, delinquency, and family instability (although good comparative data on prereservation family stability are lacking).

Yet some features of Quechan sociocultural life remained doggedly persistent throughout the 1884–1974 period. One was the function of groups of kinsmen, whether coresident/composite families or somewhat larger kinship clusters, as units of economic adaptation and political action. Despite the apparent pressures for individualization, these kinship groups—rather than individuals—seemed to be the most important economic, political, and social units involved in the dynamics of reservation life. This is not surprising in a community of this size and ethnic distinctiveness; the Quechans had no other basis for constructing adaptive units in a situation of scanty economic and political resources.

Something else persisted throughout the period of colonial manipulation: a prevailing attitude among Quechans that became a crucial factor in the attempts and pseudoattempts at Quechan community development. It was decidedly not the all-for-one-and-one-for-all communal spirit that was so fundamental to Commissioner John Collier's hopes for Indian development. It was instead a conviction, clearly reflected in Quechan leadership, that something was owed them—a collective consciousness of federal obligation to the

Quechans that was kept alive by endless public repetitions of the 1893 land fraud scenario, by hoary accounts of mistreatment at the government boarding school, and by repeated accusations against long gone superintendents. Despite the internal divisiveness, the people held in common the belief that merely being Quechans, with a designated reservation and history of federal mistreatment, entitled them to special consideration.

This attitude prevailed on two levels: the level of the community as a whole in times of turmoil over disputed land, schools, or trespassers; and the level of the community's subunits—the kinship clusters and factions—in the struggles for the pitifully scarce material and political resources available. The two levels were not always compatible with each other, or with meaningful community development; but their combined effect was to keep a constant (if often ignored) pressure on federal officials to act in the Quechans' own perceived best interests. "Quechans are so ungrateful," an Anglo official once lamented. "Instead of thanking you for something, they just take it, then turn around and demand something more, or want to know why somebody else in the tribe is getting more than they are." However much it may have chafed at the Anglo sense of proper etiquette, the behavior pattern kept outside administrators on their toes.

In sum, although certain characteristics of what has been called internal colonialism did prevail between the Quechans and the federal government, they were not always completely manifested, as in the exploitation of Quechan labor resources and the efforts at appeasing the Quechans' sense of frustrated outrage that fed intermittent attempts to resist further manipulation.

EVENTS OF 1961–1974 FROM AN INTERNAL-COLONIAL PERSPECTIVE

Federal policy of the 'sixties merely aided and abetted the internal-colonial status quo. The Economic Opportunity Act and the Manpower Development and Training Act, together with federally sponsored housing and sanitation programs, only continued the pattern of ramified welfare programs operating to appease rather than to develop. The principle of maximum feasible participation of communities in development decisions was seen by some analysts as a source of confusion at best and, at worst, a sham to hide continuing exploitation (see Moynihan 1969 and Jorgensen 1971). Then there were the land-claims settlements, hailed by assimilationist-minded lawmakers over two decades earlier as a means of eliminating the federal government as an intermediary in the manipulation of Indian resources by states and other interests.

On the other hand, these developments provided an unprecedented potential for an all-important increase in local Indian capital and political autonomy. A series of tragic clashes between minorities and law enforcement agencies in Watts, Detroit, Newark, Alcatraz, and Wounded Knee, in the late 1960s and early 1970s increased public pressure on the federal and state governments to aid American Indians and other minorities. For their own occupational survival, government officials were obliged more than ever before to listen (at least) to proposals from minority groups. Again, these combined developments merely offered a potential that had not existed before; bureaucratic control and the influence of competitive interests were still effectively present.

It was thus up to the Quechans to exploit the potential that the new developments offered and thereby to stifle the clear-cut perpetuation of the internal-colonial situation.

Their efforts in the 1960s and 1970s must be viewed in terms of what the community had become in the preceding century: a pocket of poverty. There was a large pool of unused labor desperately needing money. There was a group of community leaders eager to seize the authority so long denied them but lacking administrative sophistication and who, like their constituents, needed the cash and other benefits that the antipoverty programs might provide. Related to all these conditions was a lack of community solidarity that manifested itself in debilitating struggles among factions. Finally, there was a set of strategic precedents for coping with government development programs. Whatever the details of its historical variants, the underlying strategy was to obtain a firm government commitment by a ready acceptance of whatever benefits were offered—on terms dictated by the government, then to attempt to alter the terms to better suit the Quechans' own interests and capacities.

The difficulties that emerged after the programs were under way were the result of the Quechans' attempts to change the terms of their continuing receipt of program benefits to their own interests —political and economic. The pursuit of these interests threatened to scuttle one program (the Neighborhood Youth Corps) and seriously affected the progress of others (the mutual-help housing and the water program). Unprecedented demands for long-term community cooperation went unmet. Still, the government, deeply committed, did not cancel the benefits during this "adjustment of terms" phase.

The tribe had to keep applying for additional funding in an increasingly sophisticated manner, and by 1974, their newfound skill was being severely tested as the federal government shied away from the large-scale funding of a decade earlier. But the council had by then determined that their negotiating leverage came not so much from continuous, aggressive confrontation as from demonstrating that the funds they already had received were being put to effective use. This was one of the most crucial features of the local-level strategy for producing the transformations that were starting to occur in 1974.

What were these transformations, and why was there justification for cautious optimism when the community was still entangled in an internal-colonial situation? The bright spots—the significant enterprises—were the tomato farm and the limited start at a larger-scale tribal farming enterprise. If successfully operated and allowed to expand, these activities had the potential of becoming the basis of a tribally-owned and operated business that would provide lucrative long-term income for both the tribe as a corporation and for individual Quechans. And, if successful, the venture would represent an ultimate vindication of their ancestors' strategy for economic survival: the Quechans' traditional sustenance had come from tilling the soil, and, despite a century-long interlude of colonialistic interference, their future development would come from the same source.

National-level changes in funding and administrative policy were necessary for limited, local-level Quechan development in 1974, but were not sufficient to explain what was occurring. Whether they would perpetuate the internal-colonial manipulation of Quechan resources was an issue that would be determined in part by the Quechans themselves from the options open to them. The Quechans' strategy, in circular fashion, would continue to condition and be conditioned by future actions of the federal government and by actions of other powerful, non-Indian interests operating at the local, regional, and national levels. The basic elements in the struggle for eventual community development thus comprised a single, interacting network.

The network was volatile in 1974, subject to the effects of the continuing deterioration of the national economy. The Quechans' leverage in the interaction, though increased slightly, was far less than that of other elements. And even this modest increase was vulnerable to threats so typically posed in colonial and internal-colonial situations: the threat of a sudden, unilateral, detrimental change in federal Indian policy and the threat of collapse from internal factional competition for the still scarce economic and political resources. The fetters of internal colonialism had been loosened somewhat by the mid-1970s, but they had not been removed. True autonomy and development for the Quechan Indians were yet to come.

Notes to the Chapters

CHAPTER ONE

1. Even in the occupation of Colorado River valley lands formerly held by the Halchidomas, "the Mohave apparently did not move down into Halchidoma territory for a considerable time after they [the Halchidomas] departed for the Gila" (Fathauer 1954:112). If there had been pressure on available Mohave lands, it seems very likely that they would not have delayed their movement (unless they were simply waiting until the spring floods deposited their silt). I am assuming that the same lack of pressure prevailed among the Quechans. None of my informants or sources reported the reasons for Quechan occupation of the southern portions of this valley during this period, or whether there was a similar time lag between the evacuation by the Halchidomas and resettlement by the Quechans. Patrick Miguel, one of Forde's informants, once wrote (Miguel n.d.) that the Quechans had moved back and forth between the Colorado-Gila confluence and this northern valley prior to European contact. The reason, according to Miguel's rendering of Quechan oral tradition, was to escape the increasing pressure of years of drought and famine that followed a volcanic eruption near the mouth of the Colorado River, culminating in a severe winter that covered the confluence area with a heavy layer of snow and caused "much suffering and death." Miguel also reported that the Quechan participants in the attack on the Spanish missions in the confluence area withdrew to the Colorado River valley around the modern town of Blythe.

CHAPTER TWO

1. According to information submitted by the Quechans in one of their land claims against the government (Docket 320), Indian title to lands on

the California side of the river was extinguished "in 1853, when the whole State was taken by the Government, and on the Arizona side in 1867, when the military reservation was created." A portion of these lands was restored to Indian title when the reservation was created by executive order in 1884 ("Reply Brief of Petitioner," *Quechan Tribe v. the United States,* Docket 320, Indian Claims Commission, pp. 15–16).

2. The Miguel document was apparently prepared expressly for the tribal attorney in 1951 for possible use as evidence in the Quechan's land claims against the government (Docket 319). The general facts were corroborated by my own informants. Miguel reported yet another Quechan settlement existing directly east across the Colorado from Captain *Akes ha ar's* group, near the modern town of Ehrenberg. This settlement was led by Captain Tom (*Xo mar va vatch*) and was said to include sixty families. The site was known as *Xenyu mala vax* (big lake). Under pressure from the Anglos, some of Tom's people went to Parker, Arizona and some to Yuma, while still others moved across the river to live with *Akes ha ar's* group for several years before all remaining Quechans in this region moved south to the new Quechan reservation.

3. Patrick Miguel's unpublished report noted an interesting discrepancy between Quechan oral history and that reported by modern Anglo historians using early Spanish chronicles. Miguel wrote:

> Chief Palma's village mentioned by Forde [1931:100–101] is a myth. Forde was repeatedly informed that Palma was and is not known to the Quechan Indians and the site of his village had never been pointed out to him [Forde] by any of his informants. Likewise, Axakwethexor was not Palma's place. . . .

In another document, Miguel (n.d.) wrote: "The Quechan leader who first received the [Spanish] Missionaries for the Indians was a one-eyed man whose name was Sarhenti [cf. Spanish *sargento,* (sergeant)] and not Palma as many historians have it."

4. This privilege was claimed by the Quechans as one of the terms under which the railroad was granted a right-of-way across the reservation for its main east-west line.

5. The patent was passed on to Louis Jaeger by his father. How the father obtained it is unclear. Superintendent O'Neil noted simply that the father had obtained the patent in 1858, before the reservation was created. Quechans who attempted to unravel the history of the tract claimed, in 1974, that it had originally been given by the government to a Private John Williams, in return for Williams' service during the "Indian uprisings," although neither the date or the place of the uprisings is available. The senior Jaeger somehow received title to the property later on. This is a source of continuing interest to Quechans who suspect that the patent process on this tract was illegal.

CHAPTER THREE

1. I am unable to find information about who brought pressure for the increase in allotment size or the rationale they used. The increase was authorized in an appropriations bill for Indian affairs in 1911. It was inserted by the Senate as an amendment to the House bill H.R. 28406. The

Indians had been anxious for the increase, and the Indian office had been so informed by the Fort Yuma agent at about the time Patrick Miguel was on his way to Washington. It is unlikely that this alone was sufficient to produce the amendment. As one Quechan pointed out to me in 1974, by 1911 it really didn't matter whether the allotments were five acres or ten; the best agricultural land on the reservation (the Bard District) had already been sold to Anglos.

2. The secretary of the interior approved the new committee's organization on 22 August 1911 (stamped endorsement on a report from C. F. Hauke to interior secretary 18 August 1911).

3. In 1974, according to Fort Yuma subagency officials, some 420 acres of this land were still held by Quechan families and were incorporated as "Yuma Homestead Allotments" into the jurisdiction of the subagency. All of the land was leased to non-Indians in 1974.

4. Original construction charges on allotted lands and past due O and M charges were subsequently cancelled under the provisions of the Leavitt Act (47 Stat. 564); the government assumed responsibility for payment of O and M charges on ca. 2000 acres of unused allotments in the late 1930s (W. V. Woehlke, Memo to Commissioner 28 June 1940).

5. In 1966, the subagency superintendent was trying to induce each allottee to make a will, naming one survivor as inheritor of the tract. This would stop the burgeoning land fractionation, but probably would increase intrafamilial tensions.

6. It is not known whether the house owners received a fee for their host duties or whether there was a rotating host arrangement to equalize costs.

7. In the 1960s, older Quechans reported that Odle was assigned to a different post, then later was let out of the Indian Service.

CHAPTER FOUR

1. This law was finally amended in 1968 to require the Indians' consent before it could be applied to them by states (Officer 1971:48). In 1974, the Quechans were still undecided about whether to request retrocession of the law as it applied to them.

2. In 1954, a high school was built for the San Pasqual Unified School District just beyond the reservation's eastern boundary. There, the Quechan youths were still in a numerical minority, but only barely so; the racial balance was much more even than it had been at the Yuma High School.

3. The Mission Indian Federation claimed a larger number of members than had actually joined their organization—but so did other factional groupings in the community.

4. It is interesting to compare the text of the ratified constitution concerning the powers of the council with the realities of how those powers were regulated by the Indian office. Relevant excerpts from the constitution (Art. IV—Powers of Council, pp. 2–4) include:

> SECTION 1. The Tribal Council shall have the power:
>
> (a) to negotiate with the federal, state and local governments on behalf of the Tribe;
>
> (b) To present and prosecute any claims or demands of the Quechan Tribe; . . .

(d) To employ legal counsel for the protection and advancement of the rights of the Tribe and its members, the choice of counsel and fixing of fees to be subject to the approval of the Secretary of the Interior. . . .

SECTION 2. The Council shall have the power to prevent the sale, disposition, lease or incumbrance of tribal lands, interests in lands, or other tribal assets without the consent of the Tribe.

SECTION 3. The Council shall have the power to administer any funds or property within the control of the Tribe, but the exercise of this power shall be subject to approval by the Secretary of the Interior for a period of four years only from the date of the adoption of this Constitution. It shall also have power to advise with the Secretary of the Interior upon all appropriation estimates or Federal projects for the benefit of the Tribe prior to the submission of such estimates to the Bureau of the Budget and Congress, and to make prompt recommendations to the Secretary of the Interior or to the proper committees of Congress with respect to all such estimates and appropriations.

SECTION 4. The Council shall have the power to select subordinate boards, officials, and employees not otherwise provided for in this Constitution and to prescribe their tenure and duties. It shall have the power to make expenditures from available funds for public purposes, including salaries or other remuneration of community officials or employees subject to the restrictions in Section 3 of this article. . . .

SECTION 6. The Council shall have the power to regulate, license, and levy fees upon non-members doing business within the jurisdiction of the Tribe. This shall not apply to churches or schools. . . .

SECTION 8. The Council shall have the power to purchase under condemnation proceedings in State or Federal courts of competent jurisdiction land or other property needed for public purposes.

SECTION 9. The Council shall have power to charter subordinate organizations for economic purposes, and to regulate the activities of cooperative associations of members of the Quechan Tribe through ordinances which shall be subject to approval by the Secretary of Interior.

SECTION 10. The Council shall have the power to prescribe rules of inheritance, except concerning allotted lands under present laws, and to receive voluntary relinquishments of allotments and heirship lands and to issue assignments of land to members of the Tribe upon such conditions as may be laid down in the By-laws. . . .

SECTION 15. The Council shall have power to regulate its own procedure by ordinance or resolution.

SECTION 16. All ordinances and resolutions governing the adoption of new members (Article II, Section 2); the licensing and levying fees on non-members (Article IV, Section 6); the regulations of inheritance (Article IV, Section 10); and the appointment of guardians (Article IV, Section 13); shall be subject to the approval of the Secretary of the Interior.

> SECTION 17. The foregoing enumeration of powers shall not be construed to limit the powers of the Quechan Tribe, but all powers of local government not expressly entrusted to the Tribal Council by this Constitution shall be reserved to the people of the Quechan Tribe, and such powers may be exercised through the adoption of appropriate by-laws or constitutional amendments.
>
> SECTION 18. All ordinances or resolutions pursuant to the exercise of any power enumerated in this article shall be consistent with the laws established by the United States Government, and by the State of California and any political subdivision thereof, in so far as such laws may apply to members of the Quechan Tribe resident upon the Fort Yuma Reservation.

5. According to the recollection of some Quechans, Patrick Miguel took it upon himself to keep an eye on affairs on Indian Hill during the interregnum between Agent Jolley and Agent Cox in the early 1940s. One narrator smilingly mused in 1974:

> I can see him now—big black hat, cane, cigar 'way out to here [gesture in front of mouth]. He'd go up on the Hill every morning just to make sure everyone was doing what he was supposed to. He was more energetic than the real superintendents. They stayed in their offices all day. Patrick really walked the whole Hill! Then he'd go off somewhere, and come back for another grand tour in the afternoon.

6. The trend continued for years. In the 1967 elections, there were only seven candidates for the seven council seats; 100 votes were cast. But by December 1974, the trend seemed to have been broken. Out of a total of 386 registered voters, 307 cast votes for council members. This interesting upturn may have been due to increasing public confidence in the tribe's economic outlook.

7. This amendment was finally ratified by the electorate in the December 1974 election.

8. In 1956, the government expanded its off-reservation program to include single adults as well as families. Relocation had by then become a red flag to opponents of termination, and the program was soon rechristened the Employment Assistance and Vocational Training Program.

9. See Beals and Siegel 1966 for a more abstract discussion of the problem of sorting out clear social boundaries of groups in a situation of pervasive factionalism.

10. Often these stands featured the same types of items for sale as the others, e.g., hamburgers and soft drinks.

11. Occasionally Imperial County, California, tax assessors would venture onto the reservation and attempt to complete tax assessments on the Quechans' personal property. One such incident was reported during my stay there in 1966. The council simply turned the matter over to the Fort Yuma subagency superintendent, who reminded the county assessor's office that such property was nontaxable.

12. As of March, 1976, the return had still not been effected.

CHAPTER FIVE

1. The plans called for a motel, restaurant, and crafts shop to be built near a proposed interstate highway just south of the reservation. The highway (Interstate 8) in that area was completed by 1974.

2. These were designated as Dockets 319 and 320 for the Indian Claims Commission hearings. Docket 319 sought financial compensation for Quechan lands taken in the modern states of California and Arizona. It was settled in 1965. Docket 320 sought compensation for the proceeds of Quechan lands sold in the Bard District, but by 1974 its original objectives had been combined with attempts to obtain a return of former reservation lands and compensation for the All-American Canal right-of-way. Docket 320, as altered, was still pending in March 1976.

3. The CAP proposal was bounced back to the tribe twice, once because the tribe was referred to as "the Quechans" in one passage and "the Yumas" in another.

4. There was a technological problem involved: if all the homeowners had turned out at once, along with the supervisors, it is quite possible that construction would have been hindered by too many novices getting in each other's way.

5. There was no formal effort to measure the degree to which the Quechans understood their responsibilities in the programs. The new homeowners signed formal agreements, including labor obligations, prior to construction. In the water program the procedures had allegedly been outlined to each participant by teams of Quechan canvassers, and family heads were required to sign Public Health Service (PHS) release forms. The tribal president, after consulting with the council, signed an agreement between the tribe and the PHS that clearly stated the labor responsibilities of tribal members. It is unlikely, then, that the lack of labor was due to lack of information about what the participants were expected to provide.

6. See, for example, "The Economic Opportunity Act of 1964—Implications for American Indians" (Department of Interior 1964), and Striner 1968:319–320.

7. The figures for the State of California alone in 1966 showed an Indian dropout rate of twenty-one percent—three times higher than that of non-Indians, yet not far from the average of the group of Quechan NYC enrollees (California State Advisory Commission on Indian Affairs 1966:10). The national figures revealed in 1968 that fifty percent of Indian students drop out of school before completing high school (Johnson 1968:2; Sorkin 1971:25–26).

8. The program would feed funds into seven major areas: tribal administration ($35,000); attorney's fees ($50,000); community development—burial ground improvement, tribal equipment, arts and crafts, merchandising, maintenance fund for water system ($135,000); education ($100,000); home improvement ($100,000); land purchase ($75,000—not to exceed $10,000 per year); and a contingency trust fund of $25,000, only a third of which could be withdrawn in any one year.

9. Henry Montague succeeded Fritz Brown as tribal president in 1967. Brown became president when his predecessor died in office. He was reelected for a complete term in 1965. Montague served two terms from 1967 to 1971; in 1971 Brown again became president, was reelected in 1973, and served for a few months before resigning his office. His term was filled by Elmer Savilla, who was reelected in 1974. Both Henry Montague and Fritz

Brown were elected to several terms on the council before and after they served as council president.

10. The construction programs included three different components: Operation Mainstream (forty employees); Incentive Program (forty-four employees); and the Quechan Tribal Housing and Training Program (fourteen employees). Not all of these people were Quechans.

11. According to federal law, commodities were distributed to all qualifying families in the reservation and surrounding area; not all of the recipients were Indians.

12. According to a past tribal president in 1974, himself very knowledgeable about local agricultural technology, the "development lease" funds in the 1960s went to pay off accumulated O and M charges, so that, by the time the land was in full production, the O and M account would be current; at that time the lease rate would go up and the lessee would pay the O and M charges. The subagency superintendent reported that O and M charges and water rents in 1974 were being paid by lessees. If the land was developed but not leased, the Quechan allottee had to pay the water charges. The allottee could, however, petition the subagency office for a cancellation of the charges if he/she was unable to pay. A committee within the subagency then met to determine whether the petition would be granted.

13. Fort Yuma subagency figures revealed the increase in developed land between 1964 and 1973 (Memo to Phoenix Area Office 20 September 1973):

1964: "Irrigated land developed and leased": 4987 acres
"Irrigable land undeveloped": 3809 acres
1973: "Allotted land developed and leased": 8139 acres
"Irrigable land undeveloped": 600 acres

There is an unexplained discrepancy between the totals for the two years, so that the figures must be regarded as approximations; still, the increase is very apparent.

14. Figures compiled from CAA administration data in 1974 showed the following dispersal of individuals who had been vocational trainees in 1966–69:

Employed in off-reservation positions directly related to training: 8
Employed in positions not related to training: 13
Employed, relevance of past training unknown: 1
Unemployed in 1974 because of old age, poor health, unknown reasons, or death: 32
Still employed in on-reservation programs: 31
Whereabouts and occupation unknown: 8 (not all Quechans)

15. Fort Yuma subagency figures showed that the 1972 total "personal [allottee] income from irrigated land" amounted to $304,141. That same year, the value of crop production for non-Indian operators was estimated at $1,900,000; Indian allottees received about one-sixth of the total production income of the land for that year (memo to Phoenix Area Office 20 September 1973). These figures should reflect the lease rate increase that began modestly about a year earlier; it is probable, then, that the proportion of Indian lease income to total gross farming income was lower in the 1960s.

16. The first crop in 1974 grossed over $204,000.

17. These figures are based on analysis of data provided in "A Census of the Ft. Yuma Quechan Indian Reservation, Summer, 1972," a report prepared under the auspices of the Tribal Health Committee of the Quechan Tribal Council.

18. Based on information reported in the Quechan Tribe's *CAA Newsletter,* the December 1974 elections and subsequent contentions among council members representing opposing factions apparently did not force significant changes in the status quo as of mid-1974.

CHAPTER SIX

1. My efforts to play up the exploitative colonial nature of Quechan-federal relationships must not obscure the fact that some of the cultural and economic transformations were apparently sought by the Quechans themselves, as described in the preceding narrative.

References

Bailey, F. G.

1960 Tribe, Caste, and Nation. Manchester: University of Manchester Press.

Barnes, J. A.

1966 Indigenous Politics and Colonial Administration [originally 1960]. *In* Social Change: The Colonial Situation. I. Wallerstein, Ed. New York: John Wiley and Sons.

Barth F.

1967 On the Study of Social Change. American Anthropologist 69:661–669.

Barth, F., Ed.

1963 The Role of the Entrepreneur in Social Change in Northern Norway. Bergen: Scandinavian University Books.

Basehart, H. W., and T. T. Sasaki

1964 Changing Political Organization in the Jicarillo Apache Reservation Community. Human Organization 23:283–289.

Beals, A. R., and B. J. Siegel

1966 Divisiveness and Social Conflict. Stanford: Stanford University Press.

Bee, R. L.

1963 Changes in Yuma Social Organization. Ethnology 2:207–227.

1967 Sociocultural Change and Persistence in the Yuma

Indian Reservation Community. Unpublished Ph.D. Dissertation, University of Kansas, Lawrence.

Bennett, J. W.
1969 Northern Plainsmen: Adaptive Strategy and Agrarian Life. Chicago: Aldine Publishing Co.

Brophy, W. A., and S. D. Aberle
1966 The Indian: America's Unfinished Business. Norman: University of Oklahoma Press.

California State Advisory Commission on Indian Affairs
1966 Progress Report to the Governor and the Legislature on Indians in Rural and Reservation Areas. Sacramento: California Office of State Printing.

Castetter, E. F., and W. H. Bell
1951 Yuman Indian Agriculture. Albuquerque: University of New Mexico Press.

Deloria, V., Ed.
1971 Of Utmost Good Faith. New York: Bantam Books.

Department of Interior
1874–1900 Annual Report of the Secretary of Interior. Washington, D. C.: Government Printing Office.
1964 The Economic Opportunity Act of 1964—Implications for American Indians. Washington, D. C.: Government Printing Office.

Dobyns, H. F.
1968 Therapeutic Experience of Responsible Democracy. *In* The American Indian Today, revised edition. S. Levine and N. O. Lurie, Eds. Baltimore: Penguin books.

Dobyns, H. F., P. H. Ezell, A. W. Jones, and G. Ezell
1957 Thematic Changes in Yuman Warfare. *In* Cultural Stability and Cultural Change. V. F. Ray, Ed. Proceedings of the 1957 Annual Spring Meeting of the American Ethnological Society: 46–71.

Dowd, D. F.
1974 The Twisted Dream: Capitalist Development in the United States since 1776. Cambridge, Massachusetts: Winthrop Publishers.

Downes, R. C.
1945 A Crusade for Indian Reform, 1922–1934. Mississippi Valley Historical Review 32:331–354.

Fathauer, G. H.
1954 The Structure and Causation of Mohave Warfare. South-western Journal of Anthropology 10:97–118.

Forbes, J. D.
1965 Warriors of the Colorado. Norman: University of Oklahoma Press.

Forde, C. D.
1931 Ethnography of the Yuma Indians. University of California Publications in American Archaeology and Ethnology 28:85–278.

Hagan, W. T.
1961 American Indians. Chicago: University of Chicago Press.

Heintzelman, S. P.
1857 Report. U. S. House of Representatives Executive Document 76, 34th Congress, 3rd Session: 34–53.

Ives, J. C.
1861 Report upon the Colorado River of the West, Explored in 1857 and 1858. House Report Executive Document 90, 36th Congress, 1st Session.

Johnson, L. B.
1968 The President's Message to the Congress on Goals and Programs for the American Indian, March 6, 1968. Indian Record (March), Washington, D. C.: Government Printing Office.

Jorgensen, J. G.
1971 Indians and the Metropolis. *In* The American Indian in Urban Society. J. O. Waddell and O. M. Watson, Eds. Boston: Little, Brown and Co.
1972 The Sun Dance Religion: Power for the Powerless. Chicago: University of Chicago Press.

Kickingbird, K., and K. Ducheneaux
1973 One Hundred Million Acres. New York: Macmillan Co.

Lauderdale, J. V., and G. S. Rose
1875 Fort Yuma, California: Reports of Assistant Surgeons J. V. Lauderdale and George S. Rose, United States Army. Hygiene of the U. S. Army, Circular 8:557–564. Surgeon General's Office, Washington, D. C.: Government Printing Office.

Mekeel, S.
1944 An Appraisal of the Indian Reorganization Act. American Anthropologist 46:209–217.

Miguel, P.
n.d. The Quechan Tribe. Unpublished manuscript.

Miguel, P., Ed.
1937 An Account of the 1893 Agreement as Related by the Quechan Eye-Witnesses. Unpublished manuscript.

Moynihan, D. P.
1969 Maximum Feasible Misunderstanding. New York: The Free Press.

Officer, J. E.
1971 The American Indian and Federal Policy. *In* The American Indian in Urban Society. J. O. Waddell and O. M. Watson, Eds. Boston: Little, Brown and Co.

Ortiz, A.
1962 History and Ideology in Maricopa Chieftainship. Unpublished manuscript.

Quechan Tribal Council
1940 A Statement of Fact and a Plea for Just Consideration. . . . Unpublished manuscript.

Shames, D., Ed.
1972 Freedom with Reservation: The Menominee Struggle to Save their Land and People. Madison, Wisconsin: National Committee to Save the Menominee People and Forests.

Shepardson, M.
1963 Navajo Ways in Government. Memoirs of the American Anthropological Association 96.

Sorkin, A. L.
1971 American Indians and Federal Aid. Washington, D. C.: The Brookings Institution.

Spicer, E. H.
1962 Cycles of Conquest. Tucson: University of Arizona Press.
1969 A Short History of the Indians of the United States. New York: Van Nostrand Reinhold Co.

Steward, J. H.
1955 Theory of Culture Change. Urbana: University of Illinois Press.
1969 The Limitations of Applied Anthropology: The Case of the Indian New Deal. Journal of the Steward Anthropological Society 1:1–17.

Stewart, K. M.
1947 Mohave Warfare. Southwestern Journal of Anthropology 3:257–278.

Striner, H. E.
1968 Toward a Fundamental Program for the Training, Employment and Economic Equality of the American Indian. *In* Federal Programs for the Development of Human Resources I:293–326. Joint Economic Committee, U. S. Congress, Washington, D. C.: Government Printing Office.

Thomas, R.
1966–67 Colonialism: Classic and Internal. New University Thought 4:37–43.

Thompson, L.
1950 Culture in Crisis: A Study of the Hopi Indians. New York: Harper and Brothers.

Trippel, E. J.
1889 The Yuma Indians. Overland Monthly, Series 2, 13:561–584; 14:1–11.

Tyler, S. L.
1973 A History of Indian Policy. Bureau of Indian Affairs, Washington, D. C.: Government Printing Office.

U. S. Senate
1931 Survey of Indian Conditions in the United States, Part 17. 71st Congress, Washington, D. C.: Government Printing Office.

Zimmerman, W.
1957 The Role of the Bureau of Indian Affairs since 1933. *In* American Indians and American Life. G. E. Simpson and J. M. Yinger, Eds. The Annals of the American Academy of Political and Social Science 311:31–40.

Acknowledgments

I Wish to Express My Gratitude to the Quechans who helped me in my research by generously giving their time to answer my queries. The Quechan tribal council graciously and repeatedly allowed me to conduct my studies on the reservation. The staffs of the local Community Action Agency, the Bureau of Indian Affairs Subagency, the Public Health Service Hospital, and the Quechan-Cocopa Housing Authority also provided invaluable help.

James A. Clifton, Murray Wax, Carlyle S. Smith, and Wendell Oswalt read early drafts of some of the material included in this work, and Abraham M. Halpern offered valuable criticism of the manuscript shortly before it went into production. My thanks to them for their effort.

The research depended on financial support from several different agencies and institutions to whom I am most grateful: the National Institute of Mental Health; the Wenner-Gren Foundation for Anthropological Research; the George C. Barker, Jr., Memorial Research Fund at UCLA; and the Research Foundation of the University of Connecticut.

Raymond Blanchette of the University of Connecticut drew the maps, and Alamo Reaves of the University of Arizona Press provided her editorial expertise. I appreciate their help.

R. L. B.

Index